The Theory of
INERTIAL INFLATION

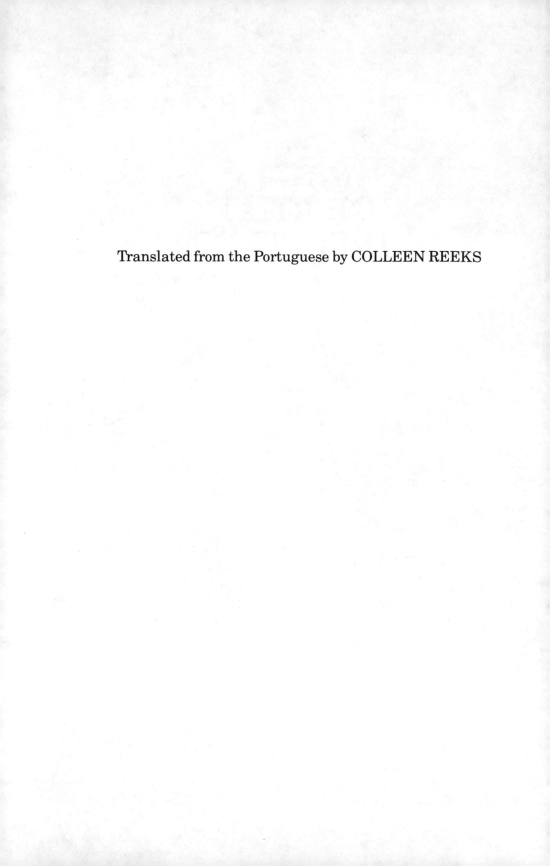

Translated from the Portuguese by COLLEEN REEKS

The Theory of
INERTIAL INFLATION
The Foundation of
Economic Reform in
Brazil & Argentina

LUIZ BRESSER PEREIRA
YOSHIAKI NAKANO
Foreword by RUDIGER DORNBUSCH

Lynne Rienner Publishers • Boulder/London

Published in the United States of Amercia in 1987 by
Lynne Rienner Publishers, Inc.
948 North Street, Boulder, Colorado 80302

An earlier version of this work was published in Portuguese as *Inflação e Recessão*.

Library of Congress Cataloging in Publication Data

Pereira, Luiz Carlos Bresser.
　The theory of inertial inflation.

　Bibliography: p.
　Includes index.
　1. Inflation (Finance)—Brazil.　2. Monetary
policy—Brazil.　3. Monetary policy—Argentina.
I. Nakano, Yoshiaki, 1944-　.　II. Title.
III.　Title: Inertial inflation.
HG835.P45　1987　　332.4'1'0981　　　86-29832
ISBN 1-55587-007-4

Printed and bound in the United States of America

The paper used in this publication meets the requirements
of the American National Standard for Permanence of
Paper for Printed Library Materials Z39.48-1984. ∞

Contents

List of Tables and Figures   vi
Foreword   *Rudiger Dornbusch*   vii
Preface   xi

1 Introduction: Inertial Inflation and the Heterodox Shock
   in Brazil   1

Part 1   The Political Economy of Inflation

2 Inflation in Oligopolistic and Technobureaucratic Capitalism   27
3 The Theory of Inertial or Autonomous Inflation   65
4 Administrative Policy: Gradualism or Shock   83
5 Inertial Inflation and the Phillips Curve   109

Part 2   The Brazilian Inflation

6 The Contradictions of Brazilian Inflation: 1964-1979   119
7 Recession and Inflation: 1981   143
8 Accelerating Factors in 1979 and 1983   151
9 Inertial Inflation on the Eve of the Shock   169
10 The Difficulties of the Cruzado and the Austral Plans   177

Statistical Appendix   185
Bibliography   187
Index   197
About the Book and the Authors   205

Tables

—————————————————— Tables ——————————————————

1.1 Annual Growth Rates for Industrial Prices 20
2.1 Inflation Rates in Central Countries 29
2.2 Inflation Rates in Underdeveloped Countries 29
2.3 Inflation in Brazil: 1964-1980 55
3.1 Central Government Deficit and the Inflation Rate 77
6.1 Inflation—Annual Rates 121
6.2 Inflation—Monthly Rates 135
7.1 Trends of the Inflation Rate 145
7.2 Wholesale Price Index (IPA)—Manufacturing 1981 146
8.1 Price Variations: 1979-1983 152
8.2 Indexes of Real Prices for the Agricultural Sector 155
8.3 Prices Controlled by the Government 161
9.1 Inflation Annual Rates 170
Statistical Appendix 1 Brazil's Internal Sector 185
Statistical Appendix 2 Brazil's External Sector 186

—————————————————— Figures ——————————————————

1.1 Conversion of Wages to Cruzados 4
1.2 Dispersion of Relative Prices 18
2.1 Inflation and Growth 30
4.1 The Phillips Curve and Autonomous Inflation 86
4.2 Indexation Based on Past Inflation 98
4.3 Indexation Based on Past and Future Inflation 99
5.1 Effect of a Supply Shock with Full Indexation 111
5.2 Effect of a Demand Shock with Full Indexation 112
5.3 Effect of Profit Margin Increases 113
8.1 Theoretical Effect on the Real Average Wage of the
    Change to Semestral Readjustments 157

Foreword

RUDIGER DORNBUSCH

Milton Friedman argues that inflation, always and everywhere, is a monetary phenomenon—too much money chasing too few goods, money burning holes in peoples' pockets. This fine book by Bresser Pereira and Nakano defends a very different view of the inflation process. The authors argue persuasively that Brazilian-style inflation must be explained mostly from the supply side. Inflation perpetuates itself as a consequence of past inflation, transmitted through formal and informal indexation of wages, public sector prices, and the exchange rate into cost and price increases today. Inflation is the result of *inertia*, not of excess demand at current prices.

That is decidedly not the theory espoused by "Chicago boys" brought up on the quantity of money and on perfect competition. It is a line of thinking developed in the setting of high inflation, indexation, and fights about income shares in Latin America in the postwar period, but especially in the past fifteen years. It is tempting to write off this approach as unsound in that it gives little room to excess demand as a central explanation for inflation. But that would be going much too far. The inertia approach does capture an extraordinarily important fact of high inflation economies, and ignoring this characteristic would lead to dramatically wrong policy advice. Where monetarists see the cure for inflation in budget tightening and monetary restraint, the inertia approach recommends incomes policy in the form of wage-price controls. The economists' scissor normally has two blades, supply and demand. But in questions of stabilization policy, that often is not the case. Monetarists want to stop inflation from the demand side only, and inertialists concentrate

vii

their attention on the control of costs and prices. There could not be a sharper contrast.

The recognition of inflation inertia is not new to some readers. The Brookings panel on economic activity has long been a forum of this approach. Students of Arthur Okun and James Tobin will remember those two's insistence that the Phillips curve is "very flat," meaning that it takes massive increases in unemployment through demand contraction to bring about even a minor reduction in the inflation rate.[1] Indeed, in 1980, under the almost Latin American title, "Inertia, Expectations and Structural Inflationary Bias," Tobin argues that it would take a decade of high unemployment to bring down U.S. inflation from its double-digit levels. As it turned out the job was done much faster and at much lower cost.

The inertia hypothesis makes for powerful politics, Roberto Campos has said that incomes policy is the aphrodisiac of politicians, and he may have understated his point. For more than a quarter of a century Latin American policy makers have been fighting inflation halfheartedly, mostly from the demand side, sometimes from the supply side. Suddenly, in the 1980s a new generation of economists proposes a coherent program of "heterodoxy": correction of fiscal deficits to pay attention to demand side problems, combined with incomes policy to stop inflation dead in its tracks. The attraction of the approach is twofold: first, incomes policy has always made for good populist politics. Second, it offers immediate results, since an inflation of 200 or 300 percent will stop from one day to the next. And there is a bonus: the heterodox approach predicts that inflation not only can be stropped, it also can be stopped with out recession.

The heterodox hypothesis has been tested in Argentina, Brazil, and Israel. The Israeli experience, after more than two years, can be pronounced a full success. Inflation has been reduced to European levels, and growth has continued throughout. The insistence in this book that heterodoxy is better than monetarism is fully vindicated by this experience. But the case of Brazil dramatizes that the demand side does matter. When incomes policy was combined with election politics that led to a massive fiscal deficit, the predictable consequence was a collapse of the Cruzado Plan. Argentina's experience has been more favorable. Inflation has been sharply reduced, but the remaining rate of 100 percent points to the need for further budget control before the next attack is staged.

What lessons are to be drawn? Should Mexico go the way of heterodoxy, or should inflation be attacked by tight monetary and fiscal policy, without incomes policy. The analysis presented in this book and the experience of Argentina and Israel clearly suggest that incomes policy should be a central pillar of stabilization. But the Brazilian experience indicates that the political euphoria of inflation stabilization removes the danger signals and hence makes overexpanding all too attractive.

Since this book was completed, the 1986 Cruzado Plan has literally blown up. Inflation in Brazil reached unprecedented levels of 20 percent per month and more in early 1987. The authors took over Brazilian economic policy in May 1987, when Bresser Pereira was nominated finance minister and Nakano joined him as chief economic advisor. Predictably, they have tried to stabilize the economy using incomes policy. The results are not in, but this valuable book offers their thinking. Much of what they will implement is already written here, but with one difference: the extra year of experience with the first Cruzado Plan has shown that, although demand side policies may not be everything, neglect them at your peril.

NOTE

1. *See* James Tobin, "Stabilization Policy Ten Years After," *Brookings Papers in Economic Activity* 1 (1980); and Arthur Okun, *Prices and Quantitites: A Macroeconomic Analysis* (Washington: Brookings, 1981).

Preface

Inflation became a central problem for the capitalist economies in the second half of the twentieth century. In the days of the gold standard and competitive capitalism, inflation was a passing phenomenon that characterized either the periods of expansion and the peaks of the economic cycle or the extraordinary upheaval of the economic system caused by catastrophies such as wars. Inflation generally alternated with periods of deflation during recessions.

However, once we entered the phase of oligopolistic and technobureaucratic capitalism, beginning after World War II and especially since the 1970s when the world economy entered a period of deceleration and crisis typical of a long Kondratieff cycle, inflation began to change. It became chronic all over the world. In some countries, principally the central countries, the rates were still moderate, although they sometimes reached levels of over 10 percent a year. Beginning in 1982, they were reduced at the cost of severe recessive policies coupled with high rates of productivity increase; however, price stability definitely no longer exists.

In many of the underdeveloped countries, the rates rose and established themselves at much higher levels, often above 100 percent. They had to be accompanied by indexation systems that moderated the distortive effects of inflation but, at the same time, accentuated its autonomous or inertial nature, thus making it more difficult to reduce. In the central capitalist countries, as well as in the periphery, the periods of deflation completely disappeared. Now we only have periods in which inflation accelerates or decelerates. Based on this broad evidence and being faced in Brazil with a permanent and accelerating inflation, we started studying inflation and writing some papers on the subject. When our ideas about autonomous or inertial inflation matured, we decided to publish this book, first in Portuguese and now in English.

During the first half of the 1980s, while Brazilian inflation rose from around 50 percent to 350 percent, to be finally stopped by a heterodox shock in February 1986, the theoretical analysis of inflation advanced significantly. Based on the Latin American structuralist theory of the 1950s and on the administered or cost push theory of the 1960s, a group of Brazilian economists criticized the monetarist and rational expectations theories and developed the theory of inertial or autonomous inflation.

The acceleration of inflation in Brazil between 1979 and 1986 did not happen gradually and linearly, but by jumps. In the second semester of 1979, inflation jumped from the 50 percent to the 100 percent level; in 1983, from the 100 percent to the 200 percent level; in the last quarter of 1984, from the 200 percent to the 280 percent level; and finally, on the eve of the shock, from the 280 percent to the 350 to 400 percent level. The theory of inertial inflation was started by making a distinction between the accelerating and the maintaining, or inertial, factors of the level of inflation. The development of the theory of inertial inflation, therefore, was deeply embedded in the Brazilian experience of inflation; however, its application can be much more generalized, including for developed economies. The basic paper, which served as matrix for the theories of this book and which corresponds to its first chapter, dealt with inflation in contemporary—technobureaucratic and oligopolistic—capitalism.

Most of the chapters in this book were first published as essays in *Revista de Economia Política*. When we got together to write Chapter 3 about the accelerating, maintaining, and sanctioning factors of inflation (1983), we decided that we would write additional essays to form a book. Its first edition was published in Brazil in 1984, with the title *Inflação e Recessão*. All chapters were written by both of us, except Chapter 2 (1981) and 6 (1980), written by Luiz Bresser Pereira, and Chapter 7 (1982), written by Yoshiaki Nakano. Chapter 4 (1984a) and Chapter 8 were written for the first Brazilian edition, and Chapter 5 (1986) for the second Brazilian edition. Chapters 1, 9, and 10 were written especially for the English edition between March and September 1986. Dates at the end of each chapter refer to the first publication except for the chapters written especially for this book for which dates refer to the moment they were completed.

The ideas developed in this book were the result of debates with many economists. To Ignácio Rangel, who developed the theory of the endogenous supply of money and gave special importance to administered inflation in Brazil, we owe a special debt. Our friends, Adroaldo Moura da Silva, André Lara Rezende, Edmar Bacha, Francisco Lafayete Lopes, Mário Henrique Simonsen, and Pérsio Arida developed, at the same time, ideas similar to the ones presented in this book. Albert Fishlow was the first economist to propose to us personally, in July 1983, the idea of an unorthodox shock. We both had been discussing this subject since we had written the second chapter of this book (first published in December 1983), and, in the second semester of 1983, we wrote Chapter 3 (first published in July 1984) proposing "the heroic solution to control inflation." We also have a debt to Celso Furtado, André Montoro Filho, Alkimar Moura, Fernando Maida Dall'Acqua, Fernão Botelho Bracher, Geraldo Gardenalli, João Sayad, José Serra, Luiz Gonzaga de Mello Belluzzo, Marcelo Antinori, Marcos Fonseca, Roberto Vellutini, Rudiger Dornbusch, and Werner Baer.

Along the line of thought that was initiated by Ignácio Rangel, we believe that, at certain points, the inverse relation between growth and inflation is more powerful than the direct relation for oligopolized economies like that of Brazil. When there is recession, inflation tends to accelerate rather than diminish because the oligopolistic corporations succeed in increasing their profit margins. At the same time, there is a reduction in the profit margins of the competitive corporations and the agricultural sector, but this reduction does not manage to make up for the increase of the markup in the oligopolist sector. The relationship between inflation and growth is more complex because there are other factors such as the variations in the rate of real wages, in the real exchange rate and in the prices of imported goods, and the measures of "corrective inflation" taken by the economic authorities, which accelerate or decelerate inflation. On the other hand, without underestimating the market, we consider that the administrative factors, derived from the monopoly power of the corporations, the trade unions, and the state, have a decisive importance in the contemporary phenomenon of inflation. In these terms, in this book we try to develop, within the wide boundries of structuralism, a theory of administered inflation that is conditioned by the power of monopoly and of inertial inflation that becomes dominant as inflation reaches high rates, resulting in the appearance of the formal and informal mechanisms of indexation.

Luiz Bresser Pereira
Yoshiaki Nakano

The Theory of
INERTIAL
INFLATION

1

Introduction: Inertial Inflation and the Heterodox Shock in Brazil

The heterodox shocks that were applied in Argentina in June 1985 and Brazil in February 1986 constitute a theoretical and practical alternative to the successive failures of the orthodox policies to control inflation in these countries. On 28 February 1986, Brazilian inflation, which was already at an annual level of approximately 360 percent, was halted by a heterodox shock. This shock consisted of a freeze in prices, wages, and the exchange rate, as well as a monetary reform that substituted the cruzado, which is intended to be strong and stable, for the devalued cruzeiro. This same phenomenon took place in Argentina nine months earlier, on 14 June 1985. In both cases, the economic policy adopted was derived directly from a new development in the Latin American structuralist theory of inflation: the theory of inertial inflation.

The object of this chapter is to make a general analysis of the shock itself, of the theory on which it was based and the way in which it was developed, and of prospects for success of both the Brazilian and Argentine shocks.

When this chapter was written, four months after the Brazilian heterodox shock, everything seemed to indicate that inflation was under control. If these early results are confirmed, and the 360 percent inflation is lowered to a reasonable level with almost no difficulties, economic theory and policy—via the theory of inertial inflation—will have taken a great step forward. Even if inflation resurges, as is happening in Argentina, these experiences in controlling high rates of inflation will have a major influence on future debates on the subject.

The neostructuralist theory of inertial inflation, which served as a foundation for the hetherodox shocks both in Argentina and in Brazil, conflicts directly with the monetarist theory of inflation based on changes

1

in the money supply and expectations. This theory, contrary to the theory of rational expectations, asserts that expectations cannot be easily modified by changes in the economic policy. Regime expectations about inflation work through the power of each economic group to protect its real income; they are based on past inflation and on the imperative of each economic agent to maintain its income share.

———————————————— 1 ————————————————

In the second semester of 1985, after four months of a partial price freeze from April to July, in which Brazilian inflation was artificially maintained at an annual level of 150 percent, it underwent a new acceleration. From a previous level of 200-230 percent a year in 1983-1984, the Figueiredo government left office with inflation at a level of 270 percent a year. At the end of 1985 and the beginning of 1986, inflation jumped from a level of 270 percent a year (almost 12 percent a month) to a new level of about 360 percent a year (about 13.5 percent a month).

When inflation (consumer price index or IPC) reached 16.2 percent in January 1985, and then 14.3 percent in February, the situation had become unbearable. The economic authorities and the president of the republic were learning all they could about the theory of inertial inflation and its implications for policy, which some Brazilian economists had developed at the beginning of the 1980s. The economists had confirmed the success of the monetary reforms and a general price, wage, and exchange rate freeze in Argentina and in Israel. It was becoming more and more clear for everyone that the only way to eliminate Brazilian inertial inflation would be by a general price freeze and a monetary reform, or, in other words, by a so-called heterodox shock. The decision to apply it on 28 February was hastened by the high inflation rate in January, which was reinforced in February.

The decision to apply a heterodox shock was also because of the failure of the recessive orthodox policies for controlling inflation that had been implemented in Brazil, beginning in the second semester of 1980. In spite of a violent contraction in demand, either due to monetary restriction or to fiscal pressure, the inflation rate, after oscillating around a level of 100 percent in the period from 1980-1982, rose to a level of 200 percent a year in 1983 and to 360 percent at the end of 1985.

The basic measures of the Stabilization Plan adopted by the government in February 1986 consisted of: (1) a price, wage, and exchange rate freeze for an undetermined length of time starting on D Day; (2) deindexation of the economy; (3) a monetary reform that introduced a new currency, the cruzado, to take the place of the cruzeiro at a parity of one thousand cruzeiros to each cruzado on D Day, and the establishment of a subsequent conversion scale based on a daily devaluation of the cruzeiro in relation to the cruzado fixed at 0.45 percent; (4) the conversion of contracts made in cruzeiros (wages, rents, school tuitions, mortgage payments, and other obligations) to cruzados via a formula that guaranteed the recomposition of their real average value. All of the other stipulations of the plan were complementary or established exceptions to these four basic guidelines.

The Cruzado Plan fits into a new economic policy that was inaugurated in August 1985, and which is based on the following directives: (1) priority for economic growth near the historic annual rates of 7 percent; (2) renegotiation of the external debt without sacrificing economic growth and without accepting the conditions of the IMF; (3) redirection of public expenditures towards social programs aimed at improving income distribution; (4) solution of the unbalanced finances of the public sector, giving priority to increasing receipts rather than cutting public expenditures.

The general freeze was accompanied by the fixing of prices for the most important consumer goods (almost 500 articles, with prices differentiated according to geographic regions). The prices were formally controlled by government enforcers, but informally by the whole population.

Wages could not be directly converted from cruzeiros to cruzados because of the different months in which wage adjustments were legally due. They also could not be readjusted by taking their peak value (100 percent of past inflation up to that date) on D Day and converting it into cruzados because, in dealing with term contracts, this would imply an increase in real wages. This, in turn, would have made the freeze unviable for businesses because it would strangle their profits. The solution that was found for this problem was a simple conversion table for the wages and benefits received in the six months before the shock that guaranteed the reconstitution of average real wages and, therefore, of the workers' buying power. The nominal wages and other remunerations effectively received between September 1985 and February 1986 were multiplied by a factor that transformed them into the real wages at the prices of February. Their total was then divided by six to obtain the average real wage. An 8 percent bonus was added to this figure to protect wages against future inflation, according to Figure 1.1.

Similar to what happened in Argentina, another conversion table was established to reduce the value of term contracts in general. Corporations

Figure 1.1 Conversion of Wages to Cruzados

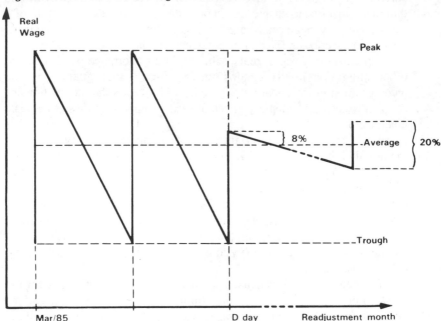

had included their expectations for future inflation in their prices for all term sales. Once prices stabilized, it became necessary to guarantee a discount for debtors that corresponded to these expectations for inflation. A daily table for converting cruzeiros to cruzados established this discount, corresponding to the geometric average of inflation in the last three months before the shock (14.65 percent). For rents, mortgage payments, and school tuitions, special formulas for conversion were established, all of which attempted to reestablish the average real value of the contracts.

The deindexation was not total, thus establishing certain guarantees for the economic agents. Monetary correction was maintained for deposits in savings accounts. The ORTNs (readjustable national treasury bonds), which served as a base for the whole indexation process, were transformed into OTNs (national treasury bonds), but they kept the guarantee of an annual correction. A "movable scale" was established for wages, guaranteeing that they would be readjusted whenever inflation reached 20 percent. When each category of workers has its annual wage negotiations, it will receive a correction equal to 60 percent of the IPC (consumer price index). This readjustment will be considered as an advance in their wages, which will be automatically corrected according to 100 percent of IPC whenever this index reaches the 20 percent trigger point.

—————————————— 2 ——————————————

The abandonment of the use of gradualism in combatting inflation and the adoption of shock measures are based on an analysis of Brazilian inflation that indicates the presence of some essential conditions that would allow for an abrupt interruption of the inflationary process. First, Brazilian inflation was predominantly inertial; that is, prices increased according to past inflation autonomously of pressures from demand or of shocks in supply. Second, given the chronic and inertial nature of inflation, the economic agents developed defense mechanisms with the goal of reaching: (1) synchronization of the readjustments of prices, wages, and the exchange rate; (2) reduction of the lags between readjustments; and (3) equilibrium in relative prices. Third, the public deficit had been significantly lowered in recent years while inflation accelerated. Fourth and last, huge superavits in the international trade balance and increasing international reserves represented a guarantee that the exchange rate freeze would be maintained.

It is not difficult to understand that, if the conditions above are fulfilled, the inflationary process could be abruptly interrupted. The deindexation, the freeze, and the monetary reform act as a synchronization mechanism that imposes a collective, coordinated decision to simultaneously interrupt the elevation of all prices and wages. If there is a perfect synchronization in the readjustments of wages and prices, if the lag between the readjustments is small, and if relative prices are balanced, the freeze would not have redistributive impacts, nor would it violate the laws of the market or, in other words, the law of value. The only function of the freeze would be to eradicate the habit of periodically readjusting prices by erasing the inflationary memory once and for all.

In the absence of the ideal conditions for a perfect synchronization of the readjustment of prices and wages, and the existence of relatively large lags in the adjustments of wages in some sectors, the heterodox shock itself tries to create these ideal conditions through administrative measures. With this in mind, wages and other incomes were converted to their real average value and the expectations for inflation that were built into contracts were neutralized by the monetary reform and the decimal table for converting cruzeiros to cruzados.

The success of the program depended mainly on one condition: that on D Day, 28 February, the freeze did not create any big winners or big losers. Relative prices had to be reasonably adjusted, without distortions caused by the previous sectorial price setting by the government. Aside from this, the lags in the price increases just before D Day had to be small enough so that, on D Day, relative prices were not unbalanced because the last adjustment was closer to or further from D Day.

If there were big winners and big losers, there would have been several correlative implications: the reform would not have respected the law of value; market prices would have deviated too much from production prices; relative prices would have been distorted, benefitting those who had increased their prices recently and penalizing those who had planned to raise their prices soon after D Day; the differences between sectorial profit rates would have increased rather than decreased; and last, wages and other term contracts would not have been converted according to their average real value. If this had happened, the pressure from the losers would have been unbearable, their prices would have to have been readjusted sooner or later, and the stabilization program would fail.

Contrary to what happened in Hungary in 1946 and in Argentina and Israel in 1985, there were no adjustments made in relative prices on the eve of D Day. The prices for the state corporations were not increased because it was thought, perhaps a bit hastily, that most of them had already been adjusted, and because it was wrongly predicted that there would be no operational public deficit in 1986. The cruzeiro, on the other hand, was not devalued before being converted into cruzados, thus not establishing a security margin in relation to the exchange rate in order to withstand a small amount of inflation in the following months.

This predicted fiscal balance came, in part, from a fiscal reform approved at the end of 1985, which increased the tax base progressively. It also came from the Stabilization Plan, which eliminated the real loss of taxes that had been caused by the difference between the moment in which taxes are computed and the moment in which they are paid. For example, in the case of the tax on industrialized products (placed on the consumer), with inflation the government was losing receipts relative to the devaluation of the cruzeiro in a three- to four-month period; with the stabilization this loss disappeared. In 1985, the operational public deficit (public sector borrowing requirements in real terms) was 3.4 percent of the GNP. After the Stabilization Plan, everything pointed in the direction of a deficit in 1986 similar to that of 1985. This kind of deficit, or one even slightly higher, was perfectly consistent with price stability; in 1986, there would be an increase in the real demand for money, which would permit the monetary authorities to issue cruzados without any pressure on aggregate demand. It was estimated that this remonetization would triple the money supply.

Two months later, however, this idea was dismissed, given new projections of a public deficit of around 5 percent of the GDP. The effects of the fiscal reform were not as positive as was previously thought: the decision to not raise the prices in the public sector immediately before the shock was a mistake, and control of public expenditures was somewhat loose.

Given the predominantly inertial nature of Brazilian inflation, the only alternative for controlling inflation was a heterodox shock. An orthodox shock, inspired by monetarist or Keynesian economics, is based on a cut in state spending and an increase in taxes, a drastic reduction of the money supply, an increase in the interest rate, and on a recession, which would have indirectly led to a reduction in wages and in profit margins. This kind of shock would not have been viable for the simple fact that inflation was inertial rather than demand push. It was necessary to break the inflationary inertia, that is, the ability of the economic agents to formally or informally index their prices, thus automatically passing their increases in costs on to prices. Indirect measures that aim to reduce this inertial increase of prices via the market are inefficient, as they present an extremely high cost-benefit relation. Actually, there are only two correct forms for controlling inertial inflation, both of which are of an administrative nature and try to directly control prices. Either a policy of gradually controlling prices, wages, and the exchange rate—in accordance with a declining future rate of inflation—is adopted, or, if the level of inflation is already very high, there is no other alternative to that of a heterodox shock.

The shock is heterodox because it is based on a price freeze and administrative measures instead of market forces to combat inflation. The former do not aim to stabilize prices by correcting, through fiscal or monetary measures, the way in which the market functions, but use direct coordination of economic relations and the imposition of decisions and actions through administrative measures dictated by a central authority. It is also heterodox because it does not provoke a recession. An orthodox shock begins with the assumption that inflation is caused by an excess of demand; for this reason, it is seen as necessary to provoke a recession that reduces demand. The heterodox shock recognizes that the market no longer functions—it no longer maintains stable prices, even though there is no excess demand—and that it is necessary to administer it. In these terms, a recession is unnecessary or even counterproductive. An expansion of the economy makes it easier to stabilize prices; the increase of income and the reduction of total fixed unit costs and the reduction of average variable costs caused by the increase in productivity make it possible to reduce average total costs, and thus neutralize the distributive conflicts.

In Argentina, the economy was already in the middle of a recession when the Austral Plan was implemented. The institution of a very high interest rate to avoid capital flight and hoarding of stocks and a very large, abrupt cut in the public deficit deepened the recession. The Stabilization Plan in Brazil was introduced in a completely different situation—when the economy was in full expansion, the external sector balanced, international reserves high, and public finances relatively under control. Aside from this, Brazil can count on a powerful industrial economy that is internationally competitive and where the opportunities for investment are enormous. For this reason, the flight of capital is a much less serious problem and, thus, does not demand the establishment of a high interest rate. Also, the risk of speculative hoarding of stocks is less in Brazil; this is another factor that helps to avoid high interest rates, because, as there were no drastic adjustments made in public prices on the eve of D Day, the economic agents did not have a special reason to expect a future increase in their prices.

3

The theory of autonomous or inertial inflation, which served as the base for the heterodox shock of 28 February 1986 in Brazil, and previously for the Argentine shock of 15 June 1985, is part of the wider structuralist theory of inflation. Actually, it could be considered as the third paradigmatic moment in the development of this theory. The first moment, which was marked by the works of the economists of CEPAL (the United Nations Economic Commission for Latin America), especially those of Juan Noyola (1956), Oswaldo Sunkel (1958), Celso Furtado (1959), Julio G. Oliveira (1964), and Aníbal Pinto (1973), introduced two basic concepts: (1) bottlenecks in supply that provoke sectorial elevations of prices, and (2) propagating effects of inflation, which spread initial price hikes to the rest of the economy. Mário Henrique Simonsen, who always uses an eclectic approach—both monetarist and structuralist—to analyze inflation, contributed to the theory of propagating effects with his concept of inflationary feedback (1970).

The second paradigmatic moment for the theory of inertial inflation was the publication of Ignácio Rangel's book, *A Inflação Brasileira* (1963). The endogenous nature of the money supply, inflation as a defense mechanism of the economy itself when faced with a chronic insufficiency of demand, and the concept of administered or oligopolistic inflation were the main ideas developed by Rangel.

The third paradigmatic moment for the theory of structural inflation took place at the beginning of the 1980s in Brazil. There are some works dealing specifically with the formulas for indexing wages, which contain some elements of the future theory of inertial inflation: André Lara Rezende (1979), André Lara Rezende and Francisco Lopes (1980), Francisco Lopes and Edmar Bacha (1981), Pérsio Arida (1982). The idea of autonomous or inertial inflation becomes more consistent with the works of Luiz Bresser Pereira (July 1981, 15-20), Adroaldo Moura da Silva (September 1981, 67-75), and Edmar Bacha (1982, ch. 7). In these, the ideas that present inflation as a mere reproduction of past inflation—that it is the result of the formal and informal indexation of the economy and, on a wider level, of the distributive conflict—begin to be defined. In Chile, Joseph R. Ramos (1977) made a pioneer contribution to the theory of inertial inflation, even though he adheres excessively to the problem of inflationary expectations. In the United States, Otto Eckstein made an important contribution to the theory of inertial inflation with his concept of "core inflation" (1981), breaking the inflation rate into three parts: core inflation, demand, and stocks in supply, making an empirical estimate with an econometric model.

The theory of inertial inflation, meanwhile, only became fully developed with the works of Bresser Pereira and Nakano (December 1983 and July 1984a), Francisco Lopes (December 1984b), Pérsio Arida (December 1984), and Lara Rezende and Pérsio Arida (December 1984). Their starting point was the concept of stagflation, that is, of the coexistence of inflation with recession, idle capacity, and unemployment. In order to explain this fact, it was necessary to construct a model of inflation that, contrary to what takes place in the Keynesian models of inflation, (1) assumes, or is compatible with, unemployment and idle capacity, and (2) does not begin from a situation of stability (zero inflation) to explain inflation, but admits that a given or going inflation rate or inflationary tendency exists.

-------------------------------- 4 --------------------------------

In order to construct a model of inertial inflation, a clear distinction—which the conventional literature on inflation does not make, or to which it does not give enough importance—between the factors that accelerate inflation (demand or supply shocks) and those that maintain it (the "trend" or "momentum," or inertial component of inflation) was necessary. By starting with zero inflation, the theories of inflation were always oriented toward explaining the causes of inflation in terms of the causes of inflationary acceleration. This resulted in a debate to determine if, in each concrete case, we were dealing with demand inflation (Keynesian, if the excess demand has a fiscal origin; monetarist, if it has a monetary origin; structuralist if the origin is sectorial), or with administered or cost inflation, provoked by the monopoly power of corporations, trade unions, or the government.

After making the distinction between the accelerating and the maintaining factors of inflation, it became necessary to clarify—when asking about the causes of inflation—if the question referred to the causes of the acceleration of inflation, or to the maintenance of the level of inflation. If one was dealing with the first question, the old debate between demand inflation and cost inflation continued to be valid. However, if one was dealing with the second question, it then became necessary to search for the causes of the autonomous or inertial nature of inflation—to know why past inflation tended to automatically reproduce itself in the present.

As the theory of inertial inflation is an advance or a new conceptual stage of the structuralist theory, it seeks its most profound cause in the distributive conflict. For the structuralists, inflation is a real phenomenon that reflects the economic structure and the power relationship in society; It is a real phenomenon that always has monetary consequences (and eventually causes). The economic agents always try, either individually or in groups, to maintain their share in the income, and, if possible, to even increase it. Also, all try to maintain a positive growth of the GDP. In the process of defending their share of the income, given the current inflation rate, economic agents increase their prices alternately and systematically. If the economy consisted of only three economic agents (A, B, and C), and if the current inflation rate were x percent, then agent A would increase its prices inertially by x percent on the first day of the month, B on the tenth, and C on the twentieth, thus causing A to increase its prices by x percent (as long as there is no new accelerating factor) on the first day of the following month, and so on. If any one of the economic agents were to stop increasing its prices, its share in the income would be reduced. All of them would be facing the prisoners' dilemma.

In his detailed model of inflation, using a Phillips curve augmented by expectations, Milton Friedman made a distinction between accelerating factors and inflationary tendency. However, as he understands inflation to be an essentially monetary phenomenon, he attributed inflation, its acceleration, and its "trend" (inertia) directly to the behavior of the money supply and indirectly to the expectations related to this money supply. As a result, the distinction between accelerating factors and maintaining factors losses its clarity, as they are all explained by the same cause: the money supply. On the other hand, by reducing the whole problem of inflation to the money supply, the monetarists, and especially the followers of the theory of rational expectations, turned inflation into a problem of expectations, and thus into a psychological problem. The determining factor for inflation became the expectations of the economic agents in relation to the money supply.

Because inflation is an economic problem, and because economics is a social science, it is a tautology that inflation is based on the behavior of individuals, their expectations for the future, their attempts to face uncertainty, and on making the most of the profits or wages they receive. Meanwhile, it is far from clear that these expectations can be easily changed by means of economic policy. Also, it is not certain that the expectations of the economic agents influence their behavior to the extent that these expectations are confirmed in practice. There are many expectations that never materialize. Albert Hirschman once defined disappointment, so common among people, as a kind of mistaken expectation. He added that "it is much more common for expectations to exceed reality than for reality to exceed expectations" (1982, 13). Because of this, the economic agents know that they cannot take their expectations too seriously.

As opposed to what the monetarist economists assert, inflation is not essentially a monetary or a psychological phenomenon, but rather a real phenomenon with monetary consequences (and, eventually, causes). Inflation is a real phenomenon directly related to the distribution of income and to class conflict. Actually, monetarists underestimate the tendency of the economic agents to defend their share of the income, because the latter base their expectations principally on past inflation, which is concrete. Instead, the monetarists believe that these expectations can be changed as a result of economic policy decisions.

According to the theory of inertial inflation, expectations are relevant, but they are based on past inflation and are a consequence of the distributive conflict. Living with chronic inflation, the economic agents try to replace their peak real income, because inflation continually corrodes the buying power of their nominal income. But it is impossible to guarantee everyone's peak real income; it is inconsistent from a distributive viewpoint, since income would then have to be greater than the product. Inflation is a mechanism that makes the distribution of income consistent via a real average income that is less than the real peak value.

In this sense, there is a radical divergence between the neostructuralist theory of inflation, based on the real distributive conflict, and the theory of rational expectations, or the Phillips curve augmented with expectations, which uses the idea that inflation is a psychological phenomenon that depends on the way the economic agents change their expectations in response to changes in the regime of economic policy.

The higher inflation is, the clearer the income effects of price increases become for all of the economic agents: the monetary illusion disappears. As a result, the distributive conflict becomes sharper and inflation more and more inertial. In the cases of hyperinflation—the study of which was very important for the formulation of the theory of inertial inflation—the inertial component of inflation becomes absolutely dominant (L. Yeager 1981). On the other hand, the dissynchronization of price increases becomes minimal and relative prices reach a reasonable balance in which no one gains or loses with inflation. Price increases become almost simultaneous. The differences between peak prices and real average prices almost disappear. For this reason, any significant exogenous factor—such as a monetary reform accompanied by the obtaining of foreign loans that guarantee the fixing of the exchange rate, as happened in the Central European countries after World War I—allows for the immediate elimination of inflation without the need for a price freeze. Taking the viewpoint of the theory of rational expectations, Sargent (1982) mistakenly attributed the end of hyperinflation to the change in the economic policy regime. Actually, inertial inflation reached such dimensions, and the time lag between price increases became so small, that inflation lost any redistributive effect and, therefore, its reason for existing. The exogenous change in economic policy was just a signal for the economic system that was ready and anxious to stop hyperinflation as long as the exchange rate was kept stable.

------------------------------ 5 ------------------------------

In the theory of inertial inflation, the money supply is considered to be a factor that sanctions inflation. The endogenous nature of the money supply was advanced by Wicksell, Bortkiewicz, Schumpeter, Keynes, and Joan Robinson in the 1930s (see Gerald Merkin, 1982), but in a very imprecise form. This idea was finally fully developed by the structuralist economists, particularly by Ignácio Rangel (1963). More recently it became popular among the post-Keynesian economists, mainly because of the contributions of Nicholas Kaldor (1970). In a capitalist economy, the need for money comes from the very process of production and capital accumulation. Basic contractual relations, such as those of wages, are fixed monetarily, and business firms and consumers need to have monetary resources and access to credit in order to make their transactions. As the value of production expands, whether because of an increase in quantity or because of an increase in prices, the demand for money increases. When business firms decide to invest, the expansion of credit is also unavoidable. In both cases, the result is an expansion of the money supply, either through the utilization of the monetary reserves of the banks and the creation of cash deposits, or by the simple issuing of money by a central bank as a form of financing an eventual budget deficit. Given the exchange equation and assuming a relative stability for the income velocity of money and the accomodative economic policy of the authorities, an inertial increase of prices necessarily leads to an increase in the money supply. It is undeniable that a central bank has or may have some role in the control of the money supply, especially through control over banking credit. But a reduction in the real money supply, that is, a nonaccommodative economic policy, leads to a crisis in liquidity, an increase in the interest rate, and to recession. This situation never lasts for long. In order to avoid a crisis and a financial collapse, the economic system tries to defend itself by increasing the nominal money supply, either directly through pressure on the monetary authorities, or indirectly through the endogenous mechanisms of the banking system, or even by creating substitutes for money in intercorporate transactions. Faced with the need to create a nominal money supply in order to prevent a reduction in the real money supply, and thus to make the volume of current production viable (macroeconomic reason), and given the liquid assets that the financially healthy corporations have at their disposal (microeconomic reason), the banking system automatically expands the nominal credit supply either by taking recourse to its idle monetary resources or by pressuring the central bank.

Naturally, there are special cases in which an increase in the money supply can transform itself into an accelerating factor for inflation. If the government decides to act in a populist way and finance its public deficit by issuing money or, more precisely, by making a real increase in the money supply, the resulting acceleration of public and private investment (given the reduction in the interest rate), would lead the economy to full employment and to a classic demand push inflation. It must be made clear, however, that the simple existence of a nominal public deficit financed by an increase in the nominal money supply does not transform this increase into an accelerating factor for inflation. Even though the money supply increases in nominal terms in order to maintain the real money supply, it will be a factor that merely sanctions inertial inflation.

—————————————————— 6 ——————————————————

Naturally, there are numerous points in common between the neostructuralist theory of inertial inflation and the post-Keynesian theory. Their basic agreement is on the endogenous nature of money. The Kaleckian theory of oligopolistic pricing based on direct costs plus a profit margin, the latter being determined by the degree of monopoly, is another point in common between the post-Keynesian and structuralist schools. Actually, the markup theory of prices that implies that prices are indexed to past prices, especially the wage rate and the exchange rate, composes the nucleus of the inertial theory of inflation. In the post-Keynesian model, however, there is no distinction between accelerating factors and maintaining factors, there is no adequate explanation for stagflation, and the distributive conflict does not receive the same emphasis. Shocks in supply are almost exclusively related to real increases in wages above productivity, thus ignoring or underestimating the oligopolistic increases in profit margins, the measures of "corrective inflation," and the differentiated behavior of the prices of the agricultural goods and mineral raw materials.

The distinction is also clear on the level of economic policy. While the monetarists are fundamentally oriented toward controlling the money supply, and the Keynesians to managing fiscal policy and income policy (thus admitting the importance of the distributive conflict), the neostructuralists emphasize administrative controls of prices, wages, and long-term policies.

If inflation is inertial, if it is not the result of an excess of demand but rather of the ability of the economic agents to automatically pass on increases in their costs to their prices, the natural way to break this cycle is administrative price controls. This solution becomes even more natural when we learn that this ability to automatically reproduce past inflation in the present would become greater, not only as inflation is higher, but also as the market for goods and services and the labor market are oligopolized and the degree of intervention of the state is increased.

Administrative wage-price controls can be carried out either gradually, in keeping with a partial deindexation through a forecast declining inflation, or abruptly, via a general freeze of prices, wages, the exchange rate, and a monetary reform. As long as inflation is at relatively low levels, it is still possible to think in terms of gradual administrative controls. However, when inflation reaches high levels (more than 300 percent in Brazil, and more than 1,000 percent in Argentina and in Israel), the only choice for abruptly cutting inflation is a freeze.

The first economist who perceived the need for an administrative type of shock treatment in order to eliminate inflation was Octávio Gouveia de Bulhões, when, at the beginning of 1983, he proposed a total deindexation of the economy. Deindexation is an administrative measure. However, as he is a monetarist and does not make use of the theory of inertial inflation, he opposed a freeze, preferring to support deindexation along with a radical reduction of the money supply.

The proposals for a freeze and deindexation are natural results of the theory of inertial inflation. Because of this, as soon as, or immediately after, the theory was formulated, proposals formulated by these previously mentioned economists appeared. Bresser Pereira and Nakano (July 1984, 123-124) proposed a "heroic solution for controlling inflation," with the choosing of a D Day for a general price freeze. Francisco Lopes (August 1984a, December 1984b) introduced the expression "heterodox shock" and made a more complete proposal along these lines, which would later serve as the main theoretical source for the Argentine and Brazilian shocks. André Lara Rezende (September 1984, 1985) and Pérsio Arida (December 1984, 5-18), both separately and together (December 1984), proposed a "monetary reform" and an "indexed currency." Mário Henrique Simonsen (November 1984) supported and further developed the original proposal of Lara Rezende. Antonio Dias Leite (January 1985) presented a proposal for "overcoming inflation in 100 days." Eduardo Modiano (1985) made a formal proposal for converting wages to an average real wage. Last, Rudiger Dornbusch (1986) proposed a freeze maintaining deindexation.

There is not enough room here to describe each one of these proposals. Taken together, they served as the base for the Austral Plan and the Cruzado Plan. In the Argentine case, there was more preoccupation with correcting relative prices and with the public deficit at the time of the shock, as had been the case in Hungary in 1946 (see Bomberger and Makinem, 1983, and Hegedus, 1986). In Brazil, the major preoccupation was with guaranteeing distributive neutrality via several formulas for conversion. In Argentina, the economy was in a recession; in Brazil, it was expanding. In both cases, however, the heterodox shock was based on the choosing of a D Day to end inertial inflation through a general price freeze. In this way, Brazil avoided the deep recession that an orthodox policy (either gradualist or by shock) for eliminating such high inflation would have provoked. Argentina was not as successful because its economy was already in recession when the shock was applied.

Now, the important question is if both of the stabilization plans will be successful or not. The orthodox economists are generally skeptical or else they pretend that there was not a heterodox shock in both countries, but rather an orthodox one. The structuralist economists are confident, because in both stabilizations, as well as in Israel, they see a confirmation of their theory of inertial inflation.

In Brazil, after four months of the Cruzado Plan, inflation was under control and prices had stabilized. In Argentina, after fourteen months of Austral Plan, inflation was 70 percent a year. The recession in Argentina was already underway before the shock; recent information indicates the beginning of a recuperation. In Brazil, there have not yet been any signs of a recession, although the interindustry conflicts over the discounts in credit sales could create obstacles to production. In both countries, meanwhile, the freeze has not yet been suspended—in Brazil, because it is still very early; in Argentina, because the government does not feel secure enough. Of course, the important question is to know what will happen after the end of the price freeze.

In terms of the inertial inflation theory, the first big risk for the plan is that the shock was not neutral enough from the distributive point of view on D Day. The second big risk is that the distortions of relative prices, which express the lack of distributive neutrality, would increase instead of decrease during the period of the freeze. In the event that these two problems converge, inflation would start to accelerate again at the moment the freeze was suspended because it had become insupportable. In Argentina, between March and June 1986, monthly inflation averaged 4.5 percent (70 percent a year). The first devaluation of the austral, of 3.75 percent, was announced at the beginning of April, anticipating monthly devaluations for the next two months of 2 percent. This relative failure is mostly a consequence of the Argentine government's delay in correcting relative prices. Certainly the public deficit and excess demand cannot be blamed for the resurgence of inflation.

No matter how inertial inflation is, on D Day there will always be some imbalance in relative prices because of controlled prices or exceptional behavior in the supply or demand of certain goods in the period immediately before the freeze. These imbalances will be frozen along with prices and, moreover, will become more visible. On the other hand, all of the formulas and tables for converting long-term contracts into australs or into cruzados will not prevent, at the start, those imbalances from increasing rather than decreasing, because of lags in the price increases and the fact that D Day is an arbitrary day among the differently timed price increases. Even though there is an attempt to convert prices to their average value and not to their peak value, there are always some prices that cannot be converted in this way or that were imperfectly converted.

In order to have an idea of behavior of relative prices in Brazil, Figure 1.2 (Fernando Maida Dall'Acqua, 1986) shows the dispersion of the annual growth rates of the main price indices collected by the Getúlio Vargas Foundation for the period from October 1982 to February 1986. It can be clearly observed that the periods with small differences in the growth rates of the relative prices, when there is a predominance of the inertial component, are followed by periods with temporarily distorted relative prices, during which the effects of shocks in supply, maxidevaluations, and corrective inflation spread through the price system. Certainly, as can be observed in Figure 1.2, between the third and fourth trimesters of 1984, there was a period of purely inertial inflation. The fluctuations in the inflation rates from one month to another in this period can be explained by seasonal effects. It can also be noted that, in February 1986, there was a large dispersion in the inflation rates. At this point, inflation was clearly passing through a phase of acceleration.

Table 1.1 only takes industrial prices into consideration, because the prices for agricultural goods and raw materials fluctuate intensely. Using the standard deviation for the analyzed inflation rates as an approximate measure of the dispersion of relative prices, it can be confirmed that the third and fourth trimesters present the smallest standard deviations, and that February 1986 showed an enormous dispersion in relative prices because of the shock of agricultural prices. This information suggests that the structure of the postfreeze relative prices should generate a dispersion in the sectorial profit rates that is inconsistent with a satisfactory long-term performance for some sectors. This means that the freeze should not last long, and that a zero inflation rate is an unattainable goal. Before the end of the freeze, however, prices should be administered, using the real prices of the second semester of 1984 as parameters.

In Brazil, in the days following the shock, there were two themes that dominated discussions. One was the maintenance of the average buying power of the last six months in the conversion of wages from cruzeiros to cruzados; the other was interindustrial relations, because there was a need for the corporations selling on credit to offer a discount relative to the inflation that was built into their selling prices. As for wages, although it was naturally difficult for the workers to accept the conversion of wages based on the average real wage rather than on the peak real wage, it seemed to be sufficiently clear that there had not been any loss for wage earners.

Figure 1.2   Dispersion of Relative Prices (%)

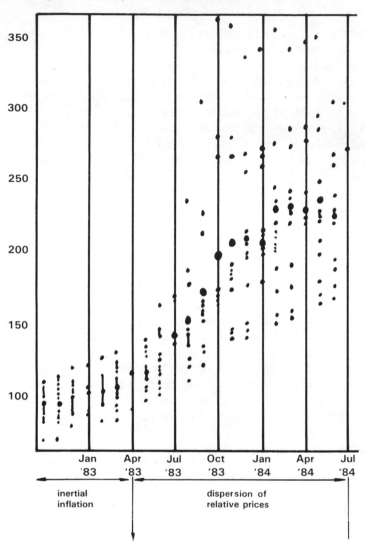

shock**s**: agriculture, exchange maxi-devaluation,
corrective inflation

Annual growth rates of the main price indicators of the economy (Consumer goods,
durable and non-durable; Capital goods, machines, vehichles and equipment, non-
edible raw materials, construction material, agricultural products, industrial products,
Cost of living index-Rio de Janeiro, National Index of Civil Construction, General
Price Index (IGP)

Source: Fernando Maida Dall'Acqua, 1986

18

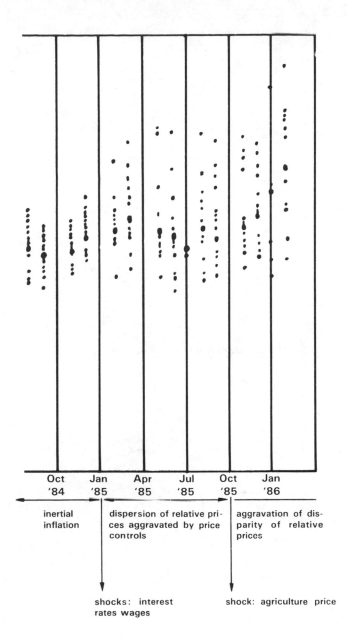

| | Oct '84 | Jan '85 | Apr '85 | Jul '85 | Oct '85 | Jan '86 |

inertial
inflation

dispersion of relative prices aggravated by price
controls

aggravation of dis-
parity of relative
prices

shocks: interest
rates wages

shock: agriculture price

Table 1.1 Annual Growth Rates for Industrial Prices (%)

	1984			1985			1985/86
	Jan/Apr	May/Aug.	Sept/Dec	Jan/Apr	May/Aug	Sept/Nov	Dec/Jan
Extractive Minerals	242	213	225	252	202	170	171
Transformation							
Metallurgy	206	210	201	210	199	216	228
Mechanical	171	211	222	260	248	244	247
Electrical Material	166	191	205	244	220	234	249
Transport Material	143	166	194	220	179	185	188
Furniture	167	190	237	297	335	327	307
Paper & cardboard	197	221	267	289	241	187	184
Rubber	173	186	219	228	214	185	168
Chemical	240	231	230	258	205	175	171
Fuel	260	221	204	244	185	156	157
Textile/clothes shoes	193	236	240	255	255	264	282
Drinks	169	195	230	257	241	257	259
Food products	232	235	223	253	228	219	303
Average	197	208	222	251	227	216	224
Standard deviation	35.1	20.0	18.7	23.2	38.7	45.0	52.0

Source: Fernando Maida Dall'Acqua, 1986

The shock maintained the relation between wages and profits more or less unaltered.

The problem of interindustrial relations is more complicated, since the government decided neither to distinguish the imbalances in the relative prices on D Day from the supervenient imbalances resulting from the inflation built into the term contracts, nor to establish a clear rule for the discounts for new supplies of merchandise sold on a credit basis. Instead, it intended to let the market resolve these two problems together through discounts freely set between the corporations. The result of this policy could be favorable, finally reducing the imbalances in relative prices, but it is more likely that it will be negative, increasing these imbalances. In the same way in which a conversion formula was set for the long term contracts in force on D Day, a formula for calculating a minimal discount for new supplies should have been adopted. In the first month after the Cruzado Plan was implemented, interindustrial relations continued to be tense: wholesalers and retailers were not accepting the discounts offered by industry; there was a shortage of merchandise in stores at the same time in which stocks were accumulating in factories. The difficulties, however, seemed to be resolved more easily than expected. As opposed to what happened in the Argentine economy, the Brazilian economy was in full expansion at the time of the shock. In spite of the interindustrial difficulties, this expansion continued after the shock, stimulated by the higher wages (since many corporations went against the conversion formula and did not reduce nominal wages when the formula called for this), by the transference of income from banks (which lost their income from cash deposits) to firms and consumers, and by the monetary illusions of the consumers. Actually this strong expansion is helping to solve the interindustrial distributive conflict, while creating demand push inflationary effects. In July 1986, the Brazilian authorities implemented a package of policies to try to control the excess consumption.

Strictly speaking, a general freeze of three to six months should be enough to break inertial inflation. A freeze for a longer period could only be justified if, during this period, the government succeeds in diminishing the imbalances in relative prices through a judicious administration of prices, and thus prevents the shock from representing large losses for some and large gains for others. It is important to note that this administration of prices is inconsistent with the goal of zero inflation for which the Brazilian government aimed just after the shock. A small amount of inflation resulting from the increase of the outdated prices is necessary. Zero inflation would only be feasible if the increases in these outdated prices were compensated for by a decrease in the prices that were changed more recently, or else if there was a large deflation in the first month.

Obviously, neither of these two alternatives is realistic. In Brazil, deflation in the first month was only 0.11 percent. In April, the second month, there was a positive inflation of 0.78 percent. The average monthly inflation up to July was around 1 percent.

In any case, the freeze cannot last long. In the first months after the shock, it would be theoretically possible to decrease the imbalances in relative prices by administrative means. In the long run, however, the risks are very great that administering prices, instead of letting them be controlled by the market, would increase rather than decrease those imbalances. For this reason, it will be necessary to suspend the freeze in time, preferably gradually, and definitely before this suspension can no longer be decided by the government but instead becomes an inevitability, imposed by the market itself, which was violated during the freeze.

As was expected, the stabilization of prices provoked a greater demand for money. The economic agents no longer needed to recycle their money quickly, preferring instead to increase their cash deposits. As a result, in the period of February-June 1986, demand deposits in the banks (commercial private banks and commercial public banks) increased 216.5 percent, the monetary base increased 134.0 percent, and the money supply (M1) 185.1 percent. For a while, until the remonetization of the economy is completed, the issuing of currency could help to finance the public deficit in a noninflationary way. It is difficult to determine the new ideal level of money with which the economy can operate. If the growth of the money supply provokes an excessive lowering of the interest rate and pressure on demand, these would be signs that it is necessary to interrupt the remonetization process. For the moment, even though there may be some excess demand, the real interest rate for depositors is being maintained at approximately the same level as before the shock: 15 percent per annum.

One month after the shock, concerns about the public deficit returned. The projections for the operational public deficit (public sector borrowing requirements in real terms) fluctuated between 3.5 percent and 5.4 percent for 1986, showing that the fiscal reform of December 1986 was not enough to balance the public budget. This deficit could be financed with the internal savings of the private sector, but it is a cause for concern in the sense that the private sector is also showing signs of wanting to recover investments. In this case, there would be fewer resources available for the public sector, thus allowing for a substantial increase in the interest rate. The compulsory loans on gasoline consumption, sales of cars, and international travel imposed in July were aimed at solving this problem.

In any case, the conditions necessary for the success of the Cruzado Plan are clear. Actually, the plan is already an extraordinary success, a great conquest by theory and economic policy. The predominantly inertial nature of Brazilian inflation before the shock is indisputable. Although the plan deserves some criticisms, especially for not having regulated interindustrial relations, it was definitely carried out with technical competence. However, there are still many decisions to be made until the moment arrives in which the market can go back to regulating the economy.

July 1986

— PART 1 —

The Political Economy of Inflation

2

Inflation in Oligopolistic and Technobureaucratic Capitalism

Inflation has accelerated and taken on new characteristics in contemporary capitalism, that is, in oligopolistic and technobureaucratic capitalism. In short, instead of being merely a monetary phenomenon, inflation has become an intrinsic element of the economic system not only of the underdeveloped countries, but also of the central countries. In this chapter, I will try to make a general analysis of the new inflationary processes. I would especially like to call attention to "administered inflation," which is administered both by large corporations and trade unions with monopoly power, and to "inertial inflation"—the reproduction today of past inflation, given expectations, and the distributive conflict in which economic agents are permanently engaged. Next, I would like to look at "compensatory inflation," which is caused by the pressures exerted on the government to guarantee the rate of accumulation and to compensate economic agents for the eventual losses caused by the recessive phases of the economic cycle. Last, I would like to look at "corrective inflation," which is produced by the government when it tries to correct the distortions caused by its own economic policy. A dialectic is set up between these three types of inflation, which, when added to structural inflation, turn inflation into a phenomenon inherent to oligopolistic capitalism or technobureaucratic capitalism, a social formation characterized by large companies, big trade unions, and the high salaries of the top executives.

This chapter is divided into fourteen sections: (1) the new inflation; (2) the exchange equation and the monetarist view that attributes inflation to the increase in the money supply; (3) the causes of the direct increase in prices that are validated by an increase in the money supply: Keynesian or demand push, structural and administered, or cost push accelerating factors of inflation; (4) a new fact: market power; (5) the neoclassic "firm" and the modern "corporation"; (6) administered inflation, markup pricing policy, and the inflation rate; (7) the idea of inertial or autonomous inflation as a result of the struggle for distribution; (8) the oil shock or inflation administered by governments; (9) the transformation of direct increases in the money supply into an endogenous variable and to the distortions caused by the economic policy that cause the state to have an unbalanced budget: compensatory inflation; (10) the political factor: inflation and legitimacy; (11) compensatory inflation in the context of the economic cycle and corrective inflation; (12) summary; (13) the recent Brazilian experience; (14) monetarist economic policy compared with administrative policy.

1

In the last ten or fifteen years, since the international capitalist system began to show the first signs of the crisis, which finally broke loose in 1973, inflation has accelerated on a worldwide level. At the same time, it took on new characteristics that suddenly made old theories obsolete. These new characteristics had been taking form for some time, but it was only at the end of the 1960s that, in the central countries, two things happened that created the need for a new explanation of the phenomenon of inflation. These two events were: (a) the coexistence of inflation and stagnation, and (b) a decisive increase in the average rate of inflation in the central capitalist countries. For years, these rates were in the range of 1 to 4 percent; then, suddenly, they tripled or even quadrupled. Double-digit inflation rates, which had been the exclusive privilege of the underdeveloped countries, became normal in the central countries. In other words, the obvious correlations of the ascendent phase of the economic cycle with inflation, and of recession (the declining phase of the cycle) with deflation, were no longer prevalent. We began to have inflation in all phases of the cycle, and now it can even accelerate during recessive periods.

After the classic analysis of Ignácio Rangel (1963), it was not only verified that in Brazil this correlation did not exist, but also, in the period 1960-1980, it was inverted. Shorter periods aside, inflation tended to decrease during prosperity (1967-1973) and to increase during recession (1960-1966, 1974-1980). Seventeen years have passed since Rangel's pioneering work, and history has only confirmed his fundamental analysis.

During this period, in Brazil as well as in the other underdeveloped countries, the average inflation rates also tended to increase. Although the inflation rates of different countries fluctuated, they definitely had a tendency to: (1) remain higher in relation to the developed countries; (2)

increase in relation to the previous period; and, (3) accentuate the lack of connection between prosperity and inflation, and between recession and deflation. In fact, the term deflation almost disappeared from the economists' vocabulary as declining prices became so rare as to be almost unheard of. Now what we have are increases or reductions in the rate of price increases, but never decreases in prices, as was common in previous crises of capitalism in the central countries.

Tables 2.1 and 2.2 present the average rates of price increases for five-year periods in some developed and underdeveloped countries.

Stagflation in the United States and the United Kingdom, for example, can be seen in the following data: in the United States, during the period from 1954 to 1958, the average annual per capita growth rate of

Table 2.1   Inflation Rates in Central Countries[a]
(Annual geometrical averages) (%)

Period	Germany	USA	France	Japan	United Kingdom
1955-59	2.1	1.7	5.3	0.6	3.0
1960-64	1.5	1.2	2.9	5.2	2.7
1965-69	2.5	3.2	3.8	5.0	4.2
1970-74	5.5	6.1	7.6	10.6	9.5
1975-79	4.1	8.0	10.0	7.2	15.5

Source of raw data: *Statistical Yearbook*, United Nations (1959 and 1977)
International Financial Statistics, IMF n° 6 (June 1980)
[a] Consumer Price Index used as deflator

Table 2.2   Inflation Rates in Underdeveloped Countries[a]
(Annual geometrical averages) (%)

Period	Brazil	Colombia	Mexico	Portugal	Venezuela
1955-59	22.5	8.6	7.8	1.4	1.4
1960-64	53.5	12.1	2.1	2.4	0.4
1965-69	35.4	9.5	3.0	5.8	1.2
1970-74	19.9	15.1	10.0	13.2	4.0
1975-79	40.9	23.5	18.9	21.3	8.9

Source of raw data: *Statistical Yearbook*, United Nations (1959 and 1977)
International Financial Statistics, IMF n° 6 (June 1980)
[a] Consumer Price Index used as deflator

the GNP was -0.2 percent and inflation was 1.5 percent. At that point, the phenomenon of stagflation did not exist. But in the period from 1969 to 1971, the yearly growth rate of the GNP was 0.7 percent against an inflation rate of 6.5 percent. This difference became even more accentuated in the period 1974-1975, when the annual rates were -1.8 percent and 9.9 percent, respectively. In the United Kingdom, from 1965 to 1969, the real per capita GNP grew only 1.8 percent against an average inflation of 4.2 percent. There we already see a moderate example of stagflation. From 1974 to 1975 there was a real decrease in production of -1.2 percent, together with a yearly price increase around 20 percent. Here the process of stagflation is very clear.[1] In Brazil, it is known that inflation rates accelerated during the cyclical declines beginning in 1962, and have continued to accelerate in new cyclical declines since 1974. Based on the original ideas proposed by Rangel, Marcos Fonseca constructed a graph that clearly shows the inverse relation between inflation and growth in Brazil since 1961 (Figure 2.1).

There are, therefore, clear indications that inflation took on new characteristics in the last ten to fifteen years: (1) the quantitative acceleration of the inflation rates was significant and implied a qualitative jump in the economic process; (2) the phenomenon of stagflation appeared, on a worldwide scale, as prices continued to increase and

Figure 2.1   Inflation and Growth

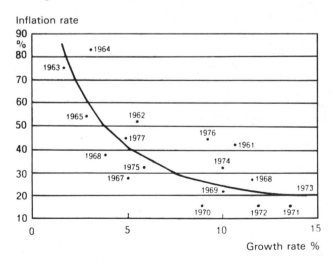

Source: Marcos Fonseca (1979)

eventually to accelerate their rate of increase while the economy itself was declining.

Given these facts, it is not only necessary to find new theories to explain this situation, but also, and more important, to determine the historical facts that cause these changes, which are transforming one of the most ancient economic phenomena in the world, inflation, into a "new inflation." Everything indicates that there has been a change in the very nature of the inflationary process. The old economic texts define inflation as a disproportionate increase in the means of payment in relationship to the national income.[2] The very etymology of the word implies this connotation. Increases in prices were thought to be the consequence of inflation, not inflation itself. It was never asked if an increase in the money supply did or did not cause a generalized increase in prices; this was an undisputed point. The question was to determine the causes of the increase in the money supply.

Today, it does not make any sense to define inflation in these terms. Inflation is simply a generalized and persistent increase in prices: it is the process that makes money lose its buying power. An increase in the money supply can be one of the causes of inflation, but it itself is no longer inflation.

The change in the definition of inflation occurred not because past economists were wrong, nor because their theories were incorrect, but because of new historical facts that modified the nature of inflation, given new decisive factors for the persistent and generalized increase in prices.

---------------------------------- 2 ----------------------------------

For traditional economic theory, whose contemporary representatives are the neoclassic or monetarist economists, the exchange equation explains the whole inflationary process.[3] According to this equation, which comes from the definition of the income velocity of money, V, as equal to nominal income Yp (real income, Y, inflated by the general price index, p) divided by the nominal money supply, M, we arrive at:

$$MV = Yp \qquad 2.1$$

If we admit, in the terms of the monetarist viewpoint, that there is a demand function for real money that is stable or, more simply, that V is constant, and that the money supply increases due to exogenous factors, an increase in M that is more than proportional to the growth of Y would necessarily cause an increase in prices. This would happen, in the first place, because this equation is definitional, making it impossible to discuss the relations between the variables. In the second place, because with an increase in M and V remaining constant, consumers would confront producers with an excess of money—they would try to buy more merchandise than was being produced, and thus would set off an inflationary spiral. Thus, with inflation resolved theoretically in these terms, the only problem the monetarists have is to determine the exogenous, extraeconomic causes for the increase of M. These are easily defined as the incompetence and populism of governments that do not resist pressures from different sectors of the economy; in more sophisticated terms, the increase in the money supply would be the result of governments' attempts to guarantee, through a Keynesian administration of effective demand, that income grew at a rate above the "natural" growth rate.[4]

In this type of analysis, using an impeccable linear logic, its authors forget or dismiss the idea that an increase in the money supply can be considered endogenous to the economic system. It also does not take into consideration that the causal relations between the variables M and p can occur as much in the sense that M determines p as that of p determining M.

If something outside the exchange equation, but endogenous to the economic system, forced prices to increase, keeping V constant, either M would have to increase or Y diminish.

Another way to see the same problem is to look at what would happen to the real money supply given the original rise of p. If one takes the real money supply as m = M/p, then when p increases and M is kept constant, the real money supply decreases. Given that the fundamental function of money is to permit transactions, this would immediately provoke a liquidity crisis. A liquidity crisis either leads to a reduction in the gross domestic product, and therefore to a crisis, or else it forces the government and banking system to increase the money supply. For a period of time, an increase in the income velocity of money, and therefore a process of reducing cash balances, could postpone an increase in M, but in the end the increase of the money supply would be inevitable. It would happen even if the state budget were to continue to be balanced. Faced with a generalized reduction in liquidity and with the menace of a recession, the monetary authorities would be obliged to issue more currency, as well as to release credit, if the banking system did not do this on its own.

It is clear that, in this case, a monetarist could assert that it was the increase in the money supply that "caused" inflation after all, but this would be confusing causes with effects. What we can confirm in this case is that the increase in currency "sanctioned" or validated inflation that had already been unleashed, making the increase in M endogenous. However, monetarist economists do not accept the argument that the increase in the money supply becomes endogenous. As they are used to thinking in terms of "must be" rather than in terms of "is," they argue that economic policy could refrain from increasing M and validating the increase in prices. The continuing recession would then control inflation. In the meantime, we can see that those who are responsible for economic policy do not in fact have this liberty, which could only be granted in terms of the voluntarist idealism of the neoclassicists. On top of that, given the monopolistic practices of the corporations and the trade unions, which refuse to reduce profit margins and wages, this eventual recession does not have the means to control prices, unless it turns into a profound and disastrous depression.

In these terms, although there may be (and in fact there is) a high correlation between M and p at any time in any country, this is not absolute proof that the monetarist theory is correct. We have heard often enough that regression analyses do not establish direct causal relationships. There is no doubt that M can cause an increase in p, as well as that p can cause an increase in M.

———————————————————— 3 ————————————————————

It obviously would be unthinkable to blame the generalized increase in inflation rates and stagflation on the incompetence and populism of governments all over the world. Therefore it would be useful for us to look for the factors that can endogenously and directly determine the initial price increases, which, in turn, provoke an increase in M, which would reinforce an increase in p. But we will not limit our analysis to the historically new factors that directly determine an increase in p, leading to the increase in M. In addition, we will examine the intrinsic and historically new factors that directly determine an increase in M, which in turn causes inflation.

There are three theories for explaining the initial increases in prices, independent of an increase in the money supply: (a) the Keynesian theory, which is based on an excess of aggregate demand over aggregate supply at the peak of the economic cycle; (b) structural inflation, caused by sectorial imbalances between supply and demand; and, (c) administered inflation, caused by the monopolistic power of corporations, trade unions, and the state.[5]

The first and second theories are, like the monetarist theory, based on demand. There is no doubt that in the ascendent phase of the cycle, and especially when, at the peak, the economy tends to reach full employment and full capacity, inflation tends to accelerate because of the pressure of aggregate demand. But it is also clear that this theory does not explain either stagflation or the recent elevation of the inflation rates.

The Keynesian theory of inflation received important empirical corroboration with the research of the British economist A. W. Phillips, who established the relationship between the unemployment rate and variation in the rate of wage in 1958. The Phillips curve shows that as the unemployment rate goes up, the rate of variation in wages goes down. If we substitute prices for wages, we would have inflation caused by the pressure of demand when the unemployment rate goes down. The Phillips curve had immense theoretical repercussions not only because it was based on solid empirical data, relative to inflation in Britain in the period 1861-1957, but also because it permitted the establishment of an "optimum" level of unemployment that would guarantee price stability.

Conservative economists, who reduced Keynesian thought to a neoclassical scheme, imagined establishing a trade-off between an acceptable unemployment rate based on the Phillips curve (which they then called the "natural rate of unemployment") and an acceptable inflation rate. Without realizing it, they were reinforcing the Marxist theory of the industrial reserve army, because they were confirming the utility of unemployment for the capitalist system. But they were also trying to confirm the thesis that recession (or output gap) would cause inflation to slow down. Next, the monetarists, who are even more conservative, found themselves in difficulties and were forced to perform a series of theoretical acrobatics in order to make the empirical data compatible with their own theories. This is because, for the pure monetarist, the Phillips curve should be completely inelastic in the long run. In other words, for them, an inverse relation between the inflation rate and the unemployment rate, and therefore the growth rate, does not exist. The "natural" growth rate would be not only compatible with full employment, but also with price stability. Any attempt to manage the aggregate demand would only be inflationary, instead of raising the long-term growth rate of GDP.

Although this discussion can be very interesting and has attracted the attention of almost all of the economists in the central countries, who are divided between Keynesians and neoclassical monetarists, the fact is that it does not help us to understand the new inflation. As Phillips's data refer to an earlier period, they are about "old inflation," and demonstrate the exact opposite of stagflation. Empirical tests referring to recent inflation do not show a correlation between the unemployment rate and inflationary deceleration. On the contrary, recession tends to provoke an elevation of the inflation rate, especially in highly oligopolized economies like Brazil's, at least in the early phases.[6]

The same thing happens with the structural theory of inflation, as this theory is limited to the problem of bottlenecks in supply and to the mechanisms by which these imbalances spread throughout the whole economy, thus remaining inside the framework of demand inflation. Structural imbalance, which arises from the imperfections of the market, is the fundamental cause of inflation, especially in the underdeveloped countries. Bottlenecks in the availability of certain products provoke price increases in those sectors. In an economy with a well-organized market, these price increases would be corrected quickly, including by falling back on imports, and prices would return to their normal level. In an underdeveloped economy, with poorly structured markets and chronic balance-of-payment problems, it takes a long time to the correct these sectorial imbalances. In the meantime, prices in those sectors remain high. The capitalists in the other sectors, forced to buy goods at higher prices, then try to increase their own prices and the workers to increase their wages, thus setting off the inflationary spiral.

Just as with the theory of inflation provoked by the excess of aggregate demand, the structural theory of inflation does not explain the recent acceleration of inflation rates coexisting with unemployment, that is, stagflation, because it does not supply us with any new information. Quite the contrary, in the underdeveloped countries that are growing, the importance of structural causes tends to diminish as their markets become better structured, thus allowing supply to respond more quickly to the stimulus of demand.[7]

4

Monetarist inflation, Keynesian employment-related cyclical inflation, and structural inflation are therefore perfectly legitimate kinds and causes of the acceleration of inflation. Cumulatively, they continue to explain the inflationary processes that occur all over the world; but, obviously, they do not explain the new inflation. They are all theories that assume demand inflation and, as such, they cannot explain stagflation. Besides, they don't concern themselves with new historical information that explains both stagflation and the decisive acceleration of the inflation rate all over the world.

In searching for new information to explain this new inflation and, consequently, in defining a new theory that takes the new historical processes into account, there seems to be no doubt that the fundamental phenomenon is the growing power of public and private enterprises, trade unions, and the state over the market.

The power of the oligopolistic corporations over the market is a decisive phenomenon of the second half of the twentieth century. Big corporations have been emerging in the central countries since the last quarter of last century, but the oligopolistic sector of the capitalist economies was still secondary to the competitive sector, especially in the United States, Britain, and France. The two countries in which the oligopolistic sector assumed an important role from the beginning of their industrialization—Germany and Japan—were not effectively integrated into the world capitalist economy until after World War II.

In general, the quantitative growth of the oligopolistic sector in central countries and in industrialized underdeveloped countries caused a qualitative jump, as shown by the definitive dominance of the oligopolist or technobureaucratic system over the competitive or market system. One integral part of the monopolistic system is the large, modern, technobureaucratic state, which, aside from its classical political functions of repression and legitimation, assumes the new economic functions of regulating the market and producing goods and services.

This process was also characterized by the advent of the multinational corporations. Just like the large producing and regulating state, multinational corporations assumed their complete form and actually spread all over the world after the end of World War II, completing the process of the internationalization of capital. At first, capital internationalized itself commercially, and then, beginning at the end of the last century, financially. However, it was only in the last thirty years that capital actually internationalized itself in the sphere of production through the multinational manufacturing corporations.

The advent of the multinationals on the international level corresponded to the decisive predominance of large oligopolistic corporations on the national level. It was only after the war that they actually assumed the character of an alternative to the market, although this process had been identified by Marx in the last century as the process of the concentration and centralization of capital. Since then, we have begun to have, in both the central and the underdeveloped industrialized economies, what Galbraith (1968) called a planning system and a market system.

Rather than sectors of contemporary capitalist economies, these systems are alternatives for controlling the economic system. The market system is a competitive system of small- and medium-sized firms that the classic and neoclassic economists take for granted in their economic models of perfect competition. The planning system is the oligopolistic system dominated not only by the large public and private corporations, but also by the large trade unions and the vast regulating state. Corporations and trade unions try to substitute themselves for the market by administering their prices. At the same time, the regulating state, faced with the relative paralysis of the mechanisms of the market, is also forced to substitute itself for it by counteradministering prices through various forms of price controls.

The advent or formation of a planning system has decisive effects on inflation, because it means that the self-regulating market does not exist anymore. It signifies that the basic definition of society would no longer be merely capitalist, based on the self-regulating market, but rather technobureaucratic-oligopolistic-capitalist. At the same time that a new class of technobureaucrats emerges in large corporations, in the state, and also in the large trade unions, the planners substitute themselves for the market. They do this by administering the system of prices, not for the whole economy, but for large, and now dominant, sectors of the economic system.

The formation and recent dominance of the oligopolistic or planning system, and therefore the transformation of capitalism into oligopolistic or technobureaucratic capitalism, is the most general and decisive new fact that can explain the new inflation of the 1970s. The attempts of the oligopolistic corporations and the trade unions to increase their participation in the income by administering prices, interest rates, and wages cause administered inflation. The tendency of the regulating state, which has become the main agent responsible for the rate of accumulation, is to control prices—given the growing incapacity of the market to do this. This, in turn, tends to provoke distortions that cause what we call "compensatory" and "corrective" inflation. On the other hand, prices administered by corporations, unions, and the state make the inertial component of inflation stronger.

—————————————————— 5 ——————————————————

With technobureaucratic capitalism and the dominance of the large corporations, inflation has become a "normal", or everpresent, phenomenon, since the regulating mechanisms of the market do not work as they are supposed to. However, new administrative forms for controlling prices that can adequately substitute for the mechanisms of the market do not appear immediately.

When the orthodox, neoclassical economists think about inflation, they still imagine a competitive market made up of an infinite number of "producers" or "firms." That is the way productive units are presented in the majority of the neoclassical microeconomics textbooks. The expression "corporation" is beginning to be used, but it has no place in the neoclassical world. The neoclassical concept of a firm is still dominant in economics textbooks, presupposing small societies of limited responsibility, or the notion of the producer—that is, of the capitalist businessperson who individually and directly runs his or her business.

In these terms, perhaps it would be more appropriate to differentiate between two types of capitalist economic units, the business firm and the corporation, rather than to speak of small companies and large companies.

The neoclassical business firm is a small unit of production that does not have any market power. It is a unit of production that limits itself to adapting to the demands of the market and attempting to maximize its productive efficiency, which translates into a reduction in costs. A firm is only managed on the production level. On the market level, it does not have any policy on prices, products, trademarks, or advertising, because it has no power to do anything in these areas. A firm has no marketing strategy besides efficiently producing a homogeneous product.

The corporation has a legal definition. In economic terms, however, it may be characterized as a production unit that has market power, which carries out a marketing strategy, has a policy on prices, and tries to set its prices by making tacit or explicit agreements with its competitors, or by setting up areas of monopoly through product and brand differention. It is generally a large production unit. However, the concepts of "small," "medium," and "large" are arbitrary. What effectively distinguishes a corporation is its market power and its ability to formulate a policy on prices, generally based on setting a margin over variable costs (markup).

The planning system is made up of corporations, the units of production with market power. Market power is a decisive factor for inflation because it permits the corporations to maintain their margins and raise their prices automatically, inertially or, in other words, independently of the market, that is, independently of the existence of an excess demand over supply. On the other hand, this signifies that the laws of the market no longer control the economy, which in fact is a tautology, since we defined the planning system, where corporations operate, as the alternative to the market system, where firms still exist.

Summing up, orthodox economic policy, based on controlling the economy through market mechanisms, has lost a large part of its validity. Monetary and fiscal policies, which are based on the self-regulating market, become inefficient because they assume that, if authorities are able to correct the market on the aggregate level (state expenditures and revenues or the money supply), the market will recover its ability to control the economy. Macroeconomic policy continues to be perfectly valid for the maket system, but it loses part of its validity in the oligopolistic system, where market mechanisms no longer function as they should. We will see that, in this sector, the consequences of the macroeconomic policies could even end up being the opposite of those desired.

─────────────────── 6 ───────────────────

The fundamental objective of the price policy of large corporations is to guarantee their profits and, second, to maximize their own expansion, or at least to maintain their participation in the market. Although, in principle, the planned rate of profits has precedence over the expansion rate, corporations are frequently driven to make a trade-off between these two objectives.

In order to understand both the basic phenomenon of stagflation and that of inertial inflation based on the price policy of the corporations, we should imagine the economy entering a recession or a descending phase of the cycle. At this point, corporations are faced with declining sales. In order to maintain their profit rates (profits divided by capital), the obvious alternative is to raise profit margins (profits divided by sales or profits divided by costs). This will necessarily signify an increase in prices because the productivity rate is considered constant for this analysis. If the recession were provoked by restrictive monetarist and fiscal policies, the response of the corporations would be even more pronounced in terms of raising prices and margins. In this situation, macroeconomic policies have the opposite effect of that desired. Corporations can raise their margins and prices because they do not have any direct competitors, or because their competitors accompany them through tacit or explicit agreements. This is how stagflation is set into motion. Acceleration of inflation and recession come together.[8]

The normal response of corporations to recession is not to raise profit margins but to keep them fixed. But even if we make the assumption that margins remain fixed during recession, stagflation, or more precisely inertial inflation, would occur.

Given the market system, what should happen as the economy slows down is not an increase or even a maintenance of margins, but rather their diminution. That is one of the basic assumptions of the orthodox economic policy about inflation. In order to try to maintain their sales, corporations should lower their margins, and thus not transfer the increases in costs on to prices. However, corporations do not belong to the market system. Their logic is the logic of the planning or oligopolistic system. So the fundamental law and practice of corporations in their price policy is that of markup pricing, of adding a fixed margin to direct costs. In this way, the corporation automatically transfers the whole increase in direct costs to prices. Margins remain fixed, and prices rise inertially.

In order to understand this phenomenon, however, it is necessary to add one more variable. The increases in costs and in prices do not all take place at the same time in all of the corporations. They alternate between one corporation and another. This lack of synchronization is a decisive factor. Let us take three corporations, A, B, and C. If these three corporations rigorously and alternately apply the policy of a fixed margin over costs, the inflation rate, once started and established at a certain level, will become permanent. The combination of fixed margins over costs, with alternating price increases, does not necessarily lead to an acceleration of the inflation rate, but rather to the maintenance of a determined level of inflation. Given the maintenance of the margins and the alternating price changes, prices will continue to grow at the same rate at which they were growing before. Any other factor that raises this level, among which could be an elevation of margins, implies the maintenance of this new level.

Thus, we have here the informal process of the indexation of the economy, with the automatic passing on of costs to prices. This is a factor that maintains inflation, or inflationary inertia, keeping inflation from falling independently of aggregate demand.

There is a third factor that should be taken into consideration: the speed with which the corporations change their prices. If this speed, which is measured by the lag between one alternation and another, is increased, it immediately has an additional inflationary effect.

At this point, we could imagine one of the corporations breaking the golden rule of the planned system—that of never getting into price competition—causing what is disparagingly called a "price war." However, unless it is supported by gains in productivity resulting from exclusive technological innovations, a decrease in prices is unthinkable for a corporation, because it knows that its competitors will follow its lead.

Inflation that is the result of the corporations' pricing policies is called "administered" or "cost" inflation. When corporations are only maintaining their margins, they are also maintaining the inflation level, as long as the speed of the price changes is maintained. This is inertial or autonomous inflation. When they manage to increase their margins in order to compensate for a fall in sales, the effect is to accelerate inflation.

However, administered inflation does not necessarily occur only in the recessive phase of the cycle. When there is relative equilibrium between supply and aggregate demand, as well as when there is prosperity, an increase in margins is an alternative that is always available for corporations. Depending on the elasticity of demand, an increase in margins could be especially advisable when the corporations' productive capacity is reaching its maximum level. Once margins are elevated, however, it will be very difficult to bring them down again; it is at this moment that the inertial component of inflation shows its weight. Thus the initial effect of an increase in margins is the acceleration of inflation and the result of fixed margins is the maintenance of inflation.

7

This analysis, especially in respect to what it has to say about the corporations A, B, and C who take turns raising their prices, assumes that inflation has very important distributive effects, making the corporations' pricing policies a form par excellence for conserving or increasing their share in total income. In general, one could say that in the world of technobureaucratic capitalism, made up of corporations, trade unions, and the state, inflation is a pitched battle between corporations, between industrial sectors, between corporations and trade unions, between social classes and even between fractions of classes, and finally between the public and private sectors, in the fight for the appropriation of the economic surplus.[9]

In competitive capitalism, inflation seemed to be an impersonal phenomenon, the result of distortions between supply and aggregate demand, for either monetary or cyclical reasons. It was never the result of isolated economic agents, because neither companies, nor workers, nor consumers were capable of making decisions or of establishing price policies. In technobureaucratic or oligopolistic capitalism, it is clear that inflation is the result of the struggle of economic agents or of associations of economic agents organized into groups, systems, or classes, to increase, or at least to maintain, their participation in the economic surplus.

In this situation, inflation is transformed into a mechanism for transferring income to the sectors that are the strongest economically or the most powerful politically. For example, as the planning system becomes economically more powerful than the market system, inflation becomes an excellent mechanism for the planning sector to appropriate part of the surplus generated in the market sector for itself. In underdeveloped countries, where the workers are unorganized, inflation functions to lower their wages and to assure high profit rates and the accumulation of capital.

However, in underdeveloped countries where the workers have already reached a higher level of political and trade union organization, inflation tends to lose this function. There, the fundamental struggle of workers is to index their wages to inflation and to introduce a productivity clause in the wage negotiation. In this way, they assure their participation in the national income, and their wages are not inflationary . However, as trade unions become stronger (and this tends to happen as the planning system expands), they tend to demand wage increases above inflation plus the rate of productivity. At this point, in view of the threat to profit rates, this also sets off inflation.[10]

It is important to take into account that even if wages are perfectly indexed, inflation can be set off by a change in the corporations' policies. This is partly what happened in Brazil after the passage of the wage law of November 1979. This law simply assured a complete semestral indexation of wages. Indexation already existed before this and, in practice, it was often semestral. But the announcement of the new law led corporations with market power to make preventive increases in their prices. This was a new inflationary factor that set off a discussion of whether inflation is or is not caused by wage policy. Actually, this discussion was not well stated: one of the causes of inflation was obviously not a real increase in wages, because they were not really increasing. But the reaction of corporations with market power to the possibility of a decrease in their profits, as a result of the new wage law, had very clear inflationary consequences. This fact reminds us that, in political economy, given the distributive conflict, what is most important for us to know is not what has already happened, but what the corporations' and consumers' expectations are.

The main thing to note is that, in technobureaucratic capitalism, the economic agents that have the will and the means to influence prices are in constant and direct, if not personal, conflict with each other. It is very different from competitive capitalism, where this conflict is watered down by the impersonality of relations between thousands and thousands of economic agents who have no other alternative than that of adjusting to the conditions of the market. Inflation is based directly on the following struggles: the class struggle, as seen in the conflict between trade unions and corporations; the inter-corporate struggle, between buyers and sellers; the struggle between sectors, as between the financial and industrial sectors; and, finally, the struggle between systems, which is the struggle between the planning and the market systems.

Even the struggle between corporations and consumers, which is unbalanced in favor of the former, is not just a struggle of a few businessmen against powerless, disorganized consumers. Consumers are beginning to form cooperatives and associations, but this is not the most important fact. What is more important is that the state, under pressure from consumers, is frequently forced to set prices for consumer goods. At this point, it takes the side of consumers against corporations. This obviously does not signify that the state is losing its fundamental characteristic of being at the service of capitalist accumulation. It only highlights the relative autonomy that is necessary for the state, which could lead it to defend, within very strict limits, workers against capitalists. This type of action by the capitalist state, which allows it to maintain an appearance of neutrality, is essential for exercising its function of legitimating the existing system of the relations of production. It also serves to emphasize the illusion that the state controls the monopolistic power of corporations.

In the context of this process, the economic agents that are in conflict over the division of the economic surplus try to administer their prices, with an eye to maintaining their participation in the income. Thus, they tend to constantly raise the inflation levels and then to conserve these new levels, giving the whole economic system a tendency toward rigidity.

8

Price administration, with its inflationary consequences, can be carried out by private corporations, state corporations, trade unions, and by the state itself. All that is necessary is for one of these types of organizations to have some power over the market, individually and/or in the form of a cartel, for price setting to be possible, and thus for administered inflation to be established.

However, there is still another possible origin of administered inflation that has taken on decisive importance in the last few years: the administration of prices for exported goods by the states themselves. There had been attempts along these lines for a long time; one example was the international agreements on the price of coffee. But it was only after OPEC's success in quadrupling the price of oil in 1973 that this form of administered inflation on the international level, directly between states, became significant.

The inflationary effects of the increase in oil prices are obvious. It implied an enormous gap between costs and prices; by dealing with a scarce, unrenewable natural resource, it was possible to completely disconnect its price from its value. This increase in margins benefitted not only the oil corporations, but especially the oil-producing states.

The most obvious inflationary effect of the oil price increase is in the corporations' practice of passing increased costs on to prices. There are also workers who consume gasoline, principally lower-level executives and technobureaucrats in all countries, who felt the need to pass their increase in expenses on to nominally higher wages and salaries. Thus, the inflationary spiral was set off, this time called "imported inflation," but which actually was an example of administered inflation, because it was the result of OPEC setting the international price of oil.[11]

The increased oil prices and the subsequent price war between the oil consumers and producers, between the intermediate and final consumers of oil, and also between those who do and those who do not directly use oil undoubtedly played an important role in the acceleration of inflation in the last decade, as well as in aggravating the phenomenon of stagflation. It is important, however, to point out that these last two phenomena had been occurring since before 1973.

In the meantime, the increase in the price of oil did not limit itself to being inflationary by provoking a price war; the corporations attempted to maintain their profit rates and the workers and technobureaucrats to maintain their wages and salaries. It was also inflationary because of its effects on the real and potential national income, the balance of payments, and the foreign debt of each country.

The sharp increase of oil prices provoked a strong deterioration in terms of trade for the oil-consuming countries. This purely and simply means that these countries became poorer; in fact, from that moment on, they had to produce more merchandise in order to buy the same amount of oil. This impoverishment could have been postponed by increasing the external debt of the consumer countries. Some countries could have managed to increase their exports in a compensatory manner by utilizing their idle capacity. All of them tried to counterattack by increasing their own prices in order to reduce their losses in terms of trade.

Although the capacity of the international financial system to recycle petrodollars is great, it is certainly limited. The utilization of idle capacity and the ability to increase exports was possible only for a limited number of countries. Increases in the prices of exports, aside from being very limited, were also counterbalanced by subsequent increases in the price of oil. In view of this, a world recession or, more specifically, the end of a long wave of investments, which had already been foreseen since the beginning of the 1970s, was sparked.

However, contrary to the predictions of neoclassical economic theory, economic deceleration did not contribute to a reduction in inflationary pressure. Corporations had to pass on to prices not only the increase in the price of oil, but also the expectations (and the reality) of a reduction in sales, due to a general, although moderate, recession of the world economy starting in 1974. Increases in, or even attempts to increase, corporations' margins at that point certainly resulted in accelerating inflation all over the world.

—————————————— 9 ——————————————

The state can play various roles in administering prices. It can be a primary cause of administered inflation by increasing its corporations' and agencies' prices, or else by making agreements like that of OPEC. It can also contribute to inflation by its policy of trying to administratively control prices and wages that are the origin of administered inflation, as it ends up legitimating prices higher than the market can allow. In this way, the state, and in particular its agency for controlling prices, is transformed into a substitute for cartels.

The state can also provoke an increase in prices when it decides to set high levels for the interest rate or for exchange rates. We will see that this happens especially when the state is led to engage in a policy of "corrective inflation."

Actually, when the state acts as the administrator of prices, it takes on a very special role. In general, its job is to hold prices down, substituting itself for the market as the only alternative for controlling prices in an economy that is dominated by the planning system. This administration of prices by the state is fundamentally an administration of profits, wages, and salaries. Therefore, it is an income policy. By administering the price of merchandise, the state tries to control the profits of the corporations; by controlling wages, the profits of the corporations and the wages of the workers; by controlling interest rates, the profits of the banks and the incomes of the financial rentiers; and by controlling rents, to control the profits of real estate rentiers.

This control has very defined limits. The state can try to control the big distortions. It cannot try to paralyze price increases at the cost of large distortions in the market. The price of merchandise should maintain its basic relationship to the amount of direct and indirect work incorporated in them. Profit rates, on the other hand, should be relatively equalized between sectors. Put another way, the market prices of merchandise should maintain their basic relationship to the prices of production; any deviation in relation to this parameter should be avoided. In the same way, wages should relate to a given profit rate that is considered "acceptable" and to a given rate of productivity. An increase in real wages, therefore, should necessarily be tied to an increase in productivity, assuming a constant profit rate. In other words, state controls cannot go against the law of value, or rather, cannot provoke serious distortions in the market. These distortions would quickly become insupportable, resulting in the emergence of free parallel markets and/or in a political and economic crisis.

In this setup, the state feels an inescapable need to control rising prices because the market mechanisms are incapable of doing this. Given this, as well as the inherent limitations of control determined by the law of value, or, which is almost the same, by the law of the need for parity in the exchange of any merchandise, another tendency appears at the heart of the state itself. This is the tendency to concentrate the negative aspects of price controls in its own hands; it makes the state assume the losses that come from the rigid control of certain prices.

The state's absorption of these distortions, which seems to be necessary in order to control prices (although they actually aren't), can take various forms. State corporations can inadequately set their own prices, or the state can control certain prices and compensate the producing corporations with subsidies. In any of these hypotheses, the state is carrying out a compensatory policy: it controls the prices of determined sectors within or without the state, and compensates for the losses that occur with ever-increasing transfers of funds. However, the limitations of this type of policy are obvious. The state corporations or agencies that produce goods or services below their value soon have deficits and need to cover these deficits with state funds. On the other hand, the private corporations that receive subsidies become a direct burden on the state treasury.

Similar processes tend to occur with the exchange rate. The exchange rate can be kept artificially high for a certain period in order to prevent an increase in the price of imported goods. Exporters, in turn, are compensated by subsidies, which again are a burden on the state budget.

After a while, the accumulation of these distortions, all of which have repercussions on the state budget, becomes unbearable. At this point, the state can issue money or go into debt internally in order to cover its deficits, with the obvious inflationary consequences. Rather than prices increasing autonomously, causing an increase in the money supply, it is the money supply that increases, causing an increase in prices. This provokes what we propose to call "compensatory inflation."[12]

Faced with an unbalanced budget, the government would perceive the need to eliminate the distortions, restoring prices to their proper places in terms of their value and, therefore, of their true costs. Here would be a policy of "corrective inflation," in which the prices of the distorted sectors are adjusted, because they had been repressed and then compensated for by state subsidies in an effort to balance the state budget.

Corrective inflation will probably accelerate inflation, unless it is extremely well balanced. Actually, it is a new form of administered inflation, characterized by a strong increase in the profit margins of the corporations whose prices had been repressed. As a result, the other corporations and the trade unions, which had already fit their profit rates and wages to the distorted prices, would immediately pass the increases in their costs on to prices, even if aggregate demand is controlled.

This process of compensatory inflation and administered inflation reinforcing each other in a phase of structural imbalance occurred in Brazil between 1974 and 1979, aggravated by a cyclical decline. Inflation in this period grew slowly from approximately 25 percent to 60 percent. At the end of 1979, the decision was made to apply corrective inflation.[13] As this consisted of administering the prices of basic products, it resulted in an explosive increase in prices, raising the level of inflation to more than 100 percent in less than one year.

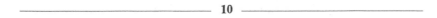

10

This analysis of the behavior of the state serves as an ideal bridge for us in analyzing the role of the increase in M as a cause of inflation. At the beginning of this chapter, we criticized the monetarist theory that states that inflation is caused by increases in M, which, in turn, are caused by exogenous factors (or, in other words, by the demagoguery and incompetence of governments) as simplistic. This does not mean that we should or could discard the idea that the increases in M that originate in government deficits could cause inflation; it is clear that an increase in the money supply above the growth rate of the GDP is inflationary, or at least reinforces inflation.

For example, in Brazil, between approximately 1966 and 1973, the federal budget was basically balanced. Nevertheless, the government was forced to issue money during this entire period in order to guarantee the liquidity of the market. This was because the market was faced with an inflation that obviously was not caused by government deficits and the issuing of currency, but rather by structural and price-control-related factors. Although the data in this respect are very vague given the separation between the fiscal and monetary budgets, everything indicates that, beginning in 1974, the government began to have growing deficits. The fiscal budget remained balanced, but the monetary budget, where more and more subsidies for agriculture based on interest rates tied to a growing inflation rate were concentrated, showed larger and larger deficits. The total economic deficit was finally acknowledged and quantified in 1979, having been estimated at about 5 percent of the gross domestic product.

There is no doubt that, in this case, the government deficit, which forced massive issues of currency, was inflationary. The increase in the money supply was not simply for reestablishing the liquidity of the financial system. It covered not only the nominal public deficit, but financed a real public deficit that sustained the economy near full employment.

In this case, however, can it be confirmed, as the monetarists propose, that the government deficits come from causes that are exogenous to the economic system, specifically from demagoguery or from government incompetence? The authoritarian government of that period certainly cannot be accused of demagoguery. As for being incompetent, it was neither more nor less so than the previous governments; therefore, it also seems unjustifiable to attribute the inflationary acceleration of this period to such a cause.

Actually, this kind of simplistic and personalized reasoning is inconsistent with the dynamics of historical processes. Demagoguery and incompetence can most certainly cause governmental financial instability. On the political level, however, it is necessary to be more careful in examining the processes that lead to this instability. Pressures are put on the government to increase its expenditures from all sectors of society. In societies that are characterized by technobureaucratic capitalism or oligopolistic capitalism, the state is a fundamental agent for the redistribution of income. Through a complex system of transfers, taxes, and subsidies, the state concentrates or redistributes income and harms or helps one class or another, one sector or another, one group or another, one region or another.

These pressures can become unbearable for a government that is politically weak or has no legitimacy in the eyes of civilian society. This happened in Brazil during the Kubitscheck government and especially during the Goulart government; it also took place during the Geisel government. The first two governments were populist democracies, the last a technobureaucratic authoritarian regime; but, all three governments' lack of legitimacy for the dominant classes, whose power is decisive in a civilian society, was clear. This lack prevents the government from limiting expenditures or from increasing taxes, which results in a deficit. At this point, compensatory inflation becomes dominant.[14]

This political analysis of inflation helps explain, among other things, why the plans for stabilization proposed by the monetarist economists are generally only viable in dictatorial regimes, which receive strong protection from the local bourgeoisie and from the interests of international capitalism. This was the case of Brazil between 1964 and 1974, of Chile from 1973 on, and of Argentina from 1977 on. Note, however, that the fact that these plans were possible does not mean that they were successful. Generally, they cause heavy recession and the failure of small- and medium-sized businesses. Also, they only have some success if they are accompanied by the political-administrative measures of wiping out trade unions and strangling wages, which has no support in the monetarist theories. Containment of inflation by democratic means generally not only implies the existence of governments with political legitimacy in the eyes of civilian society and with popular representation, but also acknowledges that an unbalanced government budget is not the only cause of inflation.[15]

—————————————————— **11** ——————————————————

According to this analysis, an unbalanced state budget is sometimes endogenous from a political point of view. Meanwhile, are there any reasons of a more strictly economic type could help explain the unbalanced state budget, making it at least partially endogenous to the economic system as well?

In the ninth section of this chapter, we looked at two fundamental economic causes that are opposites, but which complement each other. On the one hand, there is the need felt by the government to carry out price controls through the state itself, with these controls causing an unbalanced fiscal budget, which then forces it to print more and more new currency, provoking demand inflation. On the other hand, there is the tendency to apply a policy of corrective inflation, which causes cost push inflation.

The first mechanism corresponds to compensatory inflation. We can, however, examine the problem from a complementary angle. The most general cause of the tendency to have an unbalanced state budget is related to movements of the economic cycle. Our hypothesis is that it is in the declining phase of the economic cycle that the tendency toward imbalance is accentuated.

Economic deceleration is immediately and directly reflected in the collection of taxes, especially in underdeveloped countries, where indirect taxes tend to dominate. On the other hand, the vast majority of expenditures that maintain the state cannot be cut back. There may be some flexibility in expenditures for investment, but it is precisely these which should and do tend to increase at this point because of the need to counterbalance the cyclical movement in retraction. The imbalance of the state budget begins to be based on this contradiction: decreasing revenues opposed to the need to maintain, if not increase, state expenditures.

Actually, due to the (historically new) role of the state in technobureaucratic capitalism, fundamentally responsible for private accumulation and as a substitute for the market in the allocation of resources and the redistribution of income, the economic policy of the government takes on decisive significance. In this type of social formation, the state partially substitutes itself for the market in controlling or coordinating the economy. What is expected from the state is that it will limit the cyclical fluctuations that result from pure and simple coordination of the economic system by the market. One would expect compensatory action from the state when there is a declining cyclical movement.

This compensatory action can take place in two fundamental ways. One, obviously, is the Keynesian fiscal policy, which tends to be implemented not only because of the theoretical beliefs of the economists who design economic policy, but principally due to pressure from civilian society. It proposes to increase state expenditures or to cut taxes in order to induce investments, as well as to reduce unemployment and idle capacity. Theoretically, in a situation of unemployment, this policy would not be inflationary; however, if we imagine that certain sectors will reach full capacity before others, it is not difficult to link compensatory inflation to structural inflation.

There is a second, more direct, compensatory action, which is to simply subsidize certain activities or certain types of consumption. In the last analysis, this kind of compensatory action is caused by cyclical decline, as is the Keynesian fiscal policy. Its mechanisms, however, are much more casuistic, and its distortions much deeper. They are more common in underdeveloped countries, but they also occur in developed ones. In the latter, which are characterized by the welfare state, expenditures for social ends tend to increase systematically. The governments are permanently faced with pressure from the society for higher standards of living, and the alternative—private consumption through higher wages—is not only in general more expensive (therefore less efficient), but it also offers fewer opportunities for supplier contracts for capitalist corporations. During the cyclical slowdown of the economy, there is even more pressure to increase expenditures for social consumption.

One of the most common compensatory actions, which is directly related to private accumulation rather than to social consumption, is the sectorial fixation of interest rates below the existing inflation rate. This implies a subsidy for accumulation for that sector whose volume, meanwhile, is indefinite. It increases as the inflation rate increases, given a controlled interest rate. The subsidy is obviously paid from the coffers of the government, whose deficit grows.

Another compensatory action is to reduce the taxes of a sector in the name of economic planning and the need to stimulate that particular sector or region. A reduction in the state revenue is immediate and a deficit inevitable. In the same category, we find the acquisition of corporations that are in the process of bankruptcy because of cyclical retraction. Transformed into the main party responsible for the level of employment, the state has no other choice than to assume, in various forms, these debts.

Actually, in contemporary technobureaucratic capitalism, the state was made responsible for the process of capital accumulation and the rate of economic development. Thus, put at the service of private accumulation, it has no other choice than to continue to make investments itself and to finance private investments, generally by subsidizing them.

In underdeveloped industrialized countries, which tend to be strongly technobureaucratic, long-term financing is generally the direct responsibility of the state, as the private mechanisms for financing accumulation (stock markets and private banking systems, including investment banks) are unable to perform this role. If the state is made responsible for development, and if it directly controls a considerable part of investment through its own corporations, as well as the rest of investment indirectly through long term financing, it has no other choice than to compensatorily maintain the accumulation rate of the system.

Its freedom of action in this process is very limited, because the state is not an organism from outside the economic system or some kind of external regulatory agent, but rather an intrinsic part of the productive and financial economic system.[16] When the economy enters a cyclical decline, the economic policy of the state tends to become even more endogenous and immobilized. It becomes much more the result of the pressures and limitations that come from the system itself than the result of decisions of a relatively autonomous regulatory agent, as those who formulate economic policy claim.

These are characteristics of technobureaucratic capitalism, in both the developed and underdeveloped industrialized countries. They tend to be more accentuated in the latter because private interests are weakly controlled by the state, because the structural inflationary factors related to points of strangulation in supply are more accentuated, because of the frequent lack of legitimacy of governments, and finally because of the pressures that are put on the state to guarantee the accumulation of capital and the level of consumption at any price.

12

All of this analysis can lead us to various general conclusions. First, the acceleration of the inflation rates, and especially stagflation, which characterize the new inflation, are related to the substitution for competitive capitalism by technobureaucratic or oligopolistic capitalism.

Only in this type of capitalism is it possible to have inflation that maintains itself and sometimes even increases in the recessive phase of the cycle.

Second, inflation always has causes that are endogenous to the concrete social formation.

Third, these causes can, in the exchange equation, $MV = Yp$, act both directly on the money supply, provoking an increase in prices, and directly on prices, implying a need to increase the money supply in order to reestablish liquidity.

Fourth, the autonomous increases that operate directly on the level of prices are: (a) an imbalance between supply and aggregate demand at the peak of the cycle; (b) structural inflation; (c) administered inflation.

Fifth, only administered inflation is a historically new factor that can explain this new inflation.

Sixth, administered inflation is a result of the capacity of the large corporations, the trade unions, and the state itself to carry out a pricing policy in technobureaucratic capitalism—particularly in the subsystem that characterizes it, the planning system.

Seventh, this administration of prices makes it clear that inflation can be independent of excess demand. It is the result of an undeclared struggle for the division of the income between corporations, between corporations and trade unions, between corporations and consumers, and between various sectors of the economy.

Eighth, economic agents, in the distributive conflict process, change their prices alternately, one after the other, making inflation autonomous or inertial.

Ninth, the state is always an active, although at times contradictory, member in this struggle for the division of income. It tends to sustain capitalist accumulation, but its policy is the result of the class struggle.

Tenth, in this process, and particularily in the declining phase of the economic cycle, the state tends to intervene in the economy, either by controlling prices or by compensating for the losses caused by recession. In this process of intervention, the state tends to provoke distortions in the market and incur growing deficits, which are covered by an inflationary increase in the money supply.

Eleventh, governments' lack of power, which is a result of a lack of legitimacy (support from civilian society), leads them to carry out a compensatory policy in a generally irrational way, resulting in public deficits and profound distortions in the economic system.

Twelfth, correcting these distortions by using the mechanism of "corrective inflation" ends up provoking even greater inflationary pressures because the state administratively raises margins and prices, which the businesses then immediately pass on to the other areas of the economy.

Thirteenth, in an economy characterized by technobureaucratic capitalism, by price controls, and by the tendency toward compensatory distortions (which are all reflected in the public deficit), we can distinguish between the causes that maintain the inflation level and those that raise it. Administered inflation, characterized by establishment of fixed margins and wage indexation, is the main cause of the maintenance of the existing inflation level. The causes of an acceleration of inflation are: (a) prices set by the oligopolistic corporations, which succeed in increasing margins; (b) prices set by trade unions, which manage to increase their wages above the average increase in the productivity rate; (c) "corrective inflation," which is nothing more than the administered increase of repressed margins; (d) the structural sectorial imbalances between supply and demand; (e) excess demand at the peak of the cycle; (f) an excess of currency caused by compensatory deficits endogenous to the state; and (g) imported inflation.

Fourteenth, any one of these seven causes can raise the inflation level. However, once the level is raised, it becomes extremely difficult to lower it because this would imply a generalized reduction of margins, which is incompatible with the oligopolistic corporations' policies of price controls. It would mean that these corporations would be forced to pass on only part their cost increases to prices.

To sum up, inflation has numerous causes, which operate directly on the administration of prices and through the imbalance of the state budget. The new facts that explain the acceleration of the inflation rate, as well as inertial inflation and stagflation, are related to the setting of prices by large corporations and trade unions and by the corrective-distortive actions of the governments' attempts to control a process that the market no longer has the means to control.[17]

--------------------------------- 13 ---------------------------------

The model that we just developed for explaining inertial inflation and the generalized worldwide increase in the inflation rate is obviously based on the Brazilian experience during the 1970s. According to this model, there are some factors that help raise the inflation rate. Others, specifically that particular form of administered inflation that maintains fixed margins even when the economy is in a recessive phase, guarantee that once each inflation level is reached it is maintained. Inflation then becomes autonomous of demand, with prices increasing inertially.

Among the factors that accelerate inflation, there are some that act directly on prices, which then force an increase in the nominal money supply in order to maintain the liquidity of the system. Some of these, such as structural inflation and demand inflation at the peak of the cycle, appeared before technobureaucratic capitalism became dominant and continue to be active. Others are peculiar to this new social formation: inflation administered by corporations that raise their margins, by trade unions that increase their wages above productivity, by the OPEC nations that have caused the so-called imported inflation, and "corrective inflation" provoked by the government when it decides to raise the profit margins of the sectors whose prices had been repressed. On the other hand, there are those factors that act directly on the money supply, starting with state deficits, as well as pressures from the private sector to increase the money supply. These factors are especially active when there is a cyclical deceleration. In these cases, the increase in the money supply is not simply the fruit of demagoguery or of governmental incompetence. Rather it is a phenomenon endogenous to the social formations defined as technobureaucratic capitalism, in which the state is transformed into the main agent responsible for the process of accumulation.

The inflation rate in Brazil was declining from 1964 until 1972. In the first period, from 1964 to 1966, this was principally the result of a violent repression of wages, and, secondly, of some orthodox means for fighting inflation. In the second period, from 1967-1972, it was the result of administrative price controls that restrained profit margins, together with high profit rates that were possible not because of an increase in margins, but rather because of an extraordinary increase in production.

Beginning in 1973, the inflation rate began to climb again, with a decisive acceleration in its growth rhythm starting in 1979 (see Table 2.3). The change in the direction of inflation in 1973 is clearly related to a cyclical peak, with full employment and full capacity. In 1974, inflation continued to accelerate because of prices set by OPEC. Probably beginning in 1976, when deceleration became clear, growing state subsidies and pressures from the private sector provoked compensatory inflation. This process continued until the first semester of 1979. During this whole period, the government was practicing a stop-and-go policy; it would try to carry out an orthodox policy for fighting inflation, and then, being pressured by the corporations, would give up the attempt. This giving up was inevitable, because the Brazilian authoritarian state had been going through a profound political crisis of legitimacy in the eyes of civilian society since 1974. During the third period, from 1973 to 1979, there was no administered inflation characterized by an increase in the corporations' margins or caused by increases of real wages above the production rate.

Table 2.3 Inflation in Brazil: 1964 - 1980

Year	General Price Index	Cost of Living Index
1964	91.9	72.9
1965	35.5	53.9
1966	38.8	52.3
1967	24.3	25.9
1968	25.4	26.1
1969	20.2	22.3
1970	19.2	16.5
1971	19.8	24.8
1972	15.5	22.5
1973	15.7	26.7
1974	34.5	35.2
1975	29.2	28.5
1976	46.3	44.2
1977	38.8	39.2
1978	40.8	40.1
1979	77.1	70.8
1980*	110.2	93.6

Sources: General Prices Index (IGP) - Getúlio Vargas Foundation
Cost of Living Index, São Paulo - Departamento intersindical de
estatística e estudos sócio-econômicos.
Variance for the twelve months ending in October.

Inflation administered by corporations and trade unions was limited to guaranteeing the stability of each inflation level reached due to the three courses mentioned above (demand inflation in the cyclical peak, imported administered inflation, and compensatory inflation). Naturally, structural inflation should be added to this, because it did become a permanent part of the Brazilian economy, although its role did not increase.

There is a fourth period, which began in mid-1979 with a change in the economic policy. The level of inflation changed dramatically (almost doubling). The main cause of this was corrective inflation, including the maxidevaluation in December of that year. The effects of the corrective inflations were aggravated by the new wage law, which also was approved in the second semester of 1979. This law guaranteed full and semestral indexation of wages, into which production increases should be incorporated. This law did not succeed in increasing the real average wage only because corporations, faced with the perspective of a reduction of their profits, managed to increase the inflation rate, thus increasing the loss in the workers' real wages between each readjustment.[18] A third factor that increased inflation was the new increase in oil prices, which occurred in the middle of 1979.

At the end of 1980 (when this chapter was finished), a new economic policy of an orthodox nature was being presented. On the one hand, this new policy was the result of errors that had been committed previously, especially the violation of the law of value as evidenced by the preannouncing of the monetary and exchange corrections. On the other hand, it was also the result of pressures from an international financial system that could not accept not only the growing international debt, but also the constant deficits in the Brazilian trade balance. Its consequences were to raise the inflation level once more. The new economic measures, which are oriented toward freeing prices and interest rates, and a new exchange devaluation (because the economy had already accumulated profound distortions due to the extraordinary policy of preannouncing monetary corrections and exchange devaluations) clearly aim to achieve a balance-of-payments adjustment through "deflationary," recessive monetary and fiscal policy. Actually, as this policy includes new adjustments of relative prices, they show that, given a choice between balanced trade and reduced inflation, it is the former that is preferred. The result will be corrective inflation, or, in other words, a curious trade-off between inflation and a balanced trade account which neither neoclassical nor Keynesian theories can explain. Orthodox economic theory assumes that a recessive economic policy contributes to balancing international trade, as well as to decelerating inflation by increasing the hiatus of production. In an economy like Brazil's, which is dominated by oligopolies and state corporations and is full of distortions, it is very clear to everybody, including those who formulate the economic policy, that this theory is not valid. Recession could help to achieve trade balance, but it will also most certainly push inflation to a higher level.

Everything points to the fact that the government made a conscious choice for this option, giving priority to balance-of-payments adjustments at the price of an increase in the inflation rate. This reminds us that inflation is useful for capitalist accumulation; it transfers income from wage earners and the capitalist sectors that are politically weaker (or that are not considered to be a priority by the planned system) to the more dynamic and powerful capitalist sectors.

On the other hand, we should note that during the whole period that we were analyzing, the "anti-inflationary" economic policy was notable for its endogenous nature. Given the government's lack of legitimacy, as well as the lack of clear objectives of the economic authorities who (in the final analysis) were incapable of deciding if they really wanted to fight inflation or not, economic policy was no longer the result of decisions made rationally and implemented coherently. Rather, it was the result of pressures and counterpressures from the different factions into which the dominant classes are divided and, secondarily, from the pressures of the workers themselves.

14

The assertion that the market hasn't the resources to control inflation in a technobureaucratic capitalism characterized by administered prices means that the orthodox economic policies, which aim to cool off the economy and provoke a recession, are inefficient (or least insufficient) to fight inflation. If inflation tends to accelerate during a cyclical decline, either as the result of the oligopolistic corporations' mechanisms for defending their profit rates or as a result of the compensatory policies of the state, it is clear that orthodox policies, unless of an extremely severe nature, will work to stimulate rather than inhibit inflation. The simple fact is that these policies are forced to start off with corrective measures for relative prices, aiming to reestablish the truth of the market—that is, to eliminate the distortions in the law of value inherent in monopolist techno-bureaucratic capitalism. This is an indication that their character is inflationary instead of deflationary, at least in the beginning. Once the inflation level is raised in this way, it becomes most difficult to lower it unless the recession becomes a profound and long-lasting depression.

The only alternative to the orthodox policies is administrative price controls. This is extremely necessary; but we have already seen that it has narrow limits and tends to provoke distortions, which in the end are inflationary. When intervening in the price system, the state should, in principle, concentrate only on those sectors that are clearly monopolistic, able to raise their margins, or maintain them at artificially high levels. In this process, in which the state is substituting itself for the market to a certain extent, it could react selectively by stimulating certain sectors and penalizing others through a combination of income, balance-of-payments adjustment, and capital accumulation policies. The limitations, however, on the process of administering prices are narrow, not only because prices should not become disconnected from value or, more precisely, from the price of production, but also because of the administrative and political difficulties involved. On the one hand, a very complex information system is needed; on the other, the officials responsible for the controls are submitted to all kinds of pressures by the corporations, and thus they often end up simply making official the price increases. Instead of reducing the inflation rate, they stimulate it or at least maintain it at a given level.

Effective price controls would not imply that corporations should be impeded in their efforts to increase their profits margins, but rather that they should be forced to lower these margins, thus preventing them from passing on all of their increases in costs to prices. It is plain that this is not an easy task in any kind of state, and even less in those that suffer from crises of government legitimacy.

Therefore, the general conclusion about economic policy is obvious. If inflation has various causes—monetary, structural, administrative, or aggregate demand-related—which all add up, it is useless not only to pretend that there is only one correct theory for explaining inflation, but also that there is only one valid policy for fighting inflation. An anti-inflationary policy should necessarily utilize, in various degrees, all the weapons of economic policy, from the classical instruments of monetary and principally fiscal policy to the mechanisms of administering prices and wages, as well as the interest and exchange rates.

An orthodox policy for controlling inflation, which, in the last analysis, comes from the belief in the capacity of the market to control the economy, consists of: (a) decontrolling prices, interest rates, exchange rates, and (contradictorily) administratively reducing wages; (b) rapidly eliminating government deficits by reducing expenditures and increasing taxes; and (c) drastically reducing the money supply. As a result of these policies, the economy would go into a recession, and the market, given an aggregate supply greater than demand, would automatically take it upon itself to reduce wages, margins, and prices.

An administrative policy for controlling inflation would, in the first place, have to be based on a respect for the law of value. It should interfere with the four basic prices of an economy (those of merchandise, interest, exchange, and wages), but this must be done within strict limits, respecting the balance of relative prices in order to avoid distortions: high profit rates or capital gains in certain sectors and losses in others. The objective is not to guarantee equal profit rates in all sectors, since, in technobureaucratic capitalism, economic policy is used to establish a hierarchy of profit rates in keeping with the economic priorities defined by the planners. But, in the short run, difficult decisions have to be made about which sectors should suffer more and which should suffer less from the anti-inflationary policy. In other words, it has to be decided who will "pay the bill" for controlling inflation.

The only sure thing is that it is impossible to fight inflation without profits, interest rates, rents, and wages being reduced in some way. Orthodox economic policy attempts to affect all profits indiscriminately through recession. In practice, it ends up mainly affecting wages via additional means of direct control. The administrative policy should decide which ones should and will be penalized. In principle, rentiers and the business sectors that are not considered to have priority in the development process should be chosen. However, these decisions are always political and extremely difficult, not only in their making, but especially in their implementation.

We don't propose to substitute this administration for the market. We only propose that the imperfect, oligopolistic market of a techno-bureaucratic capitalism pattern function without great distortions in relative prices, thereby guaranteeing realistic and planned rates for profits and wages—an essential condition for price stability. This is possible—always respecting values and production costs, which should be taken as a referent for the main prices—by controlling the stategic prices of the economy: interest rates, the exchange rate, wages, and the prices of the cartelized oligopolistic sector. Other prices should be left to the whims of the market. It is important to note that, in technobureaucratic capitalist societies, a large part of these controls already exist to one degree or another; the difficulty lies in applying them efficiently.

This policy of price controls would naturally be complemented by fiscal policies (mainly tax increases) that would aim to balance the state budget in the medium term, as well as by a flexible monetary policy.

It is not a question of choosing between the market and administration, but of recognizing that, in oligopolistic capitalism, the market and the planning systems are both present. The problem is to know how to live with inflation, accepting that the inertial mechanisms for its maintenance are very powerful and, at the same time, to fight it, using the different policies in varying degrees of intensity, according to the needs of each situation.

The serious problem entailed in this conclusion is that the state, in charge of carrying out this economic policy, is definitely not a neutral agent. It is not a referee who can be put above society, but rather an intrinsic element of it. In oligopolistic or technobureaucratic capitalism, the state is no longer simply a basic juridical-institutional superstructure for society; it also takes part in the economic infrastructure when it acts as a producer.

Aside from this limitation, which is outside the scope of this analysis, it is certainly possible to control inflation in technobureaucratic capitalism by using an adequate economic policy. However, in order to obtain results, this policy should not only be intelligent—using flexibly any kind of instrument of economic policy—it should also be the product of a government with effective power, of a government that is legitimate in the eyes of the civil society.

There is an implicit fact behind this whole analysis that should be made explicit here. The monetarist proposal for a constant, neutral increase in the money supply in exact proportion to the increase in real income is obviously ideal. However, it is strictly out of the question in an economic system that not only develops in the midst of cycles of expansion and contraction, but also in which inflation is imbedded in an intrinsic or structural way.

Given these conditions, there are only two economic policies left for fighting inflation: either the orthodox policy of provoking recession by a drastic reduction in the money supply and state expenditures, or else the administrative policy of controlling prices through a variety of methods. These could be not only of a monetary or fiscal nature, but also of the state's firmly administering the prices of the oligopolistic sector and trying to find a medium-term solution for the bottlenecks in the economy, by moderately increasing production instead of decreasing it, and, finally, by living with a certain inflation rate.[19] An orthodox policy necessarily results in a stop-and-go process that the monetarists blame on the Keynesians, but which really is inescapable during an attempt (naturally not achieved) to apply a recessive economic policy all the way to its ultimate consequences. It results in a medium-term depression of the growth rate, rather than in a guarantee of a "natural" growth rate as the monetarists expect. An administrative policy would probably guarantee higher rates of medium-term economic growth for the system; as well, it would succeed in maintaining inflation at acceptable levels. Its assumption is that any policy for controlling inflation will only have results from success in diminishing the corporations' resistance to a reduction in their profit margins through price controls, and, at the same time, allowing the workers to limit wage demands to maintaining their real wages plus the average productivity increase. Given the market power of corporations and the growing bargaining power of workers, these two conditions for controlling inflation will be much easier to attain in a growing economy, which reduces the idle capacity and increases the employment level. That is the only way that it would be possible to make a moderate but constant increase in wages consistent with almost full employment, as well as a reduction in profit margins consistent with maintaining profit rates.

April 1981

—————————————————— Notes ——————————————————

1. The source for the data on inflation and on the growth of the GNP is the same as that for Tables 2.1 and 2.2.

2. As one person, who is both a journalist and lawyer, told me one day, quite perplexedly, "In my youth, when I studied political economy in law school, inflation was the issuing of money, it was an excess of money in circulation. Now everything has changed and I don't understand anything anymore."

3. Of course, one could make a distinction between pure neoclassicals, who are more interested in reestablishing the predominance of the competitive market, the neoclassicals who are influenced by Keynes, and the monetarists whose emphasis is on controlling the money supply.

4. The bibliography on the monetarist theory of inflation is immense, especially after Milton Friedman (1956) developed and refined the ideas of Hayek on this subject. For this type of bibliography, see Helmut Frisch (1977). It helps to note that the monetarist theory as developed by Friedman, more than being a theory on inflation, is a neoclassical alternative to Keynesian macroeconomics based on the concept of effective demand. However, this discussion is completely outside the scope of this work.

5. In this chapter, we do not intend to make a complete list of the theories on inflation. These lists have already been made, among others, by Bronfenbrenner and Holzman (1963), who did an especially interesting list of the theories of administrative inflation; Harry Johnson (1963), who emphasizes the monetarist view; Helmut Frisch, who contrasts the monetarists theory with the theories based on the Phillips curve (which, after all, is a Keynesian inspiration), in addition to presenting the structural and administrative theories and the recent attempts at synthesis; Francisco Lopes (1978), who lists the Brazilian works on inflation; and, Paul Davidson (1978), who reworks the Keynesian view.

6. Francis Cripps analyzes the Phillips curve and its monetarist revision and concludes, based on studies carried out in Britain, that the inverse relation between unemployment and nominal wages (and therefore inflation) has not been verified since World War II (1977, 109-110).

7. We will examine the different theories on inflation and bring up the basic Latin American literature on this in Chapter 4. An interesting formal exposition of the structural theory of inflation, emphasizing a survey of non-Latin American contributions on this subject, is done by André Franco Montoro Filho (1977). In this work, the author stresses that, as based on Lipsey's contribution, structural inflation can occur even when there is unemployment, because all that is needed is for one of the sectors to have reached full capacity. Note that we are limiting the concept of structural inflation to the sectoral imbalances between supply and demand. Sometimes

the concept is used to include all structural and, therefore endogenous, imbalances in the economic system that cause inflation, including the monopoly power of the business community.

8. A study carried out in the United States (Wachtel and Adelsheim, 1977), relating to the recessions of 1948-1949, 1953-1954, 1957-1958, 1960-1961, and 1969-1970, shows that the majority of the corporations, especially in the more concentrated industrial sectors, but also in the less concentrated ones, tended to increase their margins or to maintain them in those recessive periods. Among the more concentrated corporations, taking a general average, 52.6 percent increased their margins, 9.3 percent maintained them, and 38.1 percent reduced them. However, in longer periods of crisis, it is possible that the margins of the corporations ended up declining slightly, and as a result, the profit rates also went down. That is what has been happening all over the capitalist world since the second semester of 1979 despite all the inflationary resistance of the corporations.

9. André Lara Rezende (1979) and Edmar Bacha (1980) recently made two interesting formalizations of the inflationary process related to the redistributive process. According to Bacha, who even managed to incorporate administrative inflation into the model, "Inflation is an instrument for reducing the share of real wages in the income, so as to permit the capitalists to invest and consume at the levels that they want to" (p. 545). *See* also Adroaldo Moura da Silva (1978), who tries to combine various points of view on inflation into a general model.

10. James O' Connor (1977, 48) observes that usually the workers in the oligopolistic sector, being better organized, initiate an inflationary increase in wages, being followed by the workers of the public sector. An increase in wages is a way for the monopolist and public sectors to keep gains in productivity for themselves, to the detriment of the competitive sectors. But it is also a source of administered inflation.

11. Some economists have used the name "supply shock" both for phenomena like the oil price increase and for inflation that is the result of sudden and generalized deficiencies in supply, such as crop failures. Even though both phenomena occur at the level of supplies, they are very different from each other. In the firstcase, we have prices set for supply: administered or cost inflation is always "supply" inflation. In the second case, there actually is a "supply shock," but the inflation is a market inflation, as prices rise because of a drop in supply for reasons that are independent of the wishes of the business community (therefore without any "administration"), making them insufficient to meet demand.

12. For James O' Connor, this is one of the bases of fiscal crisis, whose consequences are inflationary. This fiscal crisis, which is marked by a tendency for a systematic increase in state expenditures, is structural in the capitalist system. In order to face this, the governments increase taxes or take on internal debts (which often are loans to itself, because it first permits an increase in bank deposits and therefore in the money supply).

O'Connor calls this process "inflationary finances" (1977, 54). The last resource is naturally the pure and simple issuing of money to finance the deficit in the state treasury.

13. It was José Serra who called my attention to the problem of "corrective inflation." Beginning with the first measures of Delfim Netto in the second semester of 1979, in an attempt to correct repressed prices, Serra published articles and interviews in *Folha de São Paulo*, pointing out the explosive effects that they would have on the inflation rate.

14. The first time I tried to make this analysis, which tries to make the deficits of the government and the issuing of money endogenous to the capitalist system, was in *Desenvolvimento e crise no Brasil* (1968, 59-65).

15. It is necessary, meanwhile, to point out that the tendency toward public deficit in technobureaucratic capitalism is structural, regardless of the legitimacy of the governments. James O' Connor's analysis of this subject is definitive (1973), but it is also worthwhile to quote Manuel Castells (1977, 186) here: "The socialization of prices and the privatization of profits have structural limits that the state in a monopolist capitalist society cannot overcome without provoking uncontrollable inflation." It is important to note that for "socialization of prices" Castells means the tendency of the modern state to continually increase its expenditures for social consumption, especially for the urban areas.

16. For state intervention in a state capitalist an economy, *see*, among others, Claus Offe (1977), Heinz Rudolf Sonntag, editor (1977), J. M. Vincent, J. Hirsch, M. Wirth, E. Alvater and O. Yaffe (1975), Alberto Martinelli, editor (1977), Nicos Poulantzas, editor (1977), Carlos Estevam Martins, editor (1977), Luiz Bresser Pereira (1977a), Francisco de Oliveira (1977), João Manoel Cardoso deMello (1977), Luiz Gonzaga de Mello Belluzzo (1977), Luciano Coutinho (1977), Fernando Henrique Cardoso (1977).

17. Labinini called attention to a factor that is inflationary and reduces profit rates at the same time, aside from the pressure from the workers for higher wages and the oil shocks: the elevation of indirect costs, especially the salaries of the top executives, "who set the salary levels for themselves and for other top executives in such a way that the profits of the companies are partly institutionalized and transformed into salaries for the top administrators" (1979, 13). Of course, this factor only accelerates inflation, as the corporations manage to compensate for the increased salaries with higher margins through price administration.

18. This chapter was already written when I became aware of the excellent theoretical and econometric work of Francisco Lopes and André Lara Rezende (1980) on the causes of the recent acceleration of inflation in Brazil. In this work, the authors not only show that there is no correlation between recession and inflationary deceleration, but they also construct a model that begins with the inflation level accounted for by a markup policy, and thus explain the recent acceleration of inflation by the increase in oil

prices and the new wage law. The model and their econometric tests confirm the hypothesis of this chapter. Their explicative power would have been better if they had taken the policy of the "corrective inflation" of 1979 into consideration, which actually brought about an increase in margins, thus becoming a third fundamental cause for the recent inflationary acceleration.

19. In the case of Britain, Francis Cripps notes that, because it is not the demand for workers that determines wages (as is assumed in the Phillips curve), but rather the bargaining power of the workers, recessive monetarist policies are inefficient for fighting inflation. It should be fought with production increases and a moderation of the workers' wage goals (1977, 111). In the case of Brazil, the recommendation for increasing production is the same (Ignácio Rangel 1963), it only being necessary to moderate the profit goals rather than wage goals.

3

The Theory of Inertial
or Autonomous Inflation

The inflationary process in this last quarter of the twentieth century can only be clearly undertood if we differentiate among the three mechanisms or factors that act on prices, determining that they constantly increase. These factors are: (1) those that cause the level of inflation to be maintained; (2) those that speed up (or slow down) inflation; and, (3) those that sanction or validate price hikes. The confusion and useless discussion surrounding inflation is, in large part, due to an inability to distinguish between these three mechanisms. Without a clear understanding of the concepts we are about to outline, it is not easy to distinguish the primary causes of inflation from the inertial factors that maintain the rate of inflation and those factors that sanction the current inflation rate.

The first section of this chapter examines certain assumptions concerning the nature of contemporary capitalism and the behavior of various economic agents. The next three sections examine the factors that speed up inflation (increased profit margins or increased real wages higher than productivity levels), maintain inflation (economic agents' ability to pass cost increases on to prices), and sanction inflation (particularly the increase in the nominal money supply). To the extent that the increased money supply is a mechanism that sanctions inflation, it is rather a consequence than a cause of inflation. The fifth section deals with the public sector deficit, which not only serves as a buffer in relation to economic and political tension arising from the distributional conflict, but also functions as a means to assure an increase in the money supply necessary to maintain the liquidity of the system. Sections six and seven discuss some relations between the theory developed here and the Phillips curve, as well as monetarist and Keynesian models of inflation.

---------------------------------- 1 ----------------------------------

Neoclassical and monetarist economists developed their macroeconomic policies, based on the assumption that, in capitalist economies, normally the self-correcting market mechanism leads to full employment, full capacity, and price stability. Therefore, deviations from these points of equilibrium, particularly in relation to inflation, could be easily corrected by the market itself or by an economic adjustment policy that would eliminate those inflation-causing distortions: the public deficit and an excessive money supply. Keynes dropped the basic assumptions of a self-regulating market mechanism and, thus, of full capacity and full employment from his model while working with an assumption of fixed prices. But inflation continued to be a phenomenon of excessive aggregate demand, so that the economic policy he recommended for stabilizing prices did not essentially differ from that proposed by the neoclassical economists.

Nevertheless, it has become evident in the last years that, if we consider the reality of the oligopolistic and technobureaucratic capitalism of our times, the economic models must go one step beyond Keynes and abandon the assumption of price stability. This is what we will do in this chapter. We will try to develop an analytical model of the inflationary process based on the general hypothesis that capitalist economies in the last quarter of the twentieth century have and will tend to coexist with unemployment, idle capacity, and relatively high inflation rates. This fact is not merely due to the structural imperfections of a market that is dominated by large corporations, unions, and the large technobureaucratic state, but also to the fact that, since 1970 or 1973, we have begun the phase of economic decline typical of a long Kondratieff cycle. Consequently, a radically new macroeconomic analysis has become of the utmost importance. If Keynes began to construct his model with a critique of Say's law, which automatically ensured full employment, we must now begin with a critique of Keynes, who maintained price stability as one of his basic assumptions and only allowed for demand inflation. In fact, it is only possible now to understand inflation, which became relatively autonomous in relation to the market, if we start from the assumption that its inertial component is a structural phenomenon of contemporary capitalist economies.

Besides assuming unemployment and imperfect markets, as administrative and stagflationist theories of inflation do, the model presented in this chapter starts from a third assumption: that a given rate of inflation prevails in the economy. Instead of starting from a zero rate of inflation as most models of inflation do, this analysis departs from a given and relatively high rate of inflation (two or three-digit inflation) typical of Latin American countries. Inflation in this model accelerates or decelerates starting from an inertial rate of inflation. High inflation rates are incompatible with monetary illusion, because everybody becomes aware of the distributive conflict involved in inflation.

A fourth assumption, tied to the last one, concerns the ability of the economic agents to maintain their relative shares in the income. In a modern economy, let us make the simple yet plausible assumption that workers, entrepreneurial capitalists and rentier capitalists have certain instruments at their disposal with which to defend and eventually increase their share in the national income. Workers generally defend their wages collectively, by sector, in much the same way as technobureaucrats defend their salaries. State and private enterprises seek to maintain their profit rates and profit margins separately or in oligopolistic groups. Rentiers try to maintain or increase the interest and rents they receive. This assumption generally appears in the literature concerning inflation, in terms of the theory that inflation is the result of a distributive conflict.

The fifth assumption is that these economic agents have the maintenance of a "reasonable" economic growth rate as their common objective. This means that they will be resolutely opposed to recessive economic policies. Workers and the middle class, increasingly powerful in contemporary societies, always resist recessive economic policies. Nevertheless, as Kalecki demonstrates, capitalists tend to accept recessive policies as a form of controlling union activity in a period of accelerated inflation. Yet, due to the growing inefficiency of these kinds of measures for fighting inflation, capitalists have also begun to withdraw their support for recessive policies, demanding positive and reasonably stable economic growth rates.

Based on these five assumptions stated very briefly above, we can develop a model for the inflationary process. However, it should be made clear that these assumptions do not have to be entirely realistic in order for the model to be valid. First, this model can be very useful for low rates of inflation, provided that the economic agents are not victims of monetary illusion. The higher the inflation rate, the more aware the economic agents will be of the distributive conflict, and so, less subject to monetary illusion. But even with low but persistent rates of inflation, the economic agents can be defended from monetary illusion. Second, it is not always true that the results of the distributional conflict do not favor one group or another. Third, we still have many supporters of recessive policies among the capitalist class. Yet there is no doubt that the various economic agents, whether as individuals, interest groups, classes, or nations have a much clearer notion of their own interests and continually offer greater resistance to the sacrifices imposed on them. Fourth, given cyclical fluctuations, insufficient demand, though a generalized and chronic problem, is not a permanent one. At certain moments, demand shocks instead of cost push factors can accelerate inflation.

2

First let us look at the factors that speed up and slow down inflation. If we start with an economic situation where prices are increasing at a stable rate, then inflation can only accelerate or decelerate if we have a variation in relative prices. More precisely, factors accelerating inflation in a closed economy will be (1) real average wage increases above productivity increases and/or (2) increased profit margins. In an open economy, two additional factors shall be considered: (3) real devaluations of the currency, and (4) an increase in the value of imported goods. If we consider the state's role in this model, we have one more factor to accelerate inflation: (5) an increase in taxes.

In this simplified economy, where the production price is equal to wages plus profits, and the only cost is the wage, which serves as the basis for the calculation of profit margins, the variation in prices, or the inflation rate, $\dot{p}$, will depend (1) on the variation in the wage rate, $\dot{w}$, subtracting productivity increases, $\dot{q}$, and (2) on the variation in the profit margin, $\dot{m}$ (profit over direct cost).

$$\dot{p} = \dot{w} - \dot{q} + \dot{m} \qquad\qquad 3.1$$

In this model, we can see that inflation always implies a distributional conflict. In the final analysis, the acceleration of inflation depends on the capacity of capitalists to increase their profit margins or on the ability of workers to increase their real wages. Yet this conflict can also take place within a given class, and especially among capitalist enterprises that maintain interindustrial relations.

Increased profit margins and/or real wages higher than productivity increases can result from one or more of the following four factors: (1) a generalized excess of aggregate demand in relation to supply, within a situation of full employment and little idle capacity; (2) sectorial insufficiency in supply; (3) autonomous wage or price increases due to monopoly control by corporations or unions; and, (4) reduction in labor productivity without a corresponding reduction in wages.

The first case is one of classic Keynesian inflation; the second is structural inflation; the third and fourth are administered or cost inflation. In the first case, all prices increase at about the same time. In the others, price increases in a specific sector spread to the rest of the economy as a result of the distributional conflict.

Although prices of raw materials or intermediary products are fundamental links in the propagation process of inflation, they do not appear explicitly in this simplified model because, in the final analysis, every price is the sum total of profits and wages.

Real wages can increase at the same rate as productivity increases, because what is important to corporations in determining their prices is not the wage rate but, rather, the labor unit cost. If wages and productivity are increasing at the same rate, prices can be maintained constant, and the profit-wage relation (rate of plus value) will stay constant.

If we open our model up to the international market, we should specify variations in the prices of raw materials imported in the national currency, $\dot{z}$, and the variation in the amount of raw material imported per product unit, $\dot{x}$:

$$\dot{p} = \alpha \, (\dot{w} - \dot{q}) + (1 - \alpha) \, (\dot{z} + \dot{x}) + \dot{m} \qquad 3.2$$

Variations in the price of raw materials could result from an increase in their prices in foreign exchange and/or a variation in the exchange rate above the parity rate. In the first case, we have what is called imported inflation. The wage as a part of the total cost is expressed as α, and imported raw materials as $1 - \alpha$. Increased prices for imported raw materials, as well as the devaluation of the national currency in real terms, are also factors that accelerate the inflationary process.

Corporate profit margins should not only cover the enterprise's profits, but also interest and rents paid to rentiers and taxes, as well as fixed costs and depreciation. To the extent that corporations, both in the competitive and oligopolistic sectors of the economy are able to maintain their liquid profit margins, any increase in interests, rents, taxes, or fixed costs (derived from reduced sales) implies an increase in the profit margin, and thus will serve as an accelerating factor in the inflationary process.

In the same way, measures of "corrective inflation," which aim to bring deviations in relative prices caused by price controls or by subsidies into order, cause increases in profit margins and speed up inflation.

A strictly autonomous increase (that is, independent of excess demand in relation to supply) in the profit margin would only be possible to the extent that a corporation has monopoly control over an industry. In the same way, an autonomous wage increase could only occur in a situation where workers have considerable bargaining power. The inflation rate would accelerate as a result of either of these hypotheses.

In order to maintain their rates of profit (profit over capital), oligopolist industries tend to increase their profit margins during recessions. In this way, a drop in sales is compensated for by an increased margin. However, this accelerating factor of inflation may be compensated for by the competitive sector's falling profit margins during recession.

3

Once inflation has begun because of any of these factors, there are various mechanisms that operate in modern economies that tend to perpetuate this situation, that is, that maintain the level of inflation at a relatively stable rate, even when the factors that accelerated it are no longer acting upon the economy. If increased profit margins or real wages above productivity raise the level of inflation to a higher plateau, new pressures are not necessary to maintain this new plateau. The trend is for inflation to maintain itself at that higher plateau independently of demand and in spite of a high rate of unemployment. Therefore we have a situation of stagflation that could also be called "autonomous" or "inertial" inflation.

The factor par excellence that maintains the level of inflation is the distributional conflict, that is, the fact that various corporations and unions have economic and political instruments at their disposal to help them keep their relative income share. Given the fact that, at a determined inflation level, the prices of various commodities and labor tend to adjust with time lags among them, and fact that the prices of some of these commodities are the costs of others, subsequent price and wage increases tend to occur almost automatically. In this way, every corporation and every worker or group of workers passes on its cost increases in the form of price increases.

Although this process also happens in the competitive sector, it functions more effectively in the oligopolist sector of the economy, and takes on full force in a generally and formally indexed economy like that of Brazil. In this case, cost increases are passed on according to legally defined norms and become automatic. This is true even of nonindexed prices because, when inflation is a chronic problem, the various economic agents begin to improve their defense mechanisms so that, in effect, they develop informal indexing measures. Prices are corrected more and more frequently so that there is a smaller lag between cost and price increases. Thus it is not only formal indexation, but also this informal indexing process that serve as powerful elements in the maintenance of the level of inflation, making it inertial.

It should be made clear that this generalized mechanism of formal and informal indexation does not accelerate the inflationary process, but rather maintains the existing level of inflation to the extent that it maintains profit margins, real wages, and the structure of time lags between the adjustment of prices and wages. A slowdown would only occur if the indexation of prices, wages, the exchange rate, or interest rates was partial, including a reducing coefficient, if the adjustment were made more frequently. This phenomenon could take place as a function of errors made in relation to inflationary expectations. When the various economic agents increase their prices in a chronic inflationary situation, they not only consider their current costs, but also their cost expectations. Nevertheless, we should not overestimate the importance of these forecasts in our analysis of the factors that keep up the existing inflation level. Effective cost variations always serve as the basis for these increases and consequently determine expectations.

The inflation level will be maintained to the extent that all agents working in the economy are relatively satisfied with their income share. However, if one of these groups feels that it can increase its profit margins or wages and thus increase its income share, and the other agents react by indexing their prices to the new level, the result will be the acceleration of inflation.

It should be pointed out, however, that the economic agents who took the initiative to increase their margins, interest rates, or wages would achieve a momentary increase in their share of real income even if the other economic groups passed on their respective cost increases. This is because they had the advantage of increasing their prices first and benefited from the time lag before the other prices were increased. The inflation would be more neutral if, as a reaction to the first agent's price increase, the other agents increased their prices a little bit more than their costs were increased in order to compensate for this time lag. Nevertheless, this would again result in an accelerated inflation.

Maintaining the inflation level by this process of time-lapsed price increases (generalized indexation) implies that inflation will be relatively neutral from the distributional point of view. Although this in fact is never entirely the case, it is important to consider this phenomenon in terms of our theoretical model.

These factors that maintain the inflationary level correspond to what Mário Henrique Simonsen calls "feedback components" (1970, 128-138), which in turn roughly correspond to the concept of "inflation-propagating factors" used by the Latin American structuralist economists to explain the spread of sectorial price hikes (Oswaldo Sunkel 1958, 19).

The existence of these factors that maintain the inflation level and ensure the relative stability of the various economic agents' real income makes it much more difficult to lower this inflation level. This fact has important implications in terms of economic policy.

In a fully indexed economy, any autonomous price increase (and consequently increased margins) implies increased inflation in direct relation to the original increase. This increase in the rate of inflation takes place by means of a multiplier mechanism that ends up raising all other prices proportionately.

When the price of a particular input increases originally, the prices of those products utilizing this input only increase in proportion to the first product's price hike. Nevertheless, these secondary increases have inflationary effects on other commodities, as well as on wages. These tertiary increases are reflected not only in the prices of other products, but also in an increase in the goods affected by this secondary price hike. To the extent that the prices of wage goods end up being increased, wages will also automatically increase due to indexation. The multiplier effect of the initial increase will only be exhausted when all prices have risen in the same proportion, so that the structure of relative prices remains unaltered, restoring the initial distributional equilibrium (which was only upset by the lag in the price readjustments).[1] The indexation system then guarantees the maintenance of this new level of inflation, which covers its purely inertial character.

If the economic agents who made the original price hikes are not satisfied because the entire process we described above nullified their distributional advantage, they will increase their prices again, setting off a new multiplier process and a new acceleration of inflation.

However, in an economy that is not completely indexed, the multiplier effect will not be as great because the secondary prices will increase less than proportionately to the original increase. Consequently, the initial distributional equilibrium will not be reestablished. Once the multiplier effect of the original increase is over, and the economy reaches a new level of inflation, if indexation is only partial (that is to say, if the secondary increases are less than the original ones), then the newly established inflation level will begin to decline. In this case, however, we would have to assume that the various economic agents did not maintain their respective shares in the income.

Another important consequence of generalized indexation is that it makes relative prices inflexible, creating difficultes for the process of economic adjustment of the structure of production or consumption. In other words, the role that the price mechanism plays in the process of reallocating resources becomes highly inflexible and obstinate, thus requiring the government to intervene and deindex the economy and administratively establish a new structure for relative prices.

4

Last, we will examine those factors that sanction or validate inflation. Strictly speaking, only one important factor exists in this respect: the increase in the money supply. There is no doubt about the correlation between increased prices and the money supply.[2] In a monetary economy, the real quantity of money, m, is determined by the volume of its transaction or by corresponding real income, given certain institutional factors (such as how payments are made) that determine the velocity of the circulation of money. The velocity of money can vary in the short run, as Keynes explains, depending on the motive for speculation, and, in the long run, depending on institutional changes. However, since we are not analyzing macroeconomic imbalances, but only inflation, let us simplify the matter and consider the income velocity of money to be constant.

Let us make M the nominal money supply, p the price index, and Y real income; V, the income velocity of money, is given as $V = Yp/M$, and the exchange equation, also a definition, is given as $MV = Yp$.

If V is constant, then M will be directly proportional to Yp by definition. Then it is necessary to determine the causal relationship between p and M.

An increase in the money supply would only be a factor that causes inflation, and thus, in the terminology we are using, accelerates inflation, if this increase (1) was converted into effective demand, and (2) if this effective demand was greater than aggregate demand at full employment and full capacity.

According to the Keynesian model, the conversion of the expansion of money into effective demand takes place as a result of lowered interest rates that stimulate investment. However, in order for this increased demand to imply price increases, it is essential that the economy be functioning with the full utilization of its resources. In this hypothesis, the pressure of demand would lead to increased profit margins or increased real wages. There could also be a structural kind of inflationary acceleration to the extent that only certain basic economic sectors operate at close to full capacity. In this case, even though there was not full employment, an increase in the money supply could accelerate inflation through a propagation effect.

Since approximately 1970-1973, few modern economies operate with full employment. In general, these economies are characterized by unemployment and idle capacity, given the tendency of large state and oligopolist corporations to make investments that anticipate expanded demand. Their high profit margins based on administered prices allow them to function in this way.

In these conditions, an increase in the nominal money supply cannot generally be considered to be a factor that accelerates the inflationary process. Rather, it tends to sanction inflation since, given constant price hikes, or inertial inflation, the real money supply tends to decrease, as it is defined as $m = M/p$. The decrease in the real money supply will cause a liquidity crisis and then recession. If we accept the assumption that the various economic agents seek to maintain the rate of economic growth, then there is no other alternative than to increase the nominal money supply and reestablish its real quantity.

In this case, an increased money supply could not be regarded as a cause or factor that accelerates inflation but merely one that sanctions this inflation. Monetary expansion simply keeps up with the price hikes, becoming one of the endogenous variables of the system, rather than an exogenous variable, as the linear thinking of the monetarists claims.

Although it is an endogenous variable, it should also be noted that as the money supply increases when there is generalized unemployment, as is common in contemporary economies, it can have an inflationary effect if it facilitates increased profit margins or wages in key sectors where there are insufficiencies in supply.

In periods of cyclical slowdowns, the state tends to compensate for unemployment and falling profit rates through fiscal measures, thus increasing its expenditures. This increase can be generalized or it can be put into pratice by means of a complex subsidy scheme. At any rate, it implies public deficit and an increase in the money supply (if it is not financed by the sale of public bonds). To the extent that these increased expenditures and an increase in the money supply help those enterprises or groups of workers increase their profit margins or real wages in the sectors where there are temporary shortages, we have what we called in Chapter 1 "compensatory inflation."

The money supply maintains its endogenous nature in this situation. In fact, money is the expression of a social relation and, thus, cannot be manipulated at will by those who formulate economic policy. The money supply is a function of the economy's real output and of the mechanism by which it sets its prices. On the other hand, money works as a kind of lubricant for the economic system. In this way, to the extent that inflation reduces the real money supply, society develops mechanisms to restore it.

These mechanisms may either be those that regulate the creation of money through the central bank and the commercial banks, or those of a more informal nature that create various forms of quasi-money such as credit cards, highly liquid bonds, etc.[3] In this case, an increase in the money supply is not a cause of inflation but rather a consequence, a factor that sanctions inflation while ensuring its continuity. The correlation between an increased money supply and the inflation rate is beyond all question, but the direction of the causal relation is just the opposite of what the monetarists claim.

In the kind of analysis we are presently making, the assumption is implicit that there is a strict correlation between the money supply and price level, or more precisely, nominal income. Keynes observed that the income velocity of money may vary in the short run, depending on the tendency to hoard or on the preference for liquidity, but we will consider this fact in the abstract and keep velocity constant. Milton Friedman thought he had disproven Keynes's theory in showing a stable correlation between the money supply and nominal income in the long run. However, the monetarist theory only makes sense if we consider the money supply to be a variable that is strictly exogenous to the economic system. If we postulate that the money supply is determined by monetary authorities, then we could imagine that variations in this supply would determine variations in price.

However, when we put aside this naive and linear notion that the money supply is an exogenous variable, that correlation no longer proves the monetarist hypothesis. On the other hand, if we make the assumption (which we are making in this analysis) that nominal income determines the money supply, then the correlation that has been empirically established by Friedman, among others, only serves to contradict this theory.

This notion that the money supply is endogenous to the economic system can be found in Marx when he affirms that the money supply is determined by the sum total of commodity prices, and that it is merely an illusion to think that these prices are determined by the quantity of the means of circulation (1867, Book I, 135-137). More recently, Ignácio Rangel had also made this fact clear when he explicitly inverted the causal relationship between money and prices in the exchange equation (1963), radically interpreting the thinking of both Marx and Keynes. This idea received more precise treatment in relation to Keynes's thought by Nicholas Kaldor (1970, 1982).

In the Keynesian tradition, Kaldor points out that modern capitalist economies are "credit-money economies" rather than "commodity-money economies." Thus, money is not neutral, nor can it be manipulated according to the will of economic policy. Since it is a form of credit, it is created and destroyed by the financial system in a variety of ways. On the one hand, control over cash deposits and other assets is limited; on the other, many kinds of bonds are created so that, depending on the demand for money (M_1 or M_2), its quantity will vary in time and in different countries (1982, 26-27).

Alain Lipietz adopts a similar position, starting from a modern Marxist perspective that emphasizes the credit form of money to the detriment of its merchandise form. He sees credit-money as strictly endogenous, created by banks that give loans. Thus one should not utilize the concept of a multiplier of the monetary base, but rather of the bank loans' "monetary divisor" (1982, 54).

According to this point of view, the money supply is endogenous in strictly economic terms, to the extent that the financial system creates money in the absence of or against the will of monetary authorities. Without denying this fact, there is also a political element involved in the process, in that the economic agents pressure the government when they see real liquidity diminished due to price hikes, which leads to the increase in the nominal money supply with the explicit or tacit consent of the monetary authorities.

This does not mean that the government does not have control over the money supply. Through increasingly direct or administrative means, such as the quantitative control of bank loans, or through monetary or fiscal policy affecting the interest rate, it is possible to cause modifications in the money supply for a while. Yet these changes in the quantity of money as a result of economic policy are limited in their range and duration. Heavily restrictive monetary policies not only are unable to substantially modify the money supply, but also, and more important, are unable to function for very long. These observations do not mean to deny the importance and necessity of a monetary policy in the fight against inflation, but only to point out their limitations.

5

The most linear way to explain inflation is to start with the state's budget deficit as the reason for the increase in the money supply, which in turn influences price increases. In fact, the public deficit, especially the nominal public deficit, can be considered to be an endogenous factor in the same way that money can—as a consequence of inflation rather than a cause.

The public deficit only constitutes a causal or accelerating factor of inflation if increased governmental expenditures (or decreased taxes) lead to pressure on aggregate demand in relation to supply when the economy is functioning at full capacity with full employment. Or, in other words, the public deficit is financed by an increase in the real money supply, which leads to low interest rates, high investments, and excess demand. A public deficit caused by the monetary correction of public debt is just nominal, and not a real deficit. It is a sanctioning factor of inflation, as is the increase of the money supply necessary to finance it.

The nominal public deficit facilitates the increase in the nominal money supply necessary to sanction the existing level of inertial inflation. Obviously, there are other more orthodox ways to increase the money supply. The classic formulas are for increasing credit by reducing required bank reserves in the central bank, the purchase of public bonds in the open market, and a reduction of the discount rate. Yet it is beyond question that the easiest and most convenient way for governments with a high level of inflation to increase the nominal quantity of money, and thus sanction the inflationary process, is to issue more currency.

Table 3.1 makes it very clear that there is no direct correlation between the public deficit's share in the gross domestic product and the inflation rate. There are countries with very high deficits and low inflation rates. There is some degree of correlation between the increase in the public deficit in each country and an increased inflation rate. The majority of countries had an increased public debt along with an increased rate of inflation during the 1970s. Yet, even in this case, the correlation is very

Table 3.1 Central Government Deficit and the Inflation Rate

Country	1979/81	
	Deficit as a % of the GDP	Inflation Rate
Canada	3.1	10.6
United States	2.2	11.7
Japan	8.4	5.5
France	1.7	12.5
Germany	2.1	5.2
Italy	12.0	17.9
Britain	4.9	14.4
Sweden	7.0	11.0
Brazil	7.5	82.7
Argentina	3.1	121.6
Mexico	3.2	24.2

Source: *Conjuntura Econômica*, FGV, and *International Finance Statistics*, I.M.F.

weak, since, in many cases, the deficit went down and inflation went up or vice versa.

Naturally, those countries with low inflation rates and large deficits finance their deficits through the public debt and thus discourage an increase in the money supply. Why don't the countries with high inflation rates do the same thing? It is certainly not due to a lack of avaliable domestic savings, or to a process where the private sector is crowded out by high interest rates. These problems exist in every country that has a high public deficit and seeks to finance it by using public bonds, rather than only in those with high rates of inflation. In fact, sales of open-market bonds are limited by the fact that there is a high autonomous inflation to be sanctioned by the increase of the nominal money supply.

Stating that the public deficit, as well as the increase in money supply, are factors that sanction inflation does not mean that these factors cannot also speed up the inflationary process when they pressure aggregate or sectorial demand. We also recognize the fact that the public deficit serves to mitigate the distributional conflict. When the state increases its expenditures without being able to cover this spending by its tax revenue, it serves the interest of some specific sectors and helps in maintaining aggregate demand. An acceleration of inflation may be a result of this practice. However, one of the explicit assumptions in this analysis is that, starting in 1973, if not sooner, capitalist economies have functioned with both idle capacity and unemployment. In this situation, the public deficit does not result in strong pressures on aggregate demand and thus is not the cause of increases either in profit margins or in real wages.

---------------------------------- 6 ----------------------------------

Although we consider an increased nominal money supply and the nominal public deficit to be a consequence and not a cause of inflation, this does not mean that a restrictive fiscal and monetary policy cannot serve as a tool to control inflation. It is a curious phenomenon that one can fight inflation and reduce its level by attacking its consequences (monetary expansion) rather than its original causes (increased wages and profits).

By reducing the money supply (which generally occurs together with reducing the public deficit), what one hopes to do is to reduce effective demand. As a result, competitive corporations and workers who are not very well defended by their unions are forced to lower their profit margins and wages. The oligopolistic corporations raise their profit margins in order to make up for reduced sales.[4] However, the decrease in wages and profits in the competitive sector is sufficient to cause a general drop in the inflation rate.

According to a commonly used Keynesian model, the inflation rate is directly proportional to the increases in nominal wages.[5] Returning to Equation 3.1, this means that the corporations' profit margins are constant, m = 0, so that they can be taken out of that equation; thus, the variation in prices is given by:

$$\dot{p} = \dot{w} - \dot{q} \qquad 3.3$$

The model is completed by the Phillips curve, which establishes a relation between the variation in nominal wages, $\dot{w}$, and in the unemployment rate, $\dot{d}$.

$$\dot{w} = \dot{a} + b\,\dot{d}^{-1} \qquad 3.4$$

To the extent that unemployment increases as a result of fiscal measures (preferred by the Keynesian) or of monetary measures (preferred by the monetarists), the wage rate decreases, causing a drop in the inflation level. The reduction in the money supply, which occurs in both cases, has an indirect effect on prices in that it causes unemployment and reduced wages.

However, it should be pointed out that the monetarists do not accept the Phillips curve, except as a short-term transitory phenomenon, caused by errors in relation to the expected rate of inflation (Friedman 1968, 8-9).[6] In keeping with this position, they stress monetary contraction as the means to reduce the inflationary level much more than the Keynesians. Since they deny the validity of the Phillips curve (or assume it to be completely inelastic), the more orthodox monetarists deny, in theory, that reduced inflation should be analyzed in terms of increased unemployment. Nevertheless, in pratice, the economic policy measures adopted by the monetarists are the most strongly recessive, given their radical nature in terms of reducing state expenditures and the real money supply.

By refusing to accept the Phillips curve, the monetarists tie themselves merely to the exchange equation. Yet this leaves them with no explanation for the intermediary mechanisms that link a reduction in the money supply to a reduction in prices.

---------------------------------- 7 ----------------------------------

In the continuing debate between Keynesians and monetarists, our theoretical position is radically opposed to the monetarists, and much closer to that of the Keynesians. Nevertheless, although the economic policy proposals made by each of these tendencies are quite distinct, their recessive implications often end up being quite similar.

Our critique will be limited to the simplified form of the Keynesian model we have presented here (Equations 3.3 and 3.4) since the monetarist proposal takes refuge in the universe of the Walrasian equilibrium, which has little to do with the reality of the capitalist world.

The analysis of inertial inflation that we are making differs on four points from that of the more commonly adopted Keynesian view. The first is that it considers not only the money supply, but also the public sector deficit, as endogenous variables—that is, as factors that sanction inflation. The only instance when this is not true is when the economy as a whole, or at least some of its most important sectors, is working at full capacity and/or with full employment. This situation becomes increasingly unusual as inflation becomes a generalized phenomenon in contemporary capitalism.

A second difference is that we distinguish those factors that accelerate (or cause) inflation from those that maintain the level of inflation, making it inertial. We attribute to the latter greater importance in the conditions of contemporary capitalism. The oligopolization of corporations and the strength of the trade unions, on one hand, and the indexing systems on the other, are new phenomena that tend to perpetuate inflation even when there are no factors acting to accelerate inflation. In addition, the factors that maintain inflation make it much more difficult for the inflationary level to go down. Even though they may have an effect in terms of lowering the inflation rate, recessive economic policies that seek to reduce real wages and profit margins are inefficient. The relation between the costs of this kind of policy and its results is an increasingly negative one.

The third difference is that we do not accept the assumption that profit margins are constant. Although this assumption is not essential to the Keynesian model, it is present when price increases are identified with wage increases, which make it possible to explain inflation in terms of the Phillips curve (Equations 3.3 and 3.4). In reality, profit margins are not constant, especially in times of recession. Generally speaking, the profit margin is constant when the economy develops relatively normally and uneventfully. Aside from this, it is also necessary to distinguish the competitive sector from the oligopolistic sector. Although it is always a little hazardous to generalize, it has been empirically confirmed that competitive sector corporations tend to increase their profit margins in periods of cyclical expansion, thus accelerating inflation, and tend to reduce their profit margins in recessive periods. Their counterparts in the oligopolistic sector maintain or even decrease their profit margins (if these were excessively high) in the expansive phase, and increase their margins during recession, in order to compensate for the drop in sales and to maintain their rate of profit. However, in indexed economies (such as Brazil's) the reduction in wages and profit margins during the recessionary period tends to be quite small, even in the competitive sector, due to the strength of those factors that maintain the level of inflation.

If we accept the idea of increasing inflation levels as a function of the conjugate effects of the factors that accelerate and maintain inflation, and especially of indexation's effect on the economy, then we would have to consider that the Phillips curve tends to move to the right as a fourth difference. Consequently, with the same unemployment rate, we have increased wage and inflation rates, so that the direct correlation among the three disappears. Thus, we have the phenomenon of inertial inflation and stagflation, that is, high unemployment rates in a recessionary situation together with high inflation rates.

It is necessary to add at least three more observations in relation to the underdeveloped countries: (1) because of the imperfect functioning of the market, the accelerating factors of a structural nature are more important; (2) given the trade unions' weak bargaining power and the high incidence of underemployment, the variation in the employment index has less direct influence on the inflation rate; and (3) given the imperative need to accumulate and to make up for their backward position in the world economy, the local dominant classes tend to utilize inflation as a mechanism for forced savings in the expansive phase and as a compensatory mechanism for their reduced rates of profit during periods of economic slowdown. In each case, inflation serves quite clearly to concentrate income, a phenomenon that does not necessarily tend to occur in the developed countries.

It is viable to reduce the inflation rate by recessive policies only to the extent that a reduction of profit margins in the competitive sector and of wages has a greater effect than that of increased profit margins in the oligopolist sector. However, the high economic and social cost of this kind of economic policy has become increasingly evident, both in terms of the trade unions' resistance to accepting cuts in their real wages (expressed as formal indexation), as well as in terms of the ruthless behavior of the oligopolistic enterprises.

Although we have not specifically dealt with economic policy in these remarks, we hope we have made it clear that recessive monetarist economic policies are inefficient. Monetary policy is merely one of the economic instruments that can be employed to control inflation, and its limitations are great. When monetary restrictions and recession become the main tools in the fight against inertial inflation, the result is stagflation in the industrialized countries. In those underdeveloped countries with a large industrial base, the insistent and prolonged use of these mechanisms can result in a serious process of deindustrialization.

December 1983

 NOTES

1. A formal demonstration of the multiplier in relation to wage indexation can be found in Antonio Fazio (1981, 164).

2. There is unlimited empirical proof of this fact. For example, there is Sujit S. Bhala's econometric study of twenty-nine underdeveloped countries between 1966 and 1975, in which he concludes that "the basic monetarist model of inflation performs remarkably well, given the diversity of the countries studied" (1981, 84). In fact, the monetarist model is nothing but a reproduction of the exchange equation. Empirical tests based on this equation always and necessarily show excellent results, but prove nothing since they do not define the direction of the causal relation.

3. Although this endogenous vision of money can be found in Keynes (1930, vol. II, 211), the fundamental analysis of inflation in these terms was made by Ignácio Rangel (1963). Also, *see* Basil J. Moore (1979).

4. *See* Chapter 6. Between May and June 1981, when the annual inflation rate was 85 percent in Brazil, the oligopolistic corporations raised their prices an average of 170 percent, in comparison with the competitive sector, which raised its prices by approximately 60 percent.

5. The idea can be found in Samuelson and Solow (1960).

6. Meghnad Desai has made a precise critique of the monetarist view concerning the Phillips curve (1981, 69-76).

4

Administrative Policy: Gradualism or Shock

Any policy for controlling inflation must necessarily be related to the corresponding diagnosis of the causes of the current inflationary process. If it is demand inflation, then monetary and/or fiscal policy will be indicated. If inflation is administered or autonomous, the market is imperfect, and therefore price controls and an income policy will be the natural course. If inflation is structural, it will be necessary to live with inflation for a while and, at the same time, adopt long-term measures to remove the structural bottlenecks. As these causes do not exclude each other, a combination of these policies will probably be necessary. However, emphasis should always be given to the principal cause of the continuing inflation.

The object of this chapter is to discuss the anti-inflationary policy that is needed when inflation is mainly autonomous or administered, as tends to happen more and more in the oligopolistic capitalist economies in the last quarter of the twentieth century. In these economies, be they already industrialized or be they characterized by industrialized underdevelopment, this kind of inflation became even more relevant as the world economy entered the declining phase of a Kondratieff cycle at the beginning of the 1970s. Since then, inflation has started to coexist with high unemployment rates and idle capacity, this being called stagflation and, later, inertial inflation when, independently of aggregate demand, persistent high rates of inflation became common, especially in developing countries.

In order to discuss the anti-inflationary policy needed for this kind of economic situation, in the first section of this chapter we will present an abbreviated model of inflation. In the second, third, and fourth sections we will discuss and criticize the Keynesian and monetarist policies for controlling inflation. In the following sections we will examine the "administrative" policy for controlling inflation, which is based mainly on price controls and partial deindexation of the economy, and, secondarily, on a monetary and fiscal policy. We will end by examining the "heroic" policy for controlling inflation, the freezing of prices, wages and the exchange rate.[1]

1

In any inflationary process, it is important to distinguish the factors that maintain, accelerate (or decelerate), and sanction the inflation level. The maintenance or inertial factors are a result of the economic agents' capacity to automatically pass their increases in costs on to prices, wages, and interest and exchange rates. Accelerating factors are wage increases above productivity, increases in the corporations' profit margins, and, in an open economy, a real devaluation of the currency and increases in the prices of imported components. The public deficit and an increase in the money supply, which in an economy close to full employment could be accelerating factors of inflation, are factors that merely sanction inflation in an economy with a high rate of unemployment and idle capacity. In keeping with this perspective, the inflation rate depends on the following variables: variations in the wage rate, $\dot{w}$; variations in productivity, $\dot{q}$; variations in the price of imported products in international currencies, $\dot{v}$; variations of the exchange rate, $\dot{e}$; variations in the quantity of imported raw materials per unit of production, $\dot{x}$; and, variations in the profit margins (profit above direct costs) of the corporations, $\dot{m}$:

$$\dot{p} = (\dot{w} - \dot{q}) + (1 - \alpha)(\dot{v} + \dot{e} + \dot{x}) + \dot{m} \qquad 4.1$$

In this model, the most important variables in the short run are the wage rate, the exchange rate, and profit margins. In the long run, and when inflation is not at a very high level, the rate of increase of productivity is also very relevant.

2

The aim of any anti-inflationary economic policy is to act against the components of Equation 4.1 in order to succeed in reducing its variations and, thus, in reducing the level of inflation.

Generally, the models for an anti-inflationary economic policy concentrate all of their attention on wages.[2] The reason for this is simple.

Profit margins are generally considered to be constant, or at least beyond the control of those who are responsible for economic policy. Given the need to avoid an uneven balance of payments, it is assumed that the parity exchange rate remains constant. And, by definition, those responsible for economic policy are powerless over the prices of imported goods.

The exclusion of the last variable is very natural. However, the exclusion of the variations in the real exchange rate is less acceptable, since it is common for the countries which directly control their exchange rate, not having convertible currencies, to use the valorization of the local currency as a way to combat inflation. This policy was especially used by the countries that adopted monetarist strategies based on the rational expectations theory for combatting inflation, such as Chile and Argentina at the end of the 1970s. They had hoped that by announcing beforehand the exchange rate they could establish rational parameters for their inflationary expectations. The example of Mexico at the beginning of the 1980s, however, makes it clear that the temptation to overvalue the local currency is not the prerogative of the monetarist economists.

The exclusion of profit margins does not make any sense, especially when we consider that in technobureaucratic and oligopolistic capitalism, corporations have ample opportunities to manipulate their margins.[3] Obviously, there are ideological motives for this exclusion.

The use of only nominal wages to orient an anti-inflationary policy, in accordance with the Keynesian analysis of inflation, has the advantage of simplifying things. More important, however, is that, via the Phillips curve, it is possible to relate inflation to aggregate demand, that is to the rate of unemployment that will have a direct effect on wages. On the other hand, the correlation between the variations in nominal wages and the inflation rate is always—and obviously—very high in every empirical study.

Thus, by neutralizing the other components of Equation 4.1, the inflation rate then depends exclusively on wages and on productivity:

$$\dot{p} = \dot{w} - \dot{q} \qquad\qquad 4.2$$

Productivity itself could, in the name of simplification, be ignored or put on a secondary level, especially if the inflation level is very high or if we consider that, in the short run, it is not possible to change productivity. Hence,

$$\dot{p} = \dot{w} \qquad\qquad 4.3$$

On the other hand, in accordance with the Phillips curve (1958), there is an inverse relation between the variation of the wage rate and the rate of unemployment, d (Figure 4.1). This gives us the following equation, in which a and b are constant:

$$\dot{w} = a + bd^{-1} \qquad 4.4$$

According to this, the lower the rate of unemployment, the greater the variation in the wage rate. Theoretically, we could even have wage deflation when there are extremely high levels of unemployment, as nominal wages go down and the curve crosses the abscissa.

There is a trade-off in the Phillips curve between rate of unemployment and the variation in the wage rate. These, in turn, determine variations in prices. Substituting Equation 4.4 in Equation 4.3 the inflation rate is given by

$$\dot{p} = a + bd^{-1} \qquad 4.5$$

As unemployment increases or aggregate demand slackens, the rates of both the nominal wage increase and inflation fall.

The model of the Phillips curve is adopted by the Keynesian economists, as well as by the followers of the neoclassical synthesis.

Figure 4.1 The Phillips Curve and Autonomous Inflation

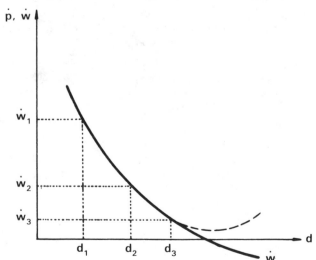

The anti-inflationary policy that obviously results from this is the reduction of aggregate demand by monetary, and preferably fiscal, measures. These are preferred because the most general assumption is that full employment and the consequential inflation are mainly caused by the public deficit or, more precisely, by the increase in public sector borrowing requirements (PSBR).

There is nothing to prevent establishing a direct relation between the variation in the inflation rate, p, and the variation in the profit margins, m in this model. However, it becomes difficult to establish, because profit margins, unlike unemployment, are not necessarily related to aggregate demand. Theoretically, one would expect that, as aggregate demand slackens, corporations would reduce their profit margins, just as the workers reduce their pressure on wages. But it is common knowledge that oligopolistic corporations tend to do the opposite.[4]

Going back to the basic model of the anti-inflationary policy based on demand management, its limitations become obvious when the economy in question does not have full employment.

First of all, as is made clear in Figure 4.1, as the unemployment rate increases, the gains in terms of reducing the inflation rate become proportionately less. Up to unemployment level d_1, the policy of controlling demand is highly efficient. Starting with level d_2, the policy of controlling demand becomes extremely inefficient. There is an intermediate situation between d_1 and d_2.

Second, there is no reason for an oligopolized economy that has high unemployment rates and idle capacity to maintain a direct correlation between the variations in wages and in prices. In order to simplify things, we will assume that this correlation exists in Figure 4.1 up to the point of unemployment d_3. After this point, however, the oligopolistic corporations begin to increase their profit margins in order to compensate for the loss in sales. As long as the increase in margins is above the decrease in wages, the price curve (which, after point d_3, separates itself from the wage curve) begins to increase as unemployment increases.

As we will see more precisely in the next chapter, this "inflection," which at first glance seems very unlikely, becomes understandable if the economy is not only oligopolized, but also large sectors are state-controlled, and especially if the economic authorities decide that, besides controlling demand, they will put into action a process of "corrective inflation" for the distorted (artificially low) prices of the goods and services produced by the state corporations. This measure, which is justified by the need to adjust relative prices, is actually imposed because of the growing fiscal difficulties in which the state and its corporations find themselves as a result of the recessive policy.

This is basically what happened in Brazil in 1983. The inflation level doubled in that year, while the economy went through a strong recession. The jump of the inflation rate was due not only to an increase in agricultural prices and the real devaluation (maxidevaluation) of the cruzeiro, but also to the "corrective inflation" measures such as the elimination of certain subsidies and the increase in the prices of the state corporations.

Third, controlling inflation by reducing demand, and consequently lowering wages, may become ineffective in terms of the Phillips curve, as the direct relation between unemployment and nominal wages is broken. There are two reasons for this break: the bargaining power of the trade unions and, especially, the need (generally translated into agreements with the unions or into laws) to index wages as a result of chronic inflation. In both cases, the Phillips curve is upwardly dislocated, that is, given the same level of unemployment, we will have a higher variation of the wage rate and of the rate of inflation. The trade unions' bargaining power can even lead to a real increase in wages, and thus to an acceleration of inflation, but what is more likely is that we will have inertial inflation with the indexation of wages. In this case Equation 4.4 takes on the following form:

$$\dot{w} = a + b\,d^{-1} + c\dot{p}_{-1} + \dot{w}_a \qquad\qquad 4.6$$

where c is the indexation coefficient, with c = 1 in the case of a full wage indexation to past prices $\dot{p}_{-1}$ and $\dot{w}_a$ represents the rate of the autonomous variation in wages due to the bargaining power of the trade unions.

To sum up, the policy of controlling inflation by demand management and a reduction of the wage rate loses its effectiveness as the oligopolist corporations raise or at least maintain their margins to compensate for the loss in sales and, especially, as the workers, given their unions and their political power, obtain the indexation of wages, leading to continuous upward dislocations of the Phillips curve.

3

The policy of demand management must be clearly distinguished from the monetarist policy. For the Keynesians (and for the middle-of-the-road adepts of the neoclassical synthesis), there is an exchange between unemployment and inflation, whereas for the monetarists this exchange does not exist, except in the short run. In the long run, the Phillips curve is inelastic, that is, vertical in relation to the horizontal axis. Strictly speaking, for the pure monetarist, the Phillips curve does not exist, so that it is theoretically possible to reduce prices without increasing unemployment.

The monetarist theory developed at the University of Chicago is naturally very complex. It is useful, therefore, to reduce it to its simplest form so that it can be more easily understood. We are not interested here in all of its nuances, as they can be found in the works of Milton Friedman and his followers.[5]

The monetarist school represents a counterrevolution against the Keynesian school; it claims to have reestablished the old neoclassical theory of general equilibrium, following Walras and Pigou. For the monetarists, money does not have any real effects on the economy. Money only determines the general level of prices, without having any influence on the level of production. This is possible because monetarist economists adopt the hypothesis of a constant relation (in the long run) between the demand for money and real income. The money demand function is converted into a nominal theory of income, postulating that the exogenous supply of money determines the nominal level of income and the price level. Therefore, for the monetarists, the process of hoarding, which was studied by Marx and Keynes, does not exist. The real rate of interest is determined in the real sector of the economy where aggregate savings determine the level of investments at the full employment level. Without going into details of the "new quantitative theory of money" developed by Milton Friedman, we can use the following equation to express their propositions:

$$M + V = Y + p \qquad\qquad 4.7$$

in which M is the rate of variation of the money supply, V the rate of variation of the income velocity of money, Y the rate of growth of real income and p the rate of increase of the price index.

As V is maintained constant in the long run, variations in M reflect ultimately on the level of prices p, for the real sector of the economy, represented by Y, is given exogenously by the natural rate of growth determined by supply factors such as the rate of population growth and technical progress. The basic argument is that, as the empirical relation between the real demand for money, M/p, and real income, Y, is stable, in the long run, prices would vary in direct proportion to the increase in the nominal money supply above the natural rate of growth of the real national income.

The basic monetarist strategy for controlling inflation is therefore very simple: stick firmly to a program of rigid control of the supply of money so that inflation will come down. In the short run, control of the money supply can have some effects on real income, but, in the long run, this will adjust to its natural level and the price level will stabilize. This control will only have real effects, bringing about a reduction in aggregate demand, as long as it is greater than aggregate supply. However, once an equilibrium between aggregate supply and aggregate demand is achieved, prices could theoretically be brought down by a continuous and programmed reduction of the money supply without affecting the employment level.

In order to understand how this would be possible, it is necessary to consider the role of expectations. For the monetarist, current inflation is basically a function of the expectations of increases in future prices, $\dot{p}^e$. Instead of writing, as would a structuralist, based on the inertial theory inflation, that present inflation is equal to past inflation, the monetarist will write:

$$\dot{p} = \dot{p}^e \qquad\qquad 4.8$$

It is important, therefore, in monetarist anti-inflationary policy, to counteract the expectations of the economic agents. For the monetarist, the basis for inflationary expectations is not past inflation, about which nothing can be done, but the expected economic policy: (1) an expected increase in the money supply, (2) expected devaluations of the currency in relation to foreign currencies, and (3) expected increases in nominal wages. Therefore, it is up to the economic authorities to act on these three variables, establishing guidelines for the corporations, the workers, and the consumers. In this way, the economic authorities should establish limits for the nominal growth of the money supply in a descending rhythm. They should also establish limits for the nominal exchange rate devaluation (announcing beforehand a declining rate of devaluations) and for nominal increases in wages, making both compatible with the reduction in the money supply and with the predicted future inflation rate.

As long as the basic guidelines are formulated correctly (have internal coherence) and as the economic authorities have credibility in the eyes of the economic agents, prices will automatically begin to fall. Although nominal wages would be going down, real wages theoretically would not go down, since the inflation rate would be reduced concomitantly. On the other hand, there would be no need for unemployment to force real wages down, since the workers and the corporations would tend to adjust themselves in a disciplined manner to the basic guidelines established by the economic authorities.

In this best of possible worlds described by the monetarist economists, in which there is no crisis because the automatic mechanism of the market permanently guarantees full employment, there is one ingredient missing: the interest rate. According to the orthodox monetarists, it would not go up as a result of the restrictive monetarist policy for two theoretical reasons: (a) because the international interest rate is the same in all countries; and (b) because, internally, the interest rate does not depend on the supply and demand for money, but rather on the supply and demand for savings.

The lack of realism in this theory is obvious. On the one hand, an *ex ante* relation as stable as the monetarists claim between the real demand for money and the production level does not exist. On the other hand, the idea that inflation is based on expectations is obvious, but the corollary that it is sufficient to establish basic guidelines that are compatible with each other, so that the economic agents will obediently reduce their expectations, is far from true. Economic agents base their expectations on past inflation (distributive conflict theory) rather than on future economic policy.

Actually, the monetarist experiments in combatting inflation generally result in a serious recession. They assume that inflation is the result of the public deficit, which provokes excess demand and an increase in the money supply. Thus, they end up adopting a policy of controlling aggregate demand. On the other hand, the policy of establishing basic guidelines for the exchange rate has the result, as was seen in Chile and Argentina, of overvaluing the local currency, with serious consequences for the balance of payments. Also, the policy of establishing basic guidelines for nominal increases of wages ends up being transformed into an authoritarian policy for a compulsory and drastic reduction of real wages.

4

Actually, the Keynesian demand management policy, which the monetarists in the end also adopt, emphasizing the control of the money supply, is perfectly acceptable when the economy is near full employment. Given this situation, restricting aggregate demand should lead to the corporations to cut their profit margins and the workers to accept cuts in their wages or, at least, not increase their wages above increases in productivity.

The greatest restriction to this kind of policy, the fact which makes it inefficient, is that its defenders tend to also use it when there is unemployment. They adopt this practice, however, because (a) to constrain demand through macroeconomic fiscal and monetary policies is politically much easier than to adopt administrative controls (in fact, monetary policies are even easier than fiscal policies because they are less discriminating); (b) because, in spite of its inefficiencies, this policy always attains some results, given the existence of competitive sectors, especially those producing agricultural and mineral raw materials and the unorganized sectors of the working class.

The strict monetarist strategy is unacceptable on all levels. The strongest argument in its favor would be the stable relationship between the money supply and the real income. But, first of all, this relation is often not verifiable. A correlation exists most of the time, but in an *ex post* form, which therefore does not establish a causal relationship. On the other hand, the concept that it is possible to reduce inflation without recession through a reduction of the money supply is strictly false, since the economic agents do not accept the basic guidelines on inflation established by the economic authorities. As a result, the monetarist strategy reduces itself in practice to a strategy of controlling aggregate demand, as reducing the money supply and the volume of internal credit provokes a recession.

Actually, the monetarist policy tends to be much more pernicious than the Keynesian policy for a number of reasons. First of all, the belief in a stable relationship between the demand for money and real income leads to much more prolonged policies to restrain the high-powered money and internal credit than the Keynesian defenders of the policies for controlling demand are disposed to adopt. Second, the resulting rise in the interest rate inhibits investments and impedes or stifles the cyclical recuperation of the economy. On this point, the Keynesian theory that the interest rate depends on the supply and demand for money is much more realistic than the classical theory, adopted by the monetarists, that the interest rate depends on the supply and demand for savings. In spite of the fall in investments, the interest rate goes up in keeping with the monetary restriction.

Autonomous or inertial inflationary pressures, being independent of excess demand, continue to manifest themselves, even in the middle of a recession, thus generating stagflation—the combination of inertial inflation with recession. In this situation, the reduction of the real money supply maintains high interest rates, favors financial speculation, and prevents or hinders the recuperation of the economy. Last, because the guidelines are not voluntarily obeyed, there is the tendency toward a real exchange rate valorization and larger deficits in the balance of payments. On the internal level, the most likely outcome will be the authoritarian imposition of limits for nominal wage increases, given the inefficiency of the monetary restrictions.

To sum up, the policy of controlling aggregate demand when there is unemployment can lead to a reduction in the inflation rate, but with a very high social and economic cost, given the inefficiency of this kind of policy for this part of the Phillips curve. The monetarist policy, in turn, only succeeds in obtaining results to the extent that it generates unemployment and, thus, confuses it with that of controlling aggregate demand. Or else, it succeeds to the extent at which authoritarian governments are able to impose a drastic reduction in real wages and/or promote an artificial valorization of the local currency.

5

We have a third type of anti-inflationary economic policy, which we will call the administrative policy for prices and incomes or, simply, the administrative policy. This kind of economic policy is based on the theoretical assumption that, in modern capitalist economies, coordination of economic activities is carried out more and more by administrative measures—by the big corporations and the state—which are partial substitutes for the market mechanisms.

Although this policy can also be useful during full employment, it is especially valid when there is unemployment and idle capacity, or when there is inertial or autonomous inflation, which comes together with administered inflation. The only efficient way to fight administered and inertial inflation is by the adoption of administrative measures—basically price controls.

The broad objective of the administrative policy is to reduce the inflation rate without either deepening the continuing recession or hurting, in terms of income distribution, the workers and the competitive sectors of the economy. Monetarist and Keynesian (demand administration) policies not only deepen the current recession, but they also tend to aggravate the concentration of income. This happens because the economic authorities only act on the economic aggregates—the money supply, public expenditures, aggregate demand—leaving the adjustment of relative prices to the market. The result is that the oligopolist sectors tend to increase their income share at the expense of the workers, the salaried middle class, and the small- and middle-sized competitive businesses. An administrative policy is used to try to make the reduction of the inflation rate compatible with controlled economic growth and, through income policy, to avoid greater distributive imbalances.

To the extent that the economy is already operating with high rates of unemployment and idle capacity, the first measure taken is to stimulate aggregate demand through a more flexible monetary policy. This also lowers the interest rate and, in consequence, increases investments and the corporations' sales. Lowering the interest rate has a directly anti-inflationary effect, as interest is a cost the corporations pass on to prices. The increase in sales, in turn, allows the corporations to lower their profit margins (profit over sales) without hurting their profit rate (profit over capital).

It is necessary, however, to note that demand should be stimulated moderately, with caution, so that the economy does not achieve full employment. If this happens, the sectors that have reached full employment will then increase their margins and wages, thus reactivating inflation.

Also, if the economy has balance-of-payments disequilibrium, an accelerated recovery would aggravate this problem because the demand for imports increases. Even though an administrative control of imports could be useful for this, its ability to restrain the increase in imports will always be relative.

6

The fundamental strategy for an administrative policy is to hinder the operation of the accelerating factors of inflation and to succeed in weakening or annulling the inertial factors that maintain the inflation level. This can be done in two alternative ways: gradually or, if inflation is already too high, by utilizing a shock strategy.

In order to make this strategy operational, the fundamental instruments are administrative price controls and a planned deindexation of the economy. Concomitantly, it would be necessary to gradually reduce the real public sector budget deficit and increase the money supply in such a way that the whole economy can adjust to progressively lower levels of inflation.

If inertial inflation, or stagflation, is accompanied by a balance-of-payments deficit, as was the case of Brazil at the beginning of the 1970s, these measures would only have results if the adjustment policy adopted is not intended to correct the distortions in relative prices by using measures of "corrective inflation." If this happens, as in Brazil in 1983, inflation will tend to accelerate rather than to reduce its rhythm. Although the orthodox adjustment policy is aimed not only at the equilibrium of the balance of payments, but also at reducing the inflation rate, its effect on inflation is the opposite of that desired. This is especially true in the first phase of the adjustment process, because of the real exchange rate devaluation and the other measures to correct relative prices, especially through the elimination of a large variety of subsidies that characterize orthodox adjustment policies.

These policies, which are supported by the monetarist and Keynesian theories, are actually extremely inefficient for combatting inertial inflation. This is because they insist on not accepting inflation as autonomous of demand and thus inertial, but rather as caused by the public deficit and an excess of available credit. The public deficit and excess supply of money would also cause the foreign trade deficit, so that the same policy would solve both of these imbalances. Aside from an exchange devaluation and adjustments in relative prices, there would also be a reduction in the absorption of external resources by a cut in the public sector borrowing requirements, or rather, in the public deficit, and a cut in the money supply, or more precisely, in banking credit. These measures would provoke an increase in the interest rate, a cut in investment, a reduction in demand, and recession. Consequently, once excess demand is eliminated, profit margins and wages would be reduced and, therefore, the result would be an inflationary deceleration, as well as a diminution in the demand for imports and an increase in the supply for export.

We have already analyzed the inadequacy of this theory for explaining inertial inflation, which is not a result of excess demand. In the same way, a balance of payments problem, expressed by a deficit in the current account balance of the country while the trade account presents a surplus, is not necessarily the result of an excess in current effective demand. The current account deficit can be derived from external causes, such as a deterioration in the terms of exchange of the country or an increase in international interest rates. It can even be provoked by interest on past debts—interest that has no relation to current aggregate demand. This was precisely the case of Brazil in the first half of the 1980s. Thus, the economy can be in a deep recession and, nevertheless, not only have inflation, but also have a deficit in its current account, which is not the result of excess current expenditure. The current amount deficit may originate from a structural imbalance due to a large interest payment on a stock of debt accumulated in the past. In this situation, cutting the absorption of goods may have little effect because the problem lies in the payment of interest.

————————————————— 7 —————————————————

Let us first examine the gradualist administrative strategy for controlling inertial inflation. Price controls and partial deindexation, or indexation according to a future declining rate of inflation, are the two basic instruments of an administrative policy for controlling inflation.

The difficulties related to administrative price controls are well known: (1) it is not possible to control all prices; (2) a very competent and big bureaucracy is necessary in order to exercise partial control; (3) the bureaucratic apparatus is easily subject to corruption; (4) the unavoidable errors when prices are administered provoke discrepencies between the set prices and equilibrium value, or, more precisely, production price, resulting in serious allocatory distortions; and (5) when setting wages, the tendency is to reduce the real wages of the workers.

Although all of these difficulties are real, administrative price controls are still recommended for the simple reason that, when there is inertial inflation and stagflation, there is no alternative. Given that prices increase autonomously of demand (inertially), we have already seen that the administration of aggregate demand is highly inefficient. Thus, there is no better strategy than that of trying to administratively control prices, especially those of the oligopolist sectors that are capable of increasing their prices independently of the existence of pressures from demand.

In order to do this, it will be necessary to create a specialized bureaucratic apparatus. This apparatus must be permanent, since the oligopolization of the economy is a permanent factor in contemporary capitalism. No doubt, this bureaucratic apparatus will undergo the risks of corruption, and it will certainly commit errors. But corruption is a phenomenon that can be partially controlled. Although the errors in setting prices can be significant, they will be fewer than those committed by an imperfect market where inertial inflation prevails.

As for errors in controlling prices, it is necessary to point out that they can be serious, provoking large distortions in the allocation of resources and in income distribution, if two basic precautions are not taken. First of all, prices must be set by a permanent process of trial and error, of successive approximations, instead of by technocratically established formulas. Second, the aim of this process of trial and error should be for the set price to come as close as possible to the production price, that is, to the price that a competitive market would tend to establish.

These two correlated precautions are essential for simultaneously (1) reducing the inflation rate, (2) guaranteeing a satisfactory allocation of resources, and (3) avoiding distortions in income distribution.

The permanent temptation to those who control prices is that of giving special treatment to the first objective to the detriment of the other two. In these terms, they confront the law of value: they artificially valorize the exchange rate, lower real wages, and maintain the prices of the state-owned corporations and some private sectors with less political power at artificially low levels.[6] As a result, aside from the distortions in relation to income distribution and the allocation of resources, there are other problems: disregarding the officially set prices, the buildup of inventories, the black market, and disorganization of the economic system. Inevitably, the short-run results will be annulled in the long run or even worsened by a new price explosion.

Administrative price and wage controls could be complemented with incentives and fiscal penalties aimed at obtaining the adherence of the corporations. These kinds of measures were suggested by Weintraub (Weintraub 1978, 153), and could be an important auxiliary instrument for directly controlling wages and profit margins. In Brazil, during the 1960s and 1970s, firms that failed to obey price controls were not only fined, but were also excluded from financing by state-owned banks and forbidden to sell to the state.

---------------------------------- 8 ----------------------------------

Once the necessary precautions are taken, administrative price controls can be successful in gradually reducing inflation by controlling the factors that accelerate and maintain the inflation level.

The basic maintaining factor of inflation, that which makes it inertial, is the formal or informal indexation of the economy or, in other words, the capacity of the economic agents to pass increases in costs on to prices independently of the existence of demand pressure. The first concern of the administrative policy should, therefore, be directed toward breaking this indexation.

The basic rule in the process of breaking the indexation process is to establish an index to correct prices in keeping not only with past inflation, but also with future inflation, which is bound to decline. The object of this type of indexation is to reestablish the average real price of either merchandise or the work force (wages), thus annulling the perverse effects of the eventual acceleration (or deceleration) of average real price inflation on them.[7]

Let us suppose that the general rate of price increases is going down because of a fall in the price of raw materials and agricultural products, which we shall assume are not indexed. The usual formula for indexing prices and nominal incomes—the application of the past inflation rate—has the effect of increasing average real prices and real incomes since the loss of value in the previous period is greater than in the current period. This idea is valid not only for the prices of goods, but also for wages and all other incomes. It can be understood more easily by looking at Figure 4.2, where we can see the usual formula for correcting prices "by peaks," that is, by the application of past inflation to reestablish the peak real prices. As inflation declines, average real prices and incomes increase, impeding the action of the anti-inflationary policy. In the axis of ordinates of Figure 4.2 are real prices or wages, p_i, (or w), in which p_i is the real price or income that corresponds to a determined indexed sector, and w is the real wage rate. In the abscissa, we have the successive periods of readjustment in which indexation was practiced. The solid line corresponds to the real price or wage, which decreases between two periods of monetary correction. The inclination of the curve is smaller between corrections, because, in the example, inflation is declining. At the end of each period, the price or income is completely corrected because the rate of inflation of the preceding period restores the real price or income of the previous peak. As a result, the dotted line, which connects the midpoints of real prices or

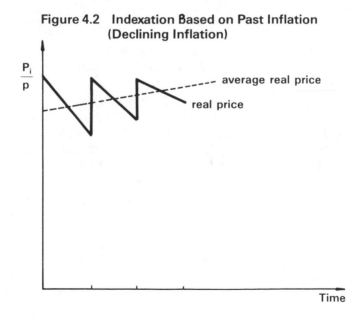

Figure 4.2 Indexation Based on Past Inflation
(Declining Inflation)

wages, corresponding to the average real price or wage, goes up. The indexation, therefore, is inconsistent because it increases rather than maintains the average real price or income. Thus, it becomes much more difficult to reduce inflation, since this kind of indexation tends to automatically reproduce the past real inflation in the present.

Actually, prices, wages, and nominal incomes are corrected periodically, but with different time lags, each one trying to recover the real peak price or income of the previous period. But, as it is distributively inconsistent to maintain real peak price or income simultaneously, inflation does its job by reducing their purchasing power.

The formula for alternative indexation, which takes into account half of the past inflation in order to reestablish the average real price, and half of the predicted future inflation, in order to guarantee that the average real price is maintained in the following period, is shown in Figure 4.3. The inflation rate undergoes the same decline in this figure as in Figure 4.2. However, as the correction is made in keeping with half of the past inflation and half of the predicted future inflation, the average real price is kept constant.

This formula can be expressed in the following way:

$$P_{t+1} = P_t(1 + 0,5\dot{p} + 0,5\,\dot{p}_f) \qquad\qquad 4.9$$

Figure 4.3 Indexation Based on Past and Future Inflation (Declining Inflation)

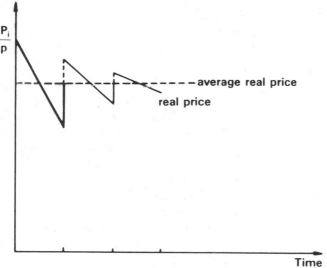

in which P is the nominal price for goods or services, p is the past inflation rate and p_f is the future predicted inflation rate.

Naturally, the difficulty with this formula is in predicting future inflation. However, it is possible to introduce corrections *a posteriori*, in order to cancel the effects of erroneous predictions.

This formula should also undergo corrections in keeping with increases in productivity. It would be necessary to increase wages in real terms in keeping with the average increase in productivity. Once this measure is adopted, and assuming that there is neutral technical progress in which the capital output ratio remains constant, the rate of surplus value, that is, the relation between profits and wages, also remains constant, and there will be no inflationary pressure.[8]

In relation to the price of goods and services, it would be necessary to consider the increase in productivity in each sector of the economy and reduce real prices correspondingly. As wages are supposed to increase according to the increase in the average productivity of the economy—rather than proportionally to the reduction of real prices due to the increase of productivity in each sector, as is assumed in pure (fundamental) economics—the reduction of real prices in each sector due to increases in sectorial productivity should be less than if there were no real increases in wages in keeping with increases of the average productivity of the economy.

To sum up, it must be emphasized that a gradual, planned deindexation should be carried out by taking into consideration a declining future inflation and variations in productivity.

9

The planned deindexation and administrative price controls should reach all sectors of the economy, including financial assets. In a formally indexed economy such as Brazil's, wages, the exchange rate, financial assets, and the prices of the state corporations are generally indexed. A planned and partial deindexation, corresponding to indexation in keeping with past inflation and predicted future inflation, should therefore reach all sectors. This is the only way that it is possible to reduce inflation without provoking serious distributive distortions.

As the prices of the corporate sector are not formally indexed, it is necessary to control them administratively. Actually, it is sufficient to control the prices—and therefore the profit margins—of the oligopolistic corporations and of some essential products. Control of the competitive sectors is, in pratical terms, impossible, given the large number of firms and of goods. Aside from this, it is not necessary because the market is capable of controlling them.

But, in relation to the essential products of the competitive sectors—especially agricultural, mineral, and animal products, it is also necessary to take two types of administrative measures: price controls and the formation of buffer stocks, emphasizing the latter measure.

All of these interventions in the market have a relatively arbitrary nature. Formulas can be applied, as referred to in the previous section, but their accuracy is always very relative. For this reason, trial and error is inevitable in the process of administering prices.

In the previous section, we referred to a method of indexation that takes future inflation into account. This kind of indexation strictly corresponds to a process of partial deindexation, to the extent at which it assumes a declining future inflation. A more direct formula for partial deindexation would be to arbitrarily establish a percent reducer for the past inflation rate (80 percent, for example) and correct prices, wages, the exchange rate, and financial activities in accordance with this formula. If inflation were declining, a reducer of this kind would correspond to the indexation formula based on future inflation. Partial deindexation and indexation based on future inflation are, therefore, very similar processes.

On the other hand, any formula for indexation or partial deindexation of prices is a form of administering prices, of an administrative control in keeping with a predetermined rules. When the inflation is autonomous in relation to demand, there is no other alternative for controlling it than to combine various types of administrative price controls, including partial deindexation and indexation based on predicted declining inflation.

10

Controlling inflation by using the formula being proposed here—a combination of administrative price controls for the oligopolistic sectors and a partial deindexation (via a reducer and/or considering a declining future inflation) with a fiscal and monetary policy that reduces the public deficit and the money supply as inflation falls—could only be successful if the government is capable of assuring a satisfactory allocation of resources and avoiding distortions in income distribution.

Obviously, this is not an easy task. It would not even present immediate results. It would be much easier to reduce inflation through a violent reduction of wages or else by harming the firms in the competitive sectors. This has happened systematically in Brazil. However, the resulting distortions in relative prices eventually need to be corrected and, when they are, space is opened for a new acceleration of inflation.

The danger of increasing the distortions in relative prices is, therefore, the biggest problem that appears when fighting inflation. Prices cannot be far from the price of production for much time. This is true for both the small competitive firms, including the agricultural ones, as well as for the large state-owned corporations. These are the two kinds of firms that tend to be used the most for combatting inflation, but, sooner or later, they are forced to reconstitute their prices in order to survive and maintain their rate of profit, thus causing new inflationary acceleration. This is because the factors that accelerate inflation—increases in profit margins and real wages—are nothing more than changes and recompositions of relative prices that come from the function of the law of value.

It should be noted that these kinds of distortions can be derived from government incompetence and political pressures put on governments. But even if there is no incompetence, the distortions will necessarily appear if the program for controlling inflation by using administrative methods has the tendency to last indefinitely. Also, new corporations' strategies for outwitting the controls are developed as the controls are prolonged.[9] Thus, it is necessary to think about administrative controls as a temporary strategy or, more precisely, as a strategy of variable rigidity, mixed with partial liberalizations—which allow the market to correct certain distortions—followed by new emphasis in the scheme of control. Otto Eckstein observed, however, that the minimum period for a price- and wage-control program should be three years (1981, 110).

11

The efficiency of administrative price and wage controls has been the subject of various studies whose results have not been absolutely conclusive, but which, in general, tend to confirm the effectiveness of this kind of policy. Otto Eckstein and James A. Girola studied five episodes in which price controls were adopted in the United States (World War I, World War II, the Korean War, wage-price guidelines of the Kennedy-Johnson administration, and the direct controls of the Nixon administration). They concluded that these controls were highly effective in retarding price increases during the two world wars and during the Nixon administration (1978, 323-333).[10]

Studies carried out in Britain and reported by Victor Argy (1981, 354) and A. J. Hagger (1977, 206) concluded that wage and price controls succeeded in controlling wages but not prices. However, according to Argy, the wage controls only succeeded in retarding wage increases in such a way that "every attempt at a prices and incomes policy [PIP] in the United Kingdom since 1965 ended in a wage explosion" (1981, 395). Hagger, in turn, concluded:

> To sum up this discussion of the findings of the various econometric studies of the effectiveness of prices and incomes policy, we may say that while the United States studies give consistent support to the view that prices and incomes policy is effective, the weight of the United Kingdom Studies appears to be fairly heavily in the other direction. (1977, 208)

These studies are undoubtedly useful because they recount experiences that had both good and bad results. They are not and cannot be conclusive because their results depend on many factors: the competence and political support of those in the government, and the favorable situation of the other economic variables, especially an increase of productivity.

In Brazil, for example, the administrative price controls established since 1967, when the Interministerial Price Council was formed, have had good results. At that time, however, the government counted on high political legitimacy (support from the civilian society), and was favored by an expansionary phase of the business cycle, during which there was a large increase in productivity. The attempt to repeat this performance in 1980 failed because the government no longer could count on the same political power, and the attempt to stimulate economic growth was artificial in that it found no support in an expansive movement of the business cycle. The measures of corrective inflation adopted in the immediately preceding period (the second semester of 1979) also had produced an inflationary acceleration that administrative controls were unable to stop.

The existence of unsuccessful experiences with administrative price controls does not condemn this kind of policy, just as the successful ones do not confirm it. They only serve to point out the errors that should not be repeated and the strategies that have been shown to be most effective. The concrete fact is that, in oligopolized and indexed economies, when there is unemployment together with stagflation, this is the only valid alternative for economic policy. Monetary and fiscal policies with demand management are also important, but they perform a complementary role. When they are put in the forefront, the result is more recession and more distortions in allocation and distribution and, in some cases (as happened in Brazil in 1983), more inflation.

———————————— 12 ————————————

Our first proposal for an anti-inflationary policy is to gradually control inflation through administrative price and income controls, including a partial and planned deindexation of the economy combined with measures to reduce the public deficit and money supply as inflation is lowered. Thus, monetary and fiscal policies appear in a subordinated form, as the money supply and the public deficit, when inflation is autonomous or inertial, and are factors that only sanction inflation.

Meanwhile, it is possible to imagine a point at which this kind of gradual policy is no longer effective. This would be when inertial inflation reaches levels that are so high, and its autonomous character is so strong that the gradual mechanisms no longer function. This will happen especially when the measures for partial deindexation and for administrative control are counterbalanced by new supply shocks, that is, by new accelerating factors resulting from disorganization of the economy, distortions in relative prices, and from the need to correct these distortions through corrective inflation. At this point, it will be necessary to think about a second and more radical alternative for fighting inflation.

The analyses of the historical experiences of controlling inflation also indicate that, in certain circumstances, a global and rapid attack is preferable to a gradualist treatment. After looking at various experiences with anti-inflationary policies, Leland B. Yeager concluded that "almost all of the successes that have come to our attention involved stopping or drastically slowing price inflation within a few months." (1981, 38).

In these conditions, a "heroic" policy of administrative price controls and the total deindexation of the economy could be the only adequate alternative. It needs to be clear that this is not the classic "shock treatment" of the orthodox economists; it is not intended for wiping out autonomous inflation by a violent repression of demand and a consequent recession. The inefficiency of this kind of policy has already been shown. For example, in 1981, a shock treatment was applied to the Brazilian economy and the rate of inflation more than doubled.

Assuming that the economy is indexed and is strongly oligopolized, what is intended is that, on a given day, a decision be made to completely deindex the economy—wages, prices, the exchange rate, rents, and interest—and then to freeze all prices from that point on. For example, if inflation is around a level of 300 percent, the most optimistic hypothesis would be that, with these measures, it would be reduced to zero the next day.

Obviously, this hypothesis is not entirely realistic. But, in order to reduce inflation substantially once the "heroic" solution is adopted, it is necessary to imagine the process in several stages.

There would be a first stage, prior to the act of deindexation, and the freeze (D Day) in which it would be necessary to make the last adjustments in relative prices. This would not be difficult for merchandise prices because, when inflation is at very high levels, business firms tend to make adjustments more and more frequently in their prices, so that the lags between the readjustments are reduced. As for wages, it would be ideal if the readjustments were already semestral or even quarterly, and would take place on the same day for all categories of workers. Then, if D Day were on a day exactly in the middle of two readjustments, the workers would receive the equivalent of the average real wage on that day. If this is not possible, it will be necessary to adopt a somewhat complicated formula (for the understanding and agreement of the workers) to convert nominal wages, with different months as the basis for indexation to the average real wage of the previous six or twelve months.

Next, on D Day, inflation would not fall to zero because it would be impossible to control all prices. There would still be some distortions in relative prices to be corrected. Also, control of the competitive sectors through administrative means is almost impossible. The important thing is for the inertial mechanism that maintains inflation to be broken, if not totally, at least in great part. A low rate of inflation will continue to exist through new accelerating factors that will be the result of the necessary adjustments in relative prices.

Finally, as a third stage, the freeze will have to be partially relaxed. At this point, however, the inflation level will probably be very low. It will continue to be reduced through the gradual administrative policy that we described earlier.

We call this policy "heroic" because it is risky. Its objective is to not provoke a recession, and it aims to not produce distortions in allocation or distribution. However, the measures are radical and can lead to the disorganization of the economic system and especially of the financial system which, in inflationary situations of this kind, is both a big beneficiary and a big factor for instability. Because of this, the heroic policy for fighting inflation can only be adopted when inflation has clearly gotten out of the control of conventional economic policy, or when civil society as a whole is convinced that the distortions caused by the high inflation rates are more serious than the eventual risks of the heroic solution.[11]

July 1984

—————————————— NOTES ——————————————

1. *See* Chapter 2 in this respect.

2. *See*, for example, A. J. Hagger (1977), who makes an excellent, didactic summary of the theories of inflation and of controlling inflation.

3. It is true that, in normal operating conditions, the oligopolies, when avoiding price competition, tend to maintain their profit margins constant; but, in an inflationary economy subject to shocks and with wider cyclical fluctuations, margins no longer continue to be constant.

4. *See* Chapter 6.

5. For a critical summary of monetarism and of its empirical tests, *see* Meghnad Desai (1981).

6. The radical economist Howard J. Sherman, after observing that Nixon, between 1971 and 1974, used wage and price controls in peacetime for the first time in the history of the United States, noted that these controls caused allocative inefficiencies and were clearly geared toward favoring the corporations, as well as toward favoring the black market (1983, 212).

7. This is basically the formula that was used by Mário Henrique Simonsen to correct wages in Brazil during the 1970s, when he was still an advisor to the planning ministry. The distortions were the result of its poor application and not of its theoretical conception.

8. Cf. Luiz Bresser Pereira (1986).

9. Cf. Charles E. Lockwood (1979, 168).

10. The failure of the policy of "wage-price guidelines" is debatable even for the Kennedy-Johnson administration. As James Tobin notes, between 1961 and 1966, unemployment was reduced from 7 percent to 4 percent, while inflation was maintained at 2 percent. In the following period, from 1966-1969, inflation grew as a result of the financing of the Vietnam War (1981, 22).

11. This chapter, including this last section proposing the "heroic solution," was written in the second semester of 1983 and published in the *Revista de Economia Política* in July 1984. In August of this year, after a great acceleration of Brazilian inflation, Francisco Lopes published a short paper proposing, not as a second alternative but as the only one, the same type of policy and calling it a "heterodox shock." When we wrote this chapter, the inflation level was changing from the 100 to the 200 percent level (*see* Chapter 7). In the second semester of 1984, the 200 percent level was well established, and new accelerating factors began to act. The

inflation rate only reached the 300 percent level in the beginning of 1986, when the Brazilian authorities opted for the shock.

5

Inertial Inflation and the Phillips Curve

The Phillips curve establishes an inverse relation between inflation and unemployment. But when the rate of unemployment and idle capacity go above a certain level, the oligopolistic corporations increase their profit margins in order to compensate for the loss of sales. As a result, the Phillips curve undergoes an "inflexion," causing inflation to accelerate as unemployment increases. Vellutini (1985) correctly observed that this inversion would be the result of successive dislocations of the Phillips curve. In this chapter, we will try to relate more systematically inertial inflation (the automatic reproduction of past inflation) and administered inflation (the acceleration of inflation because of shocks in supply provoked by the monopoly power of corporations, trade unions, and/or state) with the Phillips curve.

Inflation can be accelerated as much by an increase in demand and a consequent reduction in unemployment, which provoke movement along the Phillips curve, as by shocks in supply (or increases in the monopoly power), which momentarily raise prices above this curve. If, by considering the propagating effects of inflation, we add the inertial component—the straight reproduction of past inflation in the present—we will have an upward movement of the Phillips curve. In the first section of this chapter, we examine the case of a supply shock combined with inertial inflation. In this situation, there is one upward movement of the Phillips curve, with inflation then becoming inert at the new level. In the second section, we examine the case of demand pressure leading to a reduction in unemployment. In this situation, the maintenance or inertial factor of inflation would provoke recurring dislocations of the Phillips curve as long as the excess in demand lasts, leading to an inflationary spiral, that is, to a continuous acceleration of inflation. The "inflexion" in the

Phillips curve, which we analyze in the third section, takes place when the inflation rate accelerates because of unemployment increases. Inflation accelerates as the result of successive supply shocks, especially from autonomous increases in the profit margins that successively move the Phillips curve. Finally, in the fourth section, we develop a simple mathematical model that will combine the demand (Phillips curve) and supply shocks—the accelerating factors of inflation—with the inertial component of inflation, that is, the maintaining factor of inflation.

———————————————— 1 ————————————————

Let us begin with a simplified equation for inflation:

$$\dot{p} = \frac{A}{M} \cdot \dot{p} - 1 + \frac{B}{M} \cdot d^{-1} + \frac{H}{M} \qquad 5.1$$

In this equation A/M is the inertial or indexation coefficient. When A/M is equal to 1, past inflation, $\dot{p}_{-1}$, is reproduced wholly in the present. The second component represents the Phillips curve, with B/M being the coefficient that measures the relation between the inflation rate and the unemployment rate, d^{-1}. Last, H/M represents the impact of all of the possible kinds of supply shocks: increases in profit margins, autonomous increases of real wages above productivity, corrective inflation, imported inflation, and real (above inflation) exchange rate devaluations. Let us first take an economy in equilibrium at point d_0, where $\dot{p} = 0$, and assume that a supply shock raises the rate of price increases above the Phillips curve to the level $\dot{p}_1$ (Figure 5.1). Inflation would only be maintained at this new level if, given the existance of full indexation (A/M = 1), inflation were inertial, and if the Phillips curve moves upward to point h_1. If there are no new shocks, there will be no new upward movements of the Phillips curve. The constant unemployment rate would have no effect on wages and, thus, on prices. This case, illustrated by Figure 5.1, shows that a supply shock in a model with full indexation leads to a permanent increase in the trend rate of inflation.

———————————————— 2 ————————————————

Now let us consider a second case in which a demand shock provokes a reduction in unemployment from d_0 to d_1 as illustrated in Figure 5.2. The inflation rate then moves along the Phillips curve to the point that

Figure 5.1 Effect of a Supply Shock with Full Indexation

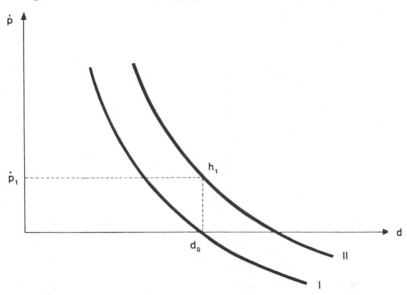

corresponds to $\dot{p}_1$. If, at that point, all economic agents are fully indexing their prices, the Phillips curve would move upward by the same value as the distance of $\dot{p}_0$ - $\dot{p}_1$, reaching inflation rate $\dot{p}_2$. Meanwhile, as pressures from demand continue and because the upward movement of the curve has already incorporated the accelerating effects provoked by the initial demand shock, inflation will accelerate again, corresponding to the distance $\dot{p}_0$ - $\dot{p}_1$, and, therefore, a new upward movement in the curve will take place. Thus the combination of excess demand with inertial inflation will provoke an inflationary spiral, causing the inflation rate to move to points A, B, C, and so on successively. This acceleration will stop only when the level of unemployment returns to d_0.

The elimination of excess demand would provoke a single reduction in the inflation rate through the movement of this rate along the Phillips curve to the $\dot{p}_2$ on the vertical axis, corresponding to d_0 on the horizontal axis. In Figure 5.2, beginning with inflation rate $\dot{p}_3$, corresponding to point C, inflation would fall to $\dot{p}_2$, corresponding to point D. At this point, inflation would remain inertial. If we want to bring the rate of inflation down to $\dot{p}_0$ by increasing unemployment, this increase would have to be very big, given the inertial character of inflation. In Figure 5.2, it is not enough to return to d_0. It would be necessary to reach very high levels of unemployment, which would be incompatible with a minimum of social

Figure 5.2 Effect of a Demand Shock with Full Indexation

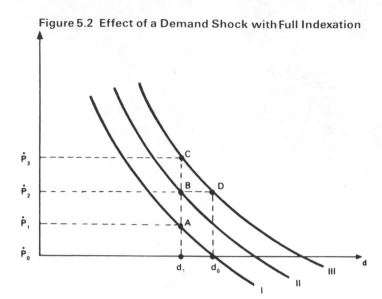

stability.

3

In this model of inflation, if there is an acceleration provoked by successive increases in the profit margins of the oligopolistic sectors aimed at neutralizing the increase in unemployment, we would have an apparent inflexion of the Phillips curve; this would result in successive upward movements of this curve. Increasing profit margins is a defense mechanism that the corporations use to protect their profit rates from recession or from a reduction in sales and the consequent increase in fixed unit costs.

In Figure 5.3, beyond the unemployment level d_1, the oligopolistic corporations would successively increase their profit margins in such a way that the Phillips curve would undergo successive dislocations. As the rate of unemployment increases from d_1 to d_2, d_3, and d_4, the Phillips curve would move upward and to the right from curve I to curves II, III, and IV. Instead of undergoing a reduction along the original curve I, the inflation rate would follow points A, B, C, and D, as if the Phillips curve were undergoing an inflexion, as represented by the dotted line. In this case, one can perceive that the inflation rate would undergo an acceleration with the increase in unemployment (idle capacity). It should become clear

Figure 5.3 Effect of Profit Margin Increases

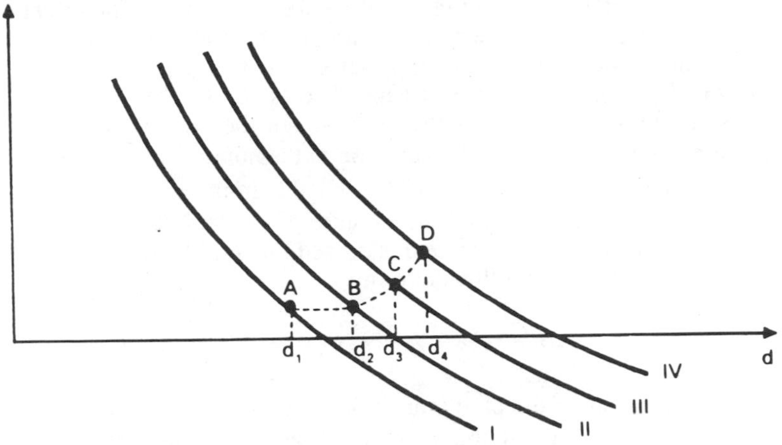

that orthodox policies for controlling inflation through recession can have adverse effects, generating stagflation.

4

This analysis could be expressed by a more disaggregated but simplified mathematical model than that represented by Equation 5.1. We will explain how the values of A, B, H, and M are determined. For this, we will make use of an equation, derived from the markup theory of prices, which represents the rate of the variation in prices, $\dot{p}$, as determined by the variation in direct costs (wages and raw materials) and the rate of the variation of the profit margin itself, $\dot{m}$.

$$\dot{p} = \dot{m} + \alpha\,(\dot{w} - \dot{q}) + (1 - \alpha)\,(\dot{v} + \dot{e} + \dot{x}) \qquad 5.2$$

In this equation, $\dot{w}$ is the wage rate, $\dot{q}$ the rate of productivity, $\dot{v}$ the price of raw material in foreign currency, $\dot{e}$ the exchange rate, and $\dot{x}$ the amount of raw material per unit produced and is the wage cost share in the total cost. The points above the letters indicate the rate of variation.

In order to make the model more complete, we can add the effect of the interest rate and of indirect taxes to the above equation. The effect of the interest rate can be represented in a simplified form if we assume that the corporations depend on loans to finance their working capital (wages and raw materials), and pass their financial costs on to prices. Given these two assumptions, the effect of the variation in the interest rate can be represented by $(\beta \dot{r})$ where $\dot{r}$ is the variation in the nominal interest rate and β is a factor of proportionality indicating the importance of loans in relation to total working capital. In the case of the indirect taxes (t), the effect of their variation is direct and is passed on entirely to prices. Thus, Equation 5.2 takes on the following form:

$$\dot{p} = \dot{m} + \alpha (\dot{w} - \dot{q}) + (1 - \alpha) (\dot{v} + \dot{e} + \dot{x}) + \beta \dot{r} + \dot{t} \qquad 5.2'$$

The mechanism of direct or indirect indexation affects this equation in three ways. First of all, if the profit margins are administered by the oligopolistic corporations, any increase in costs resulting from this administration of prices is passed on to final prices. In this way, prices are indexed to direct costs. In normal conditions of operation, the corporations keep their margins constant, but, in cases of an accentuated fall in demand, profit margins can be raised in order to protect the profitability of the corporations or to make up for the lack of demand.

The second way in which indexation affects Equation 5.2 refers to the fact that readjustments of nominal wages are automatically tied to past inflation. When there is chronic inflation, trade unions fight to reestablish the peak of real wages, which means correcting nominal wages according to 100 percent of past inflation, and to eventually obtain real wage increases. This phenomenon was represented in a very simplified form in the previous chapters by the incorporation of a component of wage indexation, $\dot{p}_{-1}$, and another of the autonomous real wage increase, $\dot{w}_a$, to the Phillips curve. Thus, the Phillips a curve took on the following form:

$$\dot{w} = a + b \, d^{-1} + c\dot{p}_{-1} + \dot{w}_a \qquad 5.3$$

In this, c is the coefficient of the indexation of wages, d the unemployment rate, and a and b the parameters of the Phillips curve.

The third way in which indexation affects our equation of the inflation rate is the mechanism of the indexation of the exchange rate. Showing the recent Brazilian experience, in which the exchange rate underwent instantaneous readjustments in relation to prices, we can express the variations in the exchange rate by:

$$\dot{e} = g\dot{p} + \text{Max} \tag{5.4}$$

In this, g represents the degree of indexation of the exchange rate in relation to current inflation and can vary according to the policy of exchange rate devaluation. "Max" represents an unexpected and real variation in the exchange rate due to a maxidevaluation.

Thus, substituting Equations 5.3 and 5.4 in Equation 5.2, and assuming that $a = \dot{q}$, we have:

$$\dot{p} = \frac{\alpha c}{1 - (1 - \alpha) g} \dot{p}_{-1} + \frac{\alpha b}{1 - (1 - \alpha) g} d_{-1}$$

$$\tag{5.5}$$

$$+ \frac{\dot{m} + (1 - \alpha)(\dot{v} + \dot{x}) + (1 - \alpha) \text{Max} + \beta \dot{r} + \dot{\iota} + \alpha \dot{w}^a}{1 - (1 - \alpha) g}$$

This equation shows explicitly the variables involved in equation 5.1, where the inflation rate is explained by three components:

I. The inertial component, represented by:

$$\frac{A}{M} = \frac{\alpha c}{1 - (1 - \alpha) g} \tag{5.6}$$

II. The demand component (Phillips curve), represented by:

$$\frac{B}{M} = \frac{\alpha b}{1 - (1 - \alpha) g} \tag{5.7}$$

III. The supply shocks component, represented by:

$$\frac{H}{M} = \frac{\dot{m} + (1 - \alpha)(\dot{v} + \dot{x}) + (1 - \alpha) \text{Max} + \dot{r} + \dot{\iota} + \alpha \dot{w}^a}{1 - (1 - \alpha) g}$$

$$\tag{5.8}$$

The inflationary multiplier (see Chapter 2, Section 3) is given by:

$$\frac{1}{M} = \frac{1}{1 - (1 - \alpha) g} \tag{5.9}$$

The inertial component defined by Equation 5.6 clearly shows that the inflation rate depends on the degree of indexation of wages, c, and of the exchange rate, g. When full indexation exists $c = 1$, and $g = 1$, and $A/M = 1$. In this case, keeping the other components neutral, the present inflation rate, $\dot{p}$, is determined by the inflation rate of the previous period, $\dot{p}_{-1}$, and is stable. Obviously a reduction of the coefficients of indexation ($c<1$ and $g<1$) can contribute to a gradual reduction in the inflation rate.

The second component of Equation 5.5 represents the demand component of inflation and is effective when unemployment is reduced and approaches the level of full employment (full utilization of the productive capacity). According to the Keynesian models, based on the Phillips curve, the inflationary effects of this component are felt first in wage cost and then in the demand for goods. It assumes that the effects of an increase in wages because of a reduction in unemployment cause an increase in prices rather than the direct pressure of aggregate demand on prices in the market for goods and services.

The various supply shocks, such as an increase in profit margins, an increase in the price of raw materials, a maxidevaluation of the exchange rate, an increase in interest rates, and an increase in indirect taxes, are represented by the third component of Equation 5.5. Any upward change in these variables has inflationary effects, and its final impact on the inflation rate is defined by two factors: (1) the incidence of the shock in total direct costs, and (2) the inflationary multiplier. This last factor, represented by Equation 5.9 and determined by the mechanism of indexation, is inherent to inertial and structural inflation. It amplifies the primary impulse caused by the shocks of costs by its propagation to the other prices. In other words, the inflationary multiplier expresses the fact that a supply shock (which, in the absence of indexation, has localized effects) has the effect of universalizing an increase in prices by the continuous passing on of costs to prices, thus tending to maintain relative prices untouched. Through this mechanism, inflation accelerates or changes to a higher inertial level.

April 1986

PART 2

The Brazilian Inflation

6

The Contradictions of
Brazilian Inflation, 1964–1979

Any analysis of Brazilian inflation should begin with the assumption that Brazil is an underdeveloped country whose capitalist market is poorly structured. This is the result both of the domination of key sectors of the economy by cartels of oligopolistic corporations and the existence of an economically strong state that has effective instruments to decisively influence the distribution of the economic surplus.

From this point of view, inflation in Brazil is a way of transferring income from the politically weaker sectors, that is, the workers, as well as from the economically less dynamic sectors, to the economically more dynamic and politically stronger sectors, which dominate the process of capital accumulation. Inflation is a battle between the dominant groups for a larger share of the economic surplus, with losses for the workers, the low- and middle-level managers, and the small- and medium-sized firms in the competitive sectors of the economy.

There is one essential condition that is necessary for carrying out this concentration of income: the possibility for the groups that benefit from inflation to intervene in the market and increase their prices, whenever possible, even more than the other groups. This intervention is made possible in Brazil by two mechanisms: (a) the organization of the oligopolistic corporations into cartels, and (b) the action of the state when it subsidizes the more powerful and dynamic segments of the economy.

In relation to the state, we are led to imagine that its objective is to control inflation, but actually it faces a permanent contradiction: the state attempts to combat inflation while it bows to the inflationary pressures of the groups that control it. As a source of inflation and of transferring income to these groups, the state can: (a) establish subsidies for these dynamic groups and then issue currency (this was the classic inflationary

119

mechanism of the populist period); (b) increase credit at negative interest rates in order to finance these dynamic groups (this was the typical mechanism used between 1967 and 1973); and (c) not control prices, or loosen the controls, to the advantage of the oligopolistic groups (this was the typical policy between 1974 and 1979).

According to this viewpoint, inflation is an economic phenomenon whose political component is essential. Inflation would accelerate in proportion to the aggressiveness of the groups that control the state and to the resistance of the dominated groups. When there is a relative balance of political forces, as in 1962-1963, inflation tends to be explosive. When the capitalist group manages to obtain unlimited domination over the workers, as was the case from 1964 to 1974, inflation tends to be reduced, with the workers paying for the deceleration of inflation with reduced wages. After the elections of 1974, when the workers regained some political weight, inflation began to grow again.

Contrary to what is predicted by orthodox economic theory, but consistent with the theory of inflation based on administered prices, inflation would tend to go up in a descendant phase of the cycle and to go down during an ascendant phase. This is because, when there is a decline, the fight to maintain a relative share in the economic surplus is much greater than during expansion. When production and productivity are growing, it is easier for some of the groups to cope with the losses that come from the policies for stabilizing prices, because, in this case, they lose only in the sense that they do not gain as much.

Implicit in this hypothesis is the assumption that an anti-inflationary policy can only succeed in Brazil when it forces one group to pay for inflation by not allowing it to raise its prices proportionately. In principle, this group has been the workers. It could be the agricultural export sector, as happened in the 1950s, small and medium companies of the traditional capitalist sectors that produce basic consumer goods, as happened after 1964, or finally public servants and lower-level military officers (or rather the low- and middle-level governmental technobureaucrats, as has happened various times).

1

The highest rates recorded for Brazilian inflation before the upsurge of the 1980s were between 1963 and 1966, reaching a peak of 91.9 percent in 1964.[1] For 1963, we can see a correlation between the high inflation rate and the political and economic disorganization of that period. However, we cannot do the same for the following years, during the Castelo Branco government, when an orthodox anti- inflationary policy was adopted based on a mistaken (demand pull) diagnosis of the basic causes of infation at that time. The costs of the restrictive monetary and fiscal policies were high in terms of unemployment and of a reduction of the growth rates. The results, in terms of deceleration of inflation, can be explained by the severe cut in real wages rather than by the orthodox economic policy.

From the moment that Delfim Netto became the minister of the treasury in March 1967, there were changes in the economic policy. Inflation was considered to be cost push, and a policy to stimulate demand and control oligopolistic prices was pursued. The inflation rate continued to fall, going from 38.8 percent to 24.4 percent from 1966 to 1967 (see Table 6.1). Once it stabilized around this rate, the government did not show much concern for reducing it to even lower levels. Beginning in

Table 6.1 Inflation - Annual Rates

Year	FGV(a)	DIEESE(b)
1960	30.5	32.9
1961	47.7	42.2
1962	51.3	62.4
1963	81.3	86.7
1964	91.9	72.9
1965	35.5	53.9
1966	38.8	52.3
1967	24.3	25.9
1968	25.4	26.1
1969	20.2	22.3
1970	19.2	16.5
1971	19.8	24.8
1972	15.5	22.5
1973	15.7	26.7
1974	34.5	35.2
1975	29.2	28.5
1976	46.3	44.2
1977	38.8	39.2
1978	40.83	40.12

December of each year over December of the preceding year.
Source: (a) Getúlio Vargas Foundation (FGV) - General Price Index - Domestic
        Availability (col. 2)
        In: *Conjuntura econômica*
        (b) DIEESE - Cost of Living Index (Inter Union Department of
        Socio Economic Statistics and Studies - DIEESE).

1967, the national product began to grow again at a considerable rate. Thus, we entered the period of the "Brazilian miracle," during which profits and salaries, as well as private and state accumulation, grew at unprecedented rates while wages stagnated.

In the 1950s, the debate on inflation was between the "monetarists" (actually, neoclassical orthodox economists) who attributed inflation to causes exogenous to the economic system that were reflected in deficits and the issuing of currency, and the structuralists, who saw inflation as a phenomenon inherent in the standard of capital accumulation of that time.[2] These positions are opposites, especially in terms of the measures they recommend for controlling inflation. The orthodox advocate the possibility of eliminating inflation, while the structuralists affirm the need to live with a moderate inflation rate. However, they do agree when they explain inflation in terms of demand. That is, both consider an aggregate demand greater than supply to be the cause of inflation. However, this does not make sense during a period of crisis or economic recession, as was the case from 1962 to 1966.

At the beginning of the 1960s, we first saw the phenomenon of the coexistence of inflation with economic recession in Brazil. This phenomenon would also occur at the end of the decade in the central countries and then be called stagflation. It was observed in Ignácio Rangel's pioneering book *A inflação Brasileira* (1963). He noted that there was a decisive cost component in Brazilian inflation. Corporations were contantly being threatened by their idle capacity and overproduction, which was caused by the unbalanced distribution of income in Brazil and especially by lack of effective demand because of the exclusion of almost the whole rural sector from the market. They were taking advantage of their oligopolistic position in the market and raising their prices autonomously, that is, without any previous increase in demand. Because the demand curve faced by the corporations as a group was inelastic, price increases implied a relatively small reduction in the amount sold. Thus, the corporations caused inflation to accelerate by increasing their markups and prices as a way to defend their profits. Therefore, we were faced with administered or cost inflation, which is perfectly compatible with recession.

However, Ignácio Rangel's analysis had few repercussions. The orthodox economists of the Castelo Branco government ignored it completely. They dealt with inflation in terms of demand and, while they called their policy "gradualist," they adopted drastic measures for reducing consumption, real wages, the working capital of the corporations, and the government deficit. Naturally, the result of all this was a recession. However, faced with pressure from business and from the middle class, they soon relaxed controls. This happened in the second semester of 1965, when the taxes for durable consumer goods were temporarily reduced. Perhaps because of this, its policy could be called "gradualist."

It was a patchy gradualism. The orthodox economic policy, copied from North American and British economic text books, had much less effect than expected, while at the same time the economy began to stagnate. Moreover, this stagnation provoked a large trade surplus in 1965 and 1966 because the industrial sector did not feel stimulated to import machines and raw materials. Ironically enough, the financing of this surplus fed back into inflation. In other words, orthodox anti-inflationary policy provoked a recession, because it led to a reduction in the demand for imports and, concomitantly, to a surplus in the balance of trade. The need to finance this surplus, that is, to buy the foreign exchange credits of the exporters, led the state to print more currency, thus sanctioning the current level of inflation.

Before Delfim Netto became treasury minister in 1967, he made a study of Brazilian inflation. He took a position different from that of the monetarists, explaining it with four variables that are independent of each other: the state deficit, wage readjustments, exchange devaluations, and the inflation of the previous year.[3] Of these, the two cost components for explaining inflation are wage readjustments and the exchange devaluation, which were not given much importance in this book.

However, when he was named as minister in 1967, he was faced with inflation and recession at the same time. In spite of being a mostly orthodox economist, he did not hesitate to emphasize the cost component in Brazilian inflation and adopted a similar diagnosis to the one elaborated by Rangel. Thus, he relaxed the credit restrictions that had been imposed earlier and went on to control the inflationary process through administrative price controls. The Interministerial Price Council (CIP) was created to carry out this task.

His acceptance of the concept of administered inflation was clear. The government even stated it in its own development program (*Programa Estratégico de Desenvolvimento*) in July 1967: "In this latest phase, inflation has continued, in spite of a retraction in demand, because of the influence of certain costs, the increase in interest rates, the increase in average prices resulting from lower sales, and the reaction to expectations."

As a result of this analysis, the government changed its strategy for fighting inflation, clearly subordinating it to the greater objective of promoting the accumulation of capital. When inflation has a cost component, it is basically functioning as a defense mechanism for the monopolistic or oligopolistic corporations against a retraction in demand. Therefore, it was necessary to stimulate demand and to stimulate economic activity. This was done by a more liberal credit policy for the private sector, stimulating investment, and by an increase in the salaries of the technobureaucrats, and stimulating consumption, especially of durable goods.

Although the government did not present large budget deficits, it continued to increase the levels of credit and to issue currency to avoid an economic recession. The nominal increase in the money supply contributed to maintaining inflation at a annual rate of around 20 percent.

On the other hand, since administered inflation is based on autonomous price increases that do not reflect an increase in demand, it depends on the dominance of oligopolistic or monopolistic markets. In these markets, competition does not function. This explains the great emphasis the government gave to the CIP. Instead of controlling prices at the retail level, which was totally inefficient, the CIP went to the source of the high prices and initially began by controlling the prices of the 350 largest Brazilian corporations, a number which increased over the years. In other words, the CIP began to control the prices of the oligopolistic and monopolistic corporations in Brazil. When dealing with a reduced number of corporations, administrative control is feasible. In this way, the CIP became a powerful instrument for controlling inflation. Setting the banks' interest rates can be included in the same line of action, since interests on circulating capital are costs, and banks in Brazil form an oligopoly.

In this way, the anti-inflationary policy between 1967 and 1973 had little to do with that of the previous government. It was a policy of living with inflation that was maintained at acceptable levels through the administrative control of prices and the systematic attempt to cut the workers' wages. The emphasis was put on the growth rate of the system and on increasing exports. As long as inflation provoked a reduction in wages, a moderate inflation rate particularly favored the process of accumulation.

At the beginning of the 1970s, the economy was in full expansion and could no longer count on idle capacity. The rate of capital accumulation increased at the same time that the growing salaries of the technobureaucrats stimulated the consumption of luxury industrial goods. In 1973, the pressures from an aggregate demand greater than supply were already felt. The acceleration of the inflation rate received a new impulse from an external supply shock: the increase in the prices of oil and other imported products.[4]

Because of the relatively high inflationary pressures, at the beginning of 1974 the new minister of the treasury, Mário Henrique Simonsen, decided to adopt a policy of violent credit restriction, thus returning to a diagnosis of demand inflation.

2

When studying the causes of inflation in Brazil, economists are divided into various camps. In order to analyze this problem, it is first necessary to distinguish between long- and short-term causes.

As for the long-term causes, we should return to the old, but not worn-out, debate between the structuralists and the orthodox, which takes us back to the 1950s. In the 1950s, the neoclassical orthodox economists, who are generically called "monetarists" in Latin America, were not working for the government. They explained inflation very simply. It had one exogenous cause: the demagoguery and administrative incapacity of the Brazilian governments of that time, which incurred constant budget deficits and increased credit as it tried to satisfy all classes and social groups in a populist way. This subsequently provoked the need to finance the budget deficit by a continuous expansion of money.[5]

Meanwhile, the structuralists, who generally occupied government posts, asserted that inflation was an endogenous phenomenon, resulting from the imperfections of markets typical of industrializing countries.[6] These imperfections manifest themselves as bottlenecks in supply. Given a sudden increase in demand or an unexpected fall in the production (supply) of certain goods, prices rise in these sectors. However, contrary to what happens in the advanced capitalist countries, when prices go up in a certain sector of the economy, supply does not respond immediately, either through an increase in internal production or through imports. Thus, the prices of that sector do not immediately return to their previous level, leading the other sectors that use inputs from that sector to raise their own prices so that they will not suffer losses. In this way, a sectorial price increase because of a bottleneck in supply spreads to the whole economy, causing a generalized inflationary process that forces workers to demand readjustments of their wages. At first, there is a variation in relative prices, but as these prices don't return quickly to their initial level, because of the structural deficiencies of the market, the other economic agents are led to increase their prices to defend their income share. Thus, an inflationary process is set off that can only be stopped if some sectors of the economy are prevented from defending themselves. Then these sectors absorb the price increases or, in other words, "pay the bill" for inflation. In Brazil, the propagation or feedback effect is especially significant because it is already institutionalized by the system of indexation or monetary correction of prices, interest rates, exchange rates, and wages. It is true that the monetary correction is not full and complete. If it were, inflation would be absolutely rigidly downwards because no class or sector of the economy would absorb the losses of a stabilization policy.

In these terms, once a sectorial inflationary process is set off, the propagation effect, or the feedback mechanism of inflation, generalizes and maintains inflation at a new and higher level. The economic system is turned into a battlefield on which all try to defend themselves from higher prices by passing on cost increases to prices or, whenever possible, increasing their own prices before their suppliers do.

Once these mechanisms of propagation are started, they tend to become permanent, maintaining the new level of inflation. First, they accelerate the rate of inflation, then they keep it independent of the existence of excess demand. The accelerating effect will be exhausted unless new inflationary shocks occur, either because of the monopoly power of some sectors or the appearance of new structural imbalances between supply and demand in specific sectors of the economy. As long as these new imbalances cannot be corrected immediately, and it takes time for supply to meet demand, we will have a new inflationary acceleration.

The agricultural and import sectors were cited as examples of sectors where bottlenecks in supply tend to initially occur. That is, given the permanent lack of foreign currency, which characterizes underdevelopment, especially during the import substitution phase, the tendency is for their prices to be under constant pressure to rise. Another structural cause of inflation is the political incapacity of the government to raise taxes in proportion to its increase in expenditures, which arise from the state's increasing intervention in the economy to stimulate accumulation.

As for agriculture, some structuralists pointed out the low elasticity of the supply of agricultural products, but the orthodox economists showed econometrically that this was not the case, at least in southern Brazil. In fact, there is no reason for the supply of agricultural products to be inelastic in relation to prices. The hypothesis that the agricultural sector is precapitalistic in Brazil and in the other underdeveloped countries is dubious. It is only in very economically backward areas, such as in certain regions of the northeast of Brazil, that supply does not respond well to price increases. This is mainly the result of a lack of information and, secondarily, of insufficiently developed capitalist relationships of production.[7]

Strictly speaking, for the structuralist theory of inflation, it is not necessary that the supply of agricultural products have low price elasticity. All that is needed is a time lag in the response of supply to an increase in demand. A time lag that is longer than acceptable for the other economic sectors will be enough for the prices of the other sectors to go up as well. The agricultural sector is only one example of a source of structural inflation. Any other sector in which there is a monetary bottleneck in supply can provoke inflation, as long as that time lag is long enough for the propagation effect between a sectorial price increase and the response of supply to set into motion a generalized price increase.[8]

3

The most important aspect in the debate between the monetarists and the structuralists is the question of the endogenous or exogenous character of the money supply. The money supply will be either a cause of inflation or a sanctioning factor, depending on the following alternatives: a money supply decided on by the government, or a money supply resulting from economic forces.

Monetarists consider it to be exogenous because its origins are outside of the dynamics of the economic system and in the area of politics—a decision of the government or of the central bank—as if it were possible to make a clear separation between politics and economics. As a result, they propose an obstinate battle against inflation through rigid restrictions of the money supply and a balanced government budget. When these measures, which are copied from the economic policies of the central countries, are adopted, they are not upheld for long. In the central countries, given that the workers are organized into strong unions, the only way to contain increases in wages during periods of expansion and inflation is by orthodox monetary measures that increase unemployment. But in countries like Brazil, the capitalists do not need this instrument, which is also painful for them, to control wages. That is why fiscal and monetary restrictions tend to be quickly abandoned.

On the other hand, endogenous structuralist inflation is that which results from the structure and dynamics of the economy itself. It comes from the imperfections of the market that characterize the process of accumulation in a technobureaucratic-capitalist country of the periphery like Brazil. The imperfections of the market are manifested either in sectorial bottlenecks in supply, which cause the acceleration of structural demand inflation, or in an eminently oligopolistic and cartelized economy, which create the conditions for an administered acceleration of inflation. Once reaching a certain level, inflation tends to be maintained at this level through the permanent propagation effect, given the distributive conflict. In order to avoid a liquidity crisis, the money supply should increase at the same rate as inflation.

The more oligopolized the economy, the more important will be the administered component of inflation. Although antitrust legislation formally exists in Brazil, cartels are openly tolerated, and the weight of the administered component is enormous. It becomes even greater when we remember that the state, either directly or through its corporations, also has monopoly power over the market and sizable weight in the country's economy.

Given the endogenous character of inflation, it is clear that curing it is not so simple. It is necessary to attack the bottlenecks, which is a long-term problem, and to avoid as much as possible autonomous or administered price increases, which is a difficult task. As a result, it is necessary to know how to live with inflation. This does not mean that there is any positive correlation between development and inflation, or any negative one, unless it becomes explosive. It does not mean that monetary and fiscal policies should not be used against inflation, as long as they are moderate. It only means that a certain inflation rate acts as a lubricant for the economic system. Since the economy resists recession very much—on one hand, there are no unemployment benefits; on the other, capitalists do not need recession to lower wages, which are already very low—the nominal money supply increases endogenously in order to maintain the level of the real money supply. If the government does not issue currency, the banking system increases its nominal credit supply to its good clients.

4

Although administered inflation is related to the structural imperfections of the market, it differs from the structuralist approach because the accelerating factors are sectorial supply shocks instead of sectorial demand shocks. It is caused by the capacity of corporations and of organized workers to increase profit margins or real wages above the increase in productivity, even if demand is weak. The essential condition for this kind of inflation is the existence of monopolistic power. Then inflation can occur, even during an economic retraction, as happened in Brazil in 1962 and 1966 and in the central countries at the end of the 1960s and in 1974.

This kind of inflation is also known as cost inflation, although this is not a correct name and is marked by strong ideological connotations. It was coined in the central countries and suggests that inflation is caused by an increase in the costs of the corporations. Strictly speaking, there are only two kinds of costs in an economy: wages and profits (profit is a cost within the system). Wages would be the only cost of the corporations that is not determined by them. Thus, this type of inflation would be determined mainly by the actions of the trade unions. If this idea is only partially true for the central countries where the trade unions are strong, in underdeveloped countries like Brazil it is unfounded, given the subordination of the workers' organizations to state control.

By defending their profits during recession and increasing them during prosperity, the oligopolistic corporations autonomously increase their prices, and the banks, which are also oligopolistic, their interest rates. If we consider profit to be a cost, we can adopt the name of cost inflation. In the meantime, administered inflation seems to be a less ambiguous name. When the large corporations have monopoly power, they administer their prices, and thus set off inflation. The state also does this, not only through its corporations, but also by directly setting prices. A tax increase is theoretically anti-inflationary. However, if it is used to increase state expenditures, it becomes inflationary. Increases in the charges for public services also have a very clear inflationary effect.

Intervention by the government to set prices, which in principle are defined by the market, are more significant and paradoxical. The asserted objective of these interventions is to control prices and inflation. There are certain moments, however, when a real wage increase, such as that declared by the Brazilian government in November 1974, just before its defeat in the elections, has a clearly inflationary character. In the same way, the government policy of systematically reducing wages, which was enforced up to that year, was anti-inflationary. Also, the CIP itself, which was created to prevent autonomous price increases, can, at certain times, end up stimulating and sanctioning them.[9] It all depends on the power of the different economic sectors in relation to the state.

When, as in the case of Brazil, inflation has a strong price administration component, there tends to be a clear inverse relation between the growth rate of the economy and the inflation rate. This is a fact that was clearly perceived by Ignácio Rangel, and which has been recently confirmed. In 1962, a process of economic crisis began in Brazil, at the same time in which the inflation rate was going up. Then, between 1967 and 1974, inflation decelerated while the country experienced extraordinary growth rates. When the economy decelerated, between 1975 and 1979, it was accompanied again by a clear acceleration of inflation.

Anti-inflationary policies work better during expansive phases of the cycle for two reasons: because the bottlenecks of the economy are partially overcome, and because, at these moments, it becomes viable to reduce the inflation rate without needing to choose a group to absorb all the costs of an anti-inflationary policy. This is possible as long as the increases in production allow this absorption to occur without resistance from those who suffer the losses, or as long as everyone is benefitting from the increase in productive efficiency.

───────────────────────────── 5 ─────────────────────────────

These kinds of inflation are not exclusive. There is no reason for the accelerating causes of inflation to be only structural, Keynesian demand push, or administered. A generalized and persistant increase in prices can easily be determined by a combination of these causes. During prosperity, the first two should be dominant; during a recession, it is administered inflation that should play a more important role. But there is nothing to prevent the occurrence of bottlenecks during a recession. On the other hand, while during prosperity it becomes even easier for the oligopolistic corporations to increase their profits margins, they probably will not do that, as this is behavior typical of firms in the competitive sector. But in special situations, oligopolistic corporations can also increase profit margins during the expansive phase of the economic cycle.

We can mention other secondary causes for the acceleration of inflation. There is imported inflation, when the prices of imported goods rise rapidly. For example, with the increase in the price of oil in 1973, all of the oil-importing countries imported inflation. There are people who talk about psychological inflation, characterized by inflationary expectations, that leads some corporations to increase their prices before the others.

This psychological inflation caused by expectations, however, is not exactly a cause for the acceleration of inflation, but rather a euphemism for expressing a very simple fact. No matter what the causes of inflation are—structural, monetary, or administrative—it will always have a basic cause: the struggle by corporations and social groups to increase their share of the surplus. Inflation is the result of a fierce battle for the division of the economic surplus. Those who are capable of increasing their prices more and before the others, those who take the front line in the inflationary process, will certainly be its beneficiaries. Once inflation reaches a given level, it can attribute its maintenance at this level to expectations. But, contrary to what monetarists think, expectations in this case are based on past inflation and thus on the distributive conflict.

This conflict takes place on a broader level between social classes. In the underdeveloped countries, inflation itself is the way in which capitalists reduce the real wages of the workers. They create what their ideologues call "forced savings," but which are really an increase in the corporations' profit rates.

During the import substitution period in Brazil, inflation was also used to transfer income from the exporting sector to the industrial sector, using the exchange rate as an intermediary mechanism. It had been maintained at a fixed rate for long periods, while internal inflation progressed at an accelerated rhythm. This resulted in an artificial valorization of the national currency and a transfer of income from exporters to importers. Later, in the 1970s, when exports received priority, a real devaluation of the cruzeiro became necessary. Although this devaluation did not take place, another way was found to promote exports: by reducing real wages, using the acceleration of inflation. This policy was not necessarily deliberate on the part of government officials, but it reflected the power of the different pressure groups.

It is significant that between the 1950s and the 1970s a curious inversion took place. Inflation was basically an instrument that the capitalists and technobureaucrats used to reduce the workers' wages. However, the official version was something else. Wage increases were considered to be a cause of inflation. Administrative control of wages and of the salaries of the lower-level government employees was defined as the way par excellence to fight inflation. In the meantime, the high salaries of the upper-level technobureaucrats were left free to grow, according to the political power of the technobureaucrats and to their relative scarcity. If we assume that the share of salaries in the income remained constant, then during certain periods, that of profits must have increased as wages were reduced.

Up until the mid-1950s, aside from transferring income from the workers to the capitalists through the lowering of real wages, inflation also transferred income from the exporting sector—the coffee growers—to the industrial sector and to the state itself via the exchange system. At this time, with the progressive exhaustion of the import substitution model at the same time in which the export system entered a crisis, the local industrial bourgeoisie consolidated itself at the top of the dominant class, the multinational manufacturing corporations entered the country en masse, and the *estado cartorial* transformed itself into a state that produces and regulates the economy.[10] Hence a new pattern of accumulation was defined: the underdeveloped industrialized model. In this setting, beginning with the Kubitschek government, inflation played the role of transferring income to the dynamic sectors of the economy, not only through a reduction of real wages, but also through the mechanism of subsidized credits.

This system generalized itself after 1964 when the state became stronger politically. It put together an extraordinary system of fiscal and credit subsidies in order to favor those sectors or activities that were considered as priorities by those who were formulating economic policy. Since they were exempt from monetary correction, the credit subsidies were especially dependent on the inflation rates. Exporters of manufactured goods, big farmers, producers of capital goods and raw materials, supermarkets, and the food industry are among those who received subsidized credits. Bankrupt financial institutions also received them. Personal criteria were added to the impersonal criteria of economic policy. Usually it was the larger corporations in each sector that benefitted the most, as they had the best administrative conditions and more political influence at their disposal.

Because interest rates were fixed in nominal terms, the higher inflation went the lower or more negative was the real rate, and the greater the subsidies. For the beneficiary sectors, the higher the inflation rate went, the better it was. The transfer of surplus to these dynamic or influential sectors was in direct proportion to the inflation rate. In these terms, by waving a magic wand, Brazilian state capitalism changed inflation from a dangerous evil to a political and economic instrument aimed at maximizing the accumulation rate of the sectors that had priority in the economy.

The pressures that were put on the state to maintain an elevated inflation rate did not come only from the need to keep the real money supply stable and from the interests of the industrial sector in maintaining the level of investments of the state at a high level. They also come from the interests of the corporations that were favored by subsidized credits at negative real interest rates. Inflation was thus built into the very logic of the model of industrialized underdevelopment.

Inflation was the result of a strategy of the more dynamic capitalist groups to increase their profits and their rate of accumulation.[11] While the technobureaucrats developed an eminently administrative strategy for increasing their share of the total income, attempting to directly increase their salaries, the capitalists used inflation to reduce the wages of the workers and to neutralize salary increases, and thus to increase their profits.

--------- 6 ---------

The structural nature of Brazilian inflation has become clearer in recent years. Here we are giving the term "structural" a wider meaning than just that which identifies the causes of inflation with sectorial bottlenecks in the supply of goods. Inflation in Brazil is structural because it is built into and is inherent in the present pattern of accumulation. It is structural because it is the outcome of a permanent distributive conflict. The imperfections in the market and the imbalances of political power between the different social and economic groups tend to accelerate inflation. In order to not lose in the distributive conflict, those who can, automatically pass on cost increases to prices, which rigidly maintains the given level of inflation.

Because the monetary authorities since 1974 did not understand the complex and structural nature of Brazilian inflation, they did not achieve the results they desired with the measures they adopted. Inflation actually recovered its ascending rhythm in 1973 after a long period of decline. At this point, demand inflation and administered inflation joined forces.[12]

The new government, which was installed in 1974, was counting on a minister of the treasury with an orthodox neoclassical orientation, Mário Henrique Simonsen. His position, at least at the beginning of this government, was to not believe in administrative mechanisms for controlling inflation, but rather to prefer the classical mechanisms of fiscal and monetary restrictions. In keeping with this position—which later became more flexible—in the first months of his administration he decided to undertake a policy of restricting credit. As a result, the Brazilian economy underwent a recession during the second half of 1974 and the first half of 1975. It was not a very deep economic crisis, but one in which the inflation rate continued to grow. The liquidity index of the economy fell precipitously until February 1975, when the government, faced with pressure from the corporations, decided to release credit again, mainly by compensatory refinancing. Thus, a phase of large profits for the banks and an acceleration of inflation began. The economic system itself did not react right away. But in the second half of 1975 it had already entered into a new cycle of prosperity. We found ourselves in the midst of a stop-and-go policy.

In the middle of 1975, we were still in an economic recession. The government continued to try stimulating demand in spite of the eventual acceleration of inflation. The new expansion was only perceived by the economic authorities in January or February 1976. Once more, inflation was immediately diagnosed as being of demand. As a result, new measures were imposed to restrict credit. However, these measures had little effect for one year; this time they did not even manage to control inflation, much less reduce economic activity. Although the index of the real liquidity of the economy began to go down again in January 1976, the large amount of speculation, as verified in the open market, increased the circulation of money and cancelled the monetary restrictions imposed by the government. It was only in the first half of 1977 that the economy began to show signs of cooling off. Industrial production, which according to the FIBGE showed a growth rate of 12.85 percent and 12.33 percent in December 1976 and January 1977, respectively, in relation to the previous twelve months, had already gone down to 8.41 percent and 7.48 percent in May and June 1977, respectively. Meanwhile, until May 1977, the inflation rate continued to rise, undergoing its first reduction only in June. This reduction confirmed itself in July and August when the inflation rate went from a monthly average of above 4 percent to a rate of 1.3 percent (see Table 6.2). This strong reduction in the inflation rate followed a series of heterodox administrative measures, which Simonsen finally took in May 1977. Among these was a freeze in the price of gasoline, a very firm action on the part the CIP, and the limitation of the price increases of the state corporations to 25 percent a year.

All of these facts contribute to making it very clear that there is a strong component of costs, or administered inflation, in Brazilian inflation, notwithstanding the component of demand. Therefore, it is necessary to make clear that demand inflation and administered inflation are compatible. They can both overlap and strengthen each other.

Demand inflation does not occur only because of an excess of money or because of sectorial shortages in supply. There is also Keynesian inflation, which occurs when the real aggregate demand exceeds supply at the peak of an economic cycle. This was probably what happened in Brazil in 1973. There are various reasons for real aggregate demand exceeding supply: (a) large investments made by the government; (b) large investments made by the private sector; (c) optimism and an increase in consumption by consumers. Any of these can cause the economy to warm up and then go on to grow rapidly. As the idle capacity disappears, and as the increase in production does not manage to accompany the increase in demand, profit margins and wages begin to rise in an inflationary manner. From 1974 to 1976, investments by the state continued to sustain a strong expansion of aggregate demand by putting pressure on prices while private investments were falling off. At the beginning of 1977, when the government noticed that the state financial resources, which had been abundant from 1967 to 1973, were beginning to be short at the same time that they were feeding inflation, a big cut in investments was announced. While this cut was sponsored by the ministry of the treasury, it was opposed by the other areas of the government, especially the public corporations. All sorts of pressures were put into action again, in order to sustain the economic activity, profits, and salaries.

Aside from being demand administered, Brazilian inflation in 1976 also had a component that was related to the real wage increases of 1975. These increases were inflationary because the corporations were not, and never are, willing to reduce their profit margins. Wage increases above the increase in productivity can only be absorbed without being inflationary if the corporations reduce their profits.

Because Brazilian inflation is a structural process endogenous to the system, it is dangerous to think that it can be done away with in a short

Table 6.2 Inflation - Monthly Rates

Month	1974		1975		1976		1977		1978	
	FGV(a)	DIEESE(b)	FGV	DIEESE	FGV	DIEESE	FGV	DIEESE	FGV	DIEESE
Jan.	2.77	2.07	2.24	2.63	3.18	4.80	3.66	5.29	2.67	4.33
Feb.	2.69	3.89	2.19	2.18	4.07	5.82	3.24	2.47	3.40	4.11
March	4.53	4.69	1.61	2.39	3.77	3.85	4.07	4.75	3.27	3.57
Apr.	5.25	5.13	1.76	2.85	3.64	4.96	4.08	6.36	3.38	1.62
May	3.47	1.84	2.07	0.72	3.5	2.32	3.58	1.59	3.20	2.68
June	1.88	0.64	2.20	2.83	2.66	0.71	1.97	1.24	3.62	4.07
July	1.23	1.45	2.15	3.45	3.77	2.40	2.10	1.81	2.85	3.42
Aug.	1.21	1.89	2.76	3.66	4.09	4.21	1.27	1.10	2.67	2.40
Sept.	1.80	2.46	2.37	1.93	3.38	2.77	1.80	2.95	2.56	1.59
Oct.	1.38	2.46	2.16	1.71	2.43	2.37	2.69	1.78	2.83	3.01
Nov.	1.55	1.84	2.26	0.35	1.85	1.49	2.62	2.69	2.75	2.26
Dec.	2.29	2.25	2.07	0.66	2.33	1.62	2.11	1.69	1.54	1.21

Sources: (a) Getúlio Vargas Foundation (FGV) - General Price Index, Domestic Availability (col. 2) In: Conjuntura econômica, n° 3, Vol. 30, March, 1976; n° 7, Vol. 31, July, 1977. (b) DIEESE - Cost of Living Index (Interunion Department of Socioeconomic Statistics and Studies - DIEESE, 1977).

135

period of time. If inflation is structural, the Brazilian economy must live for years with a certain inflation rate. Obviously, however, there is no need for this rate to be 40 percent per annum. Rates of 15 percent to 20 percent are sufficient for making the adjustments in the system.

7

In order to control inflation, it is undoubtedly necessary to adopt the classic means of fiscal and credit restrictions, with moderation, when the demand component is obvious. On the other hand, when the government has a budget deficit while the economy is functioning at almost full capacity, it is necessary to reduce expenditures, or, preferably, to selectively increase taxes. Tax increases have the advantage of being able to be less indiscriminate, thus making a better distribution of the income possible. Aside from this, government investments can be maintained while the consumption of luxuries is cut. Meanwhile, it is necessary to make it clear that, while contractionary monetary and fiscal measures are only justified when there is pressure from demand and an unbalanced budget, administrative price control is necessary under any circumstances in a cartelized economy like that of Brazil.

Certainly, it is theoretically possible to reduce inflation by using only monetary means. Money is the oxygen and lubricant of the economy. If the monetary authorities succeed in reducing the real money supply, prices become stabilized, even if inflation has structural causes or a strong component of administered prices. We know that there is a strong correlation between prices and the money supply. When prices are increasing autonomously and forcing the monetary authorities to increase the nominal money supply, if these authorities were capable of not carrying out this increase, prices would become stabilized. However, this would only be possible through the creation of an enormous liquidity crisis and a strong recession. As long as only the symptoms of inflation are prevented from appearing, rather than the causes being fought, only a serious, permanent recession can contain prices. Underdeveloped countries like Brazil have much less tolerance for recessive monetary policies than the central countries for two reasons: first, because they do not have unemployment insurance, so that large-scale unemployment is catastrophic; second, businessmen do not support the recessive measures because they do not need them to control wages. When inflation threatens to increase in the central countries during the expansive phase of the cycle, the corporations support recessive measures in order to prevent—as the industrial reserve army is eliminated—wages from growing faster than profits. In Brazil, given the existence of massive underemployment, businessmen are not afraid of an increase in wages, and so they do not support the orthodox policies for controlling inflation. On the other hand, the government has neither enough power nor enough real interest to go against the interests of the dominant class. Therefore, anti-inflationary policies have a short life span.

If inflation has administered components, the only logical way to contain it is by controlling prices. The CIP is a system that was intelligently planned, considering that its objective was to control the prices of the products of the oligopolistic corporations. However, since 1974, it has had so many of its functions taken away that it has often been unable to be an effective instrument for controlling prices. It was only in May of 1977, when the monetary authorities seemed to be desperate when faced with the systematic failure of their monetary methods for fighting inflation, that they decided to firmly adopt administrative anti-inflation methods. But in August 1977, when the general price index of the Getúlio Vargas Foundation went down 1.3 percent and the wholesale price index 0.9 percent, the president of the central bank, Paulo Lyra, in keeping with his neoclassical orientation, "named the containment of demand and the cooling off of the economy as the best reasons for anti-inflationary success. However, he recognized the importance of what is considered to be a key factor by various analysts, the rigid control of critical prices."[13]

Actually, what the anti-inflationary economic policy has clearly shown is that orthodox measures for containing credit are effective for reducing the growth rate of the economy, but not for controlling inflation. Pressure from the oligopolistic groups that make up the most dynamic sectors of the economy, as they try to increase their participation in the economic surplus, thwarts the monetary measures. What is more serious, however, is that these sectors could also thwart administrative measures while the government is under their control.

It is at this point that we perceive the political basis of Brazilian inflation. In 1977, the government limited the rate of salary increases of civil servants to 30 percent while inflation was more than 45 percent, and controlled the prices of public corporations. By this action, it seemed to have decided to make the lower- and middle-level state technobureaucrats pay the bill for controlling inflation along with the workers, since that year nominal wage increases were set by the government at rates that were lower than the increase in prices. As new elections would only take place at the end of 1978, this policy did not seem to be risky. As for making the state carry the major part of the burden of the anti-inflationary measures through a reduction in the profits and investments of the public corporations, everything shows that these are the political results of a campaign against the state-run enterprises started by the bourgoeoisie in 1975. Once more, politics and economics are dialectically interrelated, with one instance determining the other and vice versa, but always in keeping with the demands of accumulation of the Brazilian economic system, which is predominantly capitalist.

During the second semester of 1977, the clear reduction in the inflation rate was verified to be a direct result of the administration of the prices of the state corporations by the ministry of the treasury. At the end of 1978, however, the inflation rate started to accelerate again, ending the year with an increase in prices of around 40 percent. This led Minister Mário Henrique Simonsen to give interviews to journalists in which he revealed his perplexity.[14] The experience of the government forces leads one to recognize that fighting inflation is not as simple as it seems, and that its causes are not as exogenous as the monetarist analysis claims. It also makes it clear that political conditioners are inextricably built into the inflationary process. The state's attempt to divide the product into a sum of parts greater than the whole is not exogenous, as the monetarists claim, but is strictly endogenous, as in the structuralist viewpoint.

However, there is one essential component of the administrative character of Brazilian inflation that continues to be ignored: extremely high interest rates. Interest rates in Brazil were very high, and the spread between the rates paid for deposits and those charged for loans is one of the largest in the world.[15] At first, in 1974 when the government adopted a rigid orthodox economic policy, an increase in the interest rates was considered to be beneficial for controlling inflation because it would lead to a reduction in investments. However, as investments are not very sensitive to interest rates, this strategy did not help to control inflation, but only benefitted the banks and rentiers. At the beginning of 1979, when the idea that high interest rates were a fundamentally administrative component of inflation began to spread, people thought that the government would take steps to lower the interest rates. However, nothing has been done, limiting Minister Simonsen to invoke Wicksell's views on the natural rate of interest, emphasizing that "high interest cannot be a focus of cost inflation, but only the rising of the interest rate."[16] He ignored the fact that when a businessman takes out a loan from a banker at a high nominal interest rate, even if it is stable, he has to increase his prices to reduce the real interest rate to limits that are compatible with his profit rate. After all, interest is nothing more than a part of surplus value that the active capitalist pays to the inactive capitalist or rentier, using banks as intermediaries.

Actually, if inflation is a mechanism for transferring income from the workers to the capitalists, and from the "non-priority" sectors to the "priority" sectors of the national economy, it is clear that inflation is useful for the existing pattern of accumulation. However, this is no longer the case when high, increasing real interest rates turn into one of the basic causes of the maintenance and acceleration of inflation. Although investments are not very sensitive to the real interest rate, when it reaches levels as high as those in Brazil, it is obvious that productive capital begins to be affected. On the other hand, a permanent, accelerating rate of inflation threatens social stability and not only hurts the workers, but also, when the productive sectors of the dominant class cannot raise their prices quickly and frequently enough, does not stimulate capital accumulation. On the contrary, it creates problems with international credit and demoralizes the government.

In conclusion, it is not difficult to understand why anti-inflationary economic policy is rarely effective and is always insecure. It reflects the contradictory interests of the Brazilian dominant classes, the imperfections of the market, and the intrinsic contradictions of the pattern of accumulation prevalent in Brazil, which is characterized by industrialized underdevelopment.

March 1980

NOTES

1. For a historical analysis of Brazilian inflation since the middle of the last century, *see* Paulo Neuhaus (1978).
There is a basic bibliography in this book on this subject.
Between 1869 and 1939, annual inflation was less than 5 percent, except for a period during World War I when it went up to 8.5 percent. During the 1940s, it rose to more than 10 percent, and in the period from 1950 to 1976 to 25 percent (296).

2. In Brazil, the expression "monetarists," as it is used by newspapermen and politicians, means the orthodox, neoclassical economists (and eventually Keynesian economists) who attribute inflation to an increase in the supply of money or who recommend restrictive fiscal and monetary policies to control inflation. There is no distinction between Keynesian and *stricto senso* monetarists, who follow Friedman's macroeconomic model, developed in the 1950s and 1960s. Eugenio Gudin, for instance, who was not influenced by Friedman, but mostly by Gottfried Habeler, is usually considered to be the father of the Brazilian monetarist economists.

3. Antonio Delfim Netto, Afonso Celso Pastore, Pedro Cipolari, and Eduardo Pereira de Carvalho (1965).

4. As was definitely shown in 1977, the official indices for inflation for 1973, of around 16 percent, were manipulated by the government by using tabulated prices. The true inflation rate was around 26 percent, which indicates a clear increase in relation to the rate for the previous year.

5. For an interesting exposition of this position, *see* Mário Henrique Simonsen (1969). According to him: "In general terms, the sociopolitical roots of chronic inflation in the underdeveloped countries can be found in the distributive policy of the government. The different social groups show themselves to be unsatisfied with their participation in the national product and, in order to placate them, the government tries to divide the product into a number of parts greater than the whole" (124). Simonsen is an ecletic economist, using orthodox, as well as structuralist, arguments (such as the distributive conflict argument) to develop his own ideas.

6. About structural inflation *see* Juan Noyola (1956), Oswaldo Sunkel (1958), Celso Furtado (1959), Ignácio Rangel (1963), Júlio Oliveira (1964) and Aníbal Pinto (1973, 1978).

7. *See* especially Afonso Celso Pastore (1973).

8. Celso Furtado, in a work that which synthesizes the structuralist position, cites the following internal structural inflationary foci, aside from pressure to increase imports: inelasticity in the supply of agricultural products, inadequacies in the infrastructure, inadequacies in the available human resources on a short term basis, inadequacy of the fiscal structures, and an increase in the financial costs of the corporations (1976).

9. When, at the beginning of 1977, the National Association of Automobile Manufacturers showed its lack of interest in the liberalization of controls that the CIP was proposing, Eduardo Matarazzo Suplicy (1977) commented: "This organism for controlling prices (CIP) has become an administrator of the prices of the oligopolized industries in Brazil for the cartels. The actions of the CIP have been so much in line with the interests of the leading industries that produce final goods that they are afraid of a complete liberalization of prices."

10. *Estado cartorial* is an expression used by some Brazilian political scientists for the traditional Brazilian state which, aside from its classical liberal functions, also gave jobs to the middle class linked to the agrarian exporting oligarchy.

11. Carlos Eduardo Silveira observes that "inflation works in the most general manner to redistribute returns and to favor accumulation in the new dynamic center of the economy" (1974).

12. According to Luiz Antonio de Oliveira Lima, "When, at the beginning of 1973, the economy came close to a full utilization of the productive capacity, corporations with the most market power began to raise their markup" (1977).

13. *Gazeta Mercantil*, 2 September 1977.

14. *See*, among others, a long interview given to *Folha de São Paulo* (1978). This perplexity led Minister Simonsen, after being nominated to the

planning ministry, to present Congress in May 1979 with a report in which the administered components and the structural components of inflation were recognized, although timidly (Mário Henrique Simonsen, 1979). Francisco Lafayette Lopes (1978) developed a formal distinction between monetarists and structuralists, according to which, structuralists would be all of those who admit the existence of the Phillips curve, or, in other words, of an inverse relation between the inflation rate and the unemployment rate. According to this concept, the Brazilian governmental policy was structuralist. This formal distinction is not acceptable, even though it has the virtue of showing that no monetarist economist is able to remain orthodox when faced with the task of governing.

15. According to a survey of world financial markets, published by Morgan Guaranty Trust Company in May 1977, of the twenty-seven principal capitalist countries of the world, Brazil had the largest spread between interest rates given on deposits and those charged for loans: 43.8 percent for deposits and 62.0 percent for loans. In the United States, Great Britain, France, and Germany, the spreads were 1.50 percent, 1.75 percent, 3.75 percent, and 1.50 percent respectively.

16. Mário Henrique Simonsen (1979).

7

Recession and Inflation: 1981

The justification given by the neoclassical economists for the fiscal and monetary policies of controlling inflation is that a reduction in demand tends to reduce prices. This assertion can be found in any traditional textbook and is accepted by most people as an obvious truth. Nevertheless, there is nothing further from the truth than the traditional neoclassical theory of prices.

Actually, it forms a very important ideological justification, and it will continue to appear in the traditional textbooks for a long time for this reason. In this chapter, we intend to show that the monetarist economic policy implemented in late 1980, which tried to control inflation by a recession, actually accelerated it, especially in the oligopolized sectors of the economy.

By analyzing the price indices collected by the Getúlio Vargas Foundation, we can verify that the oligopolized sector of the Brazilian economy showed an acceleration in inflation during the same period in which demand underwent a very strong retraction. The fact that the annualized inflation rate verified in the May-June-July 1981 quarter in the oligopolized sectors was extremely high was a reflection of the monetarist policy. In the oligopolized sectors such as beverages this rate reached 343.5 percent, for the tobacco industry 301.0 percent, for electric materials 224.7 percent, transport material 162.9 percent, etc. At the same time, the more competitive sectors of industry, as well as the agricultural sectors and the producers of raw materials, showed much lower rates: lumber 11.32 percent, the metal industry 35.04 percent, textiles, apparel, and shoes 57.91 percent, food products 64.32 percent, agricultural products 40.38 percent, etc.

Thus the modest deceleration of inflation that occurred in 1981 was due to the fall in the rate of increase of the prices for agricultural products, raw materials, and the more competitive industrial sectors. Although output had fallen 9.6 percent in the manufacturing industry in the period from January to November 1981, compared to the same period for 1980, the wholesale price index for this sector showed a modest fall (100.3 percent in 1981 compared to 109.0 percent in 1980). In other words, the results obtained by the monetarist policy implemented since November 1980 were negligible and could be temporary. All that is needed for the inflation index to return to practically the same level as that of the previous year is for the prices of agricultural products, which increased only 70 percent in 1981, to adjust themselves to the same level as industrial prices (Table 7.1).

———————————————————— 1 ————————————————————

The most obvious thing for us to do in order to understand inflation is pay attention to the mechanism of the formation of prices. The traditional neoclassical economic theory put forth in textbooks does not clear up anything as long as it assumes that the exchange activities of abstract individuals ("producers") determine prices. On the contrary, the modern capitalist economy is dominated by big corporations that are multidivisional and monopolistic, and this institutional characteristic must be incorporated into any theory of prices. These corporations are made up of units of capital with a complex administrative structure. Actually, they are social agents dedicated to the valorization of capital, and it is in these terms that prices are determined. On top of this, the process of concentration, which is inherent in the capitalist system, permits the creation of barriers to the mobility of capital. Each corporation has a determined degree of monopoly, that is, the possibility of obtaining monopolistic profit rates. In most industrial sectors, big oligopolies dominate, and they administer their prices in the market independently of the conditions of supply and demand.

Given these conditions, it is not difficult to understand why the prices of the oligopolized sectors present behavior contrary to the neoclassical dogma, accepted as an obvious truth, that a reduction in demand provokes a reduction in prices. In practice, each oligopolistic corporation has its target profit rate, determined by its degree of monopoly. In order to reach this rate, it fixes a profit margin that, when added on to direct costs, will establish a price capable of covering the overhead costs, in addition to its target profits. Once this profit margin is calculated, it tends to remain

Table 7.1 Trends of the Inflation Rate (Annual Rates)

	12 Months from December 1980	12 Months up to December 1980	12 Months up to July 1981	6 Months up to July 1981	3 Months up to July 1981
General Price Index	108.55	95.2	110.50	105.06	84.69
Cost of Living Index	86.34	100.5	108.45	107.20	102.02
Cost of Construction Index	112.99	86.2	96.20	92.19	36.07
Wholesale Price Index	118.62	90.5	108.17	97.73	80.87
Agricultural Products	138.17	70.7	105.22	74.21	40.38
Industrial Products	110.26	99.7	108.82	108.57	101.74

Source: Conjuntura econômica; Getúlio Vargas Foundation

Table 7.2   Wholesale Price Index (IPA) – Manufacturing 1981

1. Competitive sectors that show a clear inflationary deceleration					
	12 months from December 1980	12 months up to December 1980	12 months up to July 1981	6 months up to July 1981	3 months up to July 1981
Metalurgy	102.40	83.2	79.91	64.96	35.04
Lumber	157.50	21.6	65.66	26.08	11.34
Real Estate	121.42	81.8	108.01	61.83	86.52
Leather and furs	43.97	89.1	73.61	90.82	61.02
Textiles, clothes and shoes	101.84	68.8	76.24	56.17	57.91
Food products	85.60	96.9	92.03	80.17	64.32

2. Oligopolized sectors that showed acceleration and/or hight inflationary rates	12 months from December 1980	12 months up to December 1980	12 months up to July 1981	6 months up to July 1981	3 months up to July 1981
Electrical material	106.62	135.2	129.70	178.19	224.73
Home appliances	115.13	134.0	137.34	191.65	227.27
Transport material	107.38	149.4	149.85	183.14	162.94
Motor vehicles	107.53	148.0	146.72	176.22	157.65
Paper & cardboard	95.87	120.5	110.53	102.06	157.85
Rubber	136.29	166.5	140.29	146.77	158.99
Chemicals	130.72	113.9	130.84	163.87	149.25
Beverages	118.71	127.2	141.85	127.01	343.51
Tobacco	65.39	183.0	156.28	287.73	301.00

Source: *Conjuntura Econômica*: Getúlio Vargas Foundation

relatively constant. Under normal conditions, prices are determined by adding the fixed margin to direct costs, which is why they tend to be insensitive to variations in demand. In the meantime, any variation in direct costs tends to be passed on to prices.

However, when demand falls drastically, as happened in the first semester of 1981, fixed unit costs increase, and if the profit margin does not increase, profits will be eaten away by this increase in costs. As oligopolistic corporations have control over the market, they try to recover the losses suffered from the fall in sales by increasing their profit margins. By increasing the profit margin for the remaining sales, they try to assure their projected profit rate.

This is exactly what happened in the 1981 recession. The Brazilian economy entered a process of recession after extremely restrictive monetary measures were applied beginning in the second semester of 1980. As a result, the oligopolistic sectors raised their profit margins, provoking a typical inflation of profits. It was precisely during the period of May-July 1981 when the corporations made the greatest cuts in the level of their production, laying off many workers, so that their profit margins and their prices underwent the greatest increases, as can be seen in Table 7.2. Once the margins are raised, if there is no fall in demand, there is no reason for the oligopolies to precipitate changes in prices. This explains why, in the following months when demand fell less rapidly, the rate of inflation was smaller.

----------- 2 -----------

Aside from these concentrated and oligopolized sectors, there is also a segment of the economy made up of the agricultural sector, the sector that produces raw materials, and some competitive branches of industry in which the mechanism for establishing prices is very different from that in the oligopolized sector. There is a free mobility of capital in these sectors, and thus firms do not have the power to administer their prices. Intercapitalist competition makes prices relatively flexible. When there is a drop in demand, they react by reducing their prices in order to be able to honor their financial commitments. This is clearly seen in Table 7.2, where we can verify that these competitive sectors decelerated their prices when demand underwent an accentuated fall.

However, this deceleration has its limits, because when prices cease to cover direct costs, all corporations prefer to stop production. Thus, once a level of prices is reached in which there is no profit, even the competitive corporations begin to pass the increase in their direct costs on to their prices. The recessive policy then stops working in an anti-inflationary way in these sectors.

In this way, what happens to inflation depends on the relative weight of the competitive and oligopolistic sectors in the economy. If the relative weight of the concentrated sectors is very great, the recession tends to accelerate inflation by compensating for the falls in the competitive sectors.

3

Obviously, this process of increasing profit margins has its limits. We then need to know what these limits are and when they begin to act. They depend on the degree of monopoly, that is, on the capacity of the corporations to set up obstacles to competition, such as imposing barriers for new corporations entering the sector, differentiating products, controlling technology and channels of distribution, etc. The greater their degree of monopoly, the longer the recession must last before the oligopolies no longer respond by increasing their profit margins. However, there is a moment in which this policy of raising prices no longer compensates for the fall in sales, and all of the corporations go into the red. This happens when the recession turns into a depression that is so prolonged that it destroys the whole economy, provoking generalized bankruptcy. Prices (relative to wages) also go up so much that demand becomes extremely sensitive to new increases. At this point, the unemployment level is so high that wages have already undergone big reductions and inflation thus begins to yield. In this case, the monetarist policy does have some effectiveness, but it is at the cost of a large increase in unemployment and a reduction in real wages.

A effective reduction in the inflation rate takes place especially in the next phase, when demand begins to be reactivated by the government itself because of strong social pressures. As sales begin to increase, fixed costs and profit margins may be reduced.

The above analysis clearly shows that the competitive sectors, along with the workers who lose their jobs and have their real wages reduced, pay the costs of the recessive policy adopted by the government. Only the big oligopolistic corporations are able to transfer their losses from the retraction in demand to consumers by accelerating their price increases. Sooner or later the workers and the competitive sectors will try to cope with their losses from recession and from the deceleration of their wages and prices.

April 1982

8

Accelerating Factors
in 1979 and 1983

During the period of rapid economic expansion from 1967 to 1973, Brazilian inflation was around an average annual rate of 19.5 percent.[1] In subsequent years it began to suffer from the impact of various inflationary pressures, until, in the second semester of 1983, it reached a level ten times higher.

In the first phase, the inflation rate doubled, going from an average annual rate of 19.5 percent in the period 1967-1973, to 38.7 percent in the period 1974-1978. During this period, the rise in the inflation rate was accounted for by the impact of high international oil prices. In spite of this acceleration, the inflation rate was maintained under relative control, stabilizing itself at an annual level of approximately 40 percent.

After 1979, Brazil entered a more turbulent phase, with a series of new accelerating factors (supply and demand shocks), which caused the annual inflation rate to jump to 77.2 percent in 1979 and to around 100 percent in the period 1980-1982. In 1983, new inflationary pressures caused the inflation level to double again, closing the year with an annual rate of 211 percent. The main price fluctuations that occurred in the period from 1979 to 1983 are shown in Table 8.1.

In this chapter, we will analyze the main factors that caused inflation in Brazil to soar. We will restrict the study to the period after 1979 and concentrate the analysis on two critical moments: the second semester of 1979 and the first semester of 1983. The acceleration of inflation that occurred in these two periods can be explained with the help of the model of autonomous or inertial inflation that we studied in Part 1 of this book. For these two periods, the main factors causing inflation to accelerate were: (1) price adjustments administered by the government (the so-called corrective inflation), implying an increase or recomposition of profit

Table 8.1 Price Variations: 1979 - 1983 (%)

Year	IGP-DI	Means of payment	Exchange devaluation	Monetary correction	Diesel oil on the Rotterdam market	Internal price of gasoline	Internal price of diesel oil	Nominal wages
1978	40.8	42.2	30.3	36.2	7.9	33.3	31.4	58.1
1979	77.2	73.6	103.3	47.2	145.2	169.0	160.9	67.8
1980	110.2	70.2	54.0	50.8	−0.8	125.7	66.7	109.7
1981	95.2	74.7	95.1	95.6	−5.0	66.7	150.0	96.4
1982	99.7	69.7	97.7	97.8	−0.8	96.5	104.0	107.6
1983	211.0	92.0	289.4	156.6	−15.1	166.5	194.1	121.0

Sources: Getúlio Vargas Foundation, Central Bank,
Federation of Industries of the State of São Paulo (for wages)

margins; (2) the maxidevaluations of the exchange rate; (3) shocks of agricultural prices; and (4) changes in the formula for the indexation of wages.

The assumption in this analysis is that the acceleration of inflation functions as a defense mechanism for the business sector against threats to profits. It tries to protect these profits from recession, wage increases, devaluations of the exchange rate, increases of agricultural prices, and corrective inflation. In other words, the acceleration of inflation defends the profits of the business sector, because it succeeds in increasing the profit margin or, simply because when inflation goes up, it causes the average real wage to go down.

—————————————— 1 ——————————————

When analyzing the process of the acceleration of inflation, the second semester of 1979 is an important period because it was both decisive and full of incidents and experiences that caused strong inflationary pressure. This pressure caused the inflation rate to jump from 40.8 percent in 1978 to 77.2 percent in 1979 and to 110.2 percent in 1980.

The year 1979 began with pressure from the prices of agricultural products that was the result of an inadequate expansion of cultivated area, as well as of poor harvests from 1977 to 1979. Actually, since the beginning of the 1970s, agricultural prices had been turning into an inflationary factor, but they had been repressed at the consumer level through price controls. This phenomenon can be accounted for by an insufficient supply of products for internal consumption, as well as by some cost-related pressures.

These pressures are explained by the increasing distance of the production areas from the centers of consumption, and subsequently by the expulsion from the rural frontier of the small farmers, who did not have legal rights over their land *(posseiros)*. They were also influenced by the rapid modernization of agricultural production in the Central-South region of the country. This modernizing process implied high financial outlays to make the transition from traditional, itinerant agriculture, which uses almost no industrial input, to a type of agriculture that entailed massive consumption of industrial products. It also involved a process of replacing the fertility of the soil, which was exhausted by the previous process of traditional exploitation. This all added up to the fact that, on the one hand, the increase in productivity due to modernization usually resulted in an increase in costs while, on the other hand, it interrupted the subsidy for the urban sector that was implicit in nonmonetary production costs and an underpaid work force.

The insufficient expansion of the supply of agricultural products was especially severe for products for internal consumption. This was basically because of a combination of the following factors: (1) income concentration that limited food consumption, (2) a lack of stimulation for food production because of price controls and unequal terms of trade with the oligopolistic industrial sector, (3) the stimulation and expansion of agricultural products for export, (4) heavy land speculation, and (5) an inadequate landholding structure.

As a result of these factors, the internal per capita availability of basic food—rice, beans, corn, manioc, and potatoes—suffered a 25 percent drop between 1967 and 1969. Even if one includes products of animal origin—beef, pork, poultry, milk products, and eggs—there was still a drop of -0.76 percent per year in the same period in terms of internal per capita availability.[2]

As shown in Table 8.2, in 1979 there was a factor for potential inflation: the price squeeze of agricultural products at the consumer level. The changes in the economic policy in the second semester of 1979 created a favorable environment for turning this factor into effective inflation. The average quarterly annualized rate of increase in the price of foodstuffs in 1979 jumped from 69.5 percent and 39.5 percent in the first two quarters, to 105.2 percent and 139 percent in the third and fourth quarters.

The monetary and fiscal policy in the period between 1974 and the first semester of 1979 was basically a policy of "stop and go," which maintained inflation under relative control at an annual level of a little below 40 percent. At the same time, it maintained economic growth by means of public investments financed by external debts.

In the first semester of 1979, the eruption of the war between Iran and Iraq and the new monetary policy adopted by the Federal Reserve Board of the United States gave Brazil two brutal shocks: (1) the "second oil shock," which caused the price of oil to double on the international market between the first quarter of 1979 and 1980, going from $12.63 per barrel to $21.01; and (2) the impact of the interest rate, which caused the prime rate to reach a level of 20 percent per annum, so that the real interest rate on the international market, which was around zero at the beginning of the decade, rose to a level of around 8 percent per annum at the end.

It was in this context that planning minister, Mário Henrique Simonsen, decided to implement a new orientation for the economic policy, making it more austere. He proposed budget and monetary reforms aimed at taking effective control over the expenditures of the public sector and over monetary expansion. He also took complementary steps in

Table 8.2 Indexes of Real Prices for the Agricultural Sector[a]

Year	Prices received by the farmers		Wholesale prices for foodstuffs	Consumer prices for foodstuffs for Rio de Janeiro
	Crops	Animal products		
1970	100	100	100	100
1971	110	105	107	102
1972	113	114	109	102
1973	142	142	110	102
1974	138	163	109	108
1975	149	145	110	106
1976	186	126	116	108
1977	184	129	116	110
1978	173	141	123	111
1979	161	169	126	116

Source: Getúlio Vargas Foundation.
[a] Prices deflated by the IGP-DI.

monetary and credit control by requiring that the equivalent in cruzeiros to 50 percent of foreign loans be deposited in the central bank for six months and by restricting the conditions for consumer loans.

This new policy was never implemented because it was faced with strong resistance both from inside and from outside the government. As a result, Simonsen resigned his position as planning minister in August, to be replaced by Antonio Delfim Netto.

The new minister implemented a new orientation completely contrary to that of Simonsen. Rather than decelerate the economy, he sought to expand it and, at the same time, to reduce inflation, as he had done in 1967. Thus, he adopted the following set of measures: (1) release credit and practice a looser monetary policy; (2) expand government expenditures; (3) control interest rates by applying a reducer to the prevailing rates; (4) suspend price controls for foodstuffs and for industrial products through the CIP (interministerial price control); (5) advocate a real readjustment of the prices of petroleum products, of public services, and of other prices administered by the government.

To have an idea of the impact of this "corrective inflation" policy, one only needs to remember that petroleum products, which had been readjusted by an average rate of 32.3 percent in 1978, underwent an average readjustment of 164.8 percent in 1979. Just in the month of November, gasoline was increased by 58.1 percent and diesel oil by 37.9 percent. There is no doubt that the big rise in the real price of imported energy acted as a shock, unleashing a wave of inflationary acceleration that caused inflation to double between 1970 and 1980.

At the same time, congress approved law 6708, shortening the period for readjusting wages from a one-year to one-semester basis. It also guaranteed that they would be raised to 10 percent above the inflation rate as measured by the national consumer price index (INPC) for those who made up to three minimum wages. The wage readjustments guaranteed by the law for those in the higher income brackets were progressively smaller, so that workers who earned up to 11.5 minimum wages had their real wage protected, while those above that level saw their wages decline.

There is no sufficient empirical evidence to prove the hypothesis that law 6708 increased the coefficients of indexation of the average wage to prices, or that the reduction in the period for readjusting wages had a strong inflationary impact.

There is no doubt that the new law had some inflationary impact as soon as it was enforced, but the real wage increase was almost immediately neutralized. In fact, a reduction in the period for wage readjustment would imply, in principle, an increase in the average real wage and, consequently,

Figure 8.1 Theoretical Effect on the Real Average Wage
of the Change to Semestral Readjustments

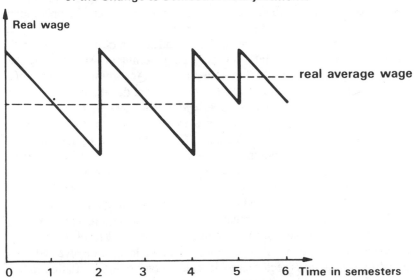

a reduction in profit margins, as we can see in Figure 8.1. To neutralize this change, the business sector's immediate solution was to accelerate the inflation rate. When faced with the simple threat of an increase in costs, business firms reacted by increasing their profit margins and prices. The resulting acceleration of inflation lowered real wages. The business sector also managed, through an increase in the turnover of workers, to reduce average real wages. Finally, the law itself, by penalizing wages above the level of 11.5 minimum wages, also helped to neutralize its own inflationary impact. As a result, there were not, according to the law, significant variations in the per unit cost of labor. See, for example, Eduardo Modiano (1983) and Paulo Vieira da Cunha (1983).

As if the inflationary impact of the previous measures was not enough, on 7 December 1979, the economic authorities carried out a maxidevaluation of the cruzeiro of 30 percent. The inflationary impact of this measure was immediate. Prices went up not only for imported products, but also for all other products because of the propagation effect. Speculation by those who held stocks of imported goods or of goods with a high content of imported components anticipated the inflationary impact.

In order to try to restrain the inflationary impact of the maxidevaluation, the government announced in advance that it would go back to administering prices and would establish limits for monetary correction and for a nominal exchange devaluation at 45 percent. It also tried to control monetary and credit policy by imposing a limit of 45 percent over the expansion of credit for the banking system for operations based on resources earned in the internal market.

When it announced a parameter for the indexation of the exchange rate that was below the actual inflation rate, the government was adopting the monetarist theory of "purchasing power parity." According to this theory, the inflation rate should adjust itself to the nominal devaluation rate of the currency. In order to do this, it is only necessary to make a prior announcement of the devaluation to a lower rate so that it can create expectations for a lower inflation rate. This is the same policy that was adopted earlier in Chile and in Argentina, based on the tablita of currency devaluation, with catastrophic consequences for these two countries.

Unfortunately, this attempt to control inflation "by decree" was a complete disaster. It was based on the assumption that the business sector would believe in the official measures and thus change its expectations, which would guarantee a drop in the inflation rate to the levels decreed by the government (50 percent). The impact of the exchange rate revealed that, in reality, the business sector bases its calculations on past inflation rather than on future rates decreed by the government, which, as a result, has no conditions to determine the expectations. After jumping from 77.2 percent to 110 percent, from 1979 to 1980, inflation stablized at this level, in spite of the preannounced exchange and monetary index. A small reduction in the inflation rate only came about in 1981, thanks to a radical contractionary policy that was adopted at that time. On the other hand, the valorization of the cruzeiro, provoked by the minidevaluations below the inflation rate, discouraged exports and encouraged imports. This, in turn, provoked a commercial deficit of almost three billion dollars in 1980, even though all of the indicators had pointed toward a policy of external adjustment since 1979. As a result, this adjustment, which was not carried out with moderation nor under Brazilian control in 1979 and 1980, was done violently and under the control of international creditors and the IMF in the following years.

--------- 2 ---------

In 1983, when the inflation rate doubled again, going from an annual rate of 99.7 percent in 1982 to 211.8 percent there were many similarities to 1979. Prices were once again submitted to a series of inflationary shocks: (1) strong pressure from the price of agricultural goods because of a reduction in the amount of cultivated land and an explosion in the price of some products, such as soya, in the international market; (2) a maxidevaluation in the exchange rate in February 1983 of 30 percent; (3) "corrective inflation" through price increases (and the elimination of subsidies) for some products and services that were controlled by the government (electric energy, steel, petroleum products, wheat, etc); and (4) a tax increase.

The first thing that differentiates 1983 from 1979 is that these inflationary shocks were now occurring in an economy that was going through its third year of recession. This was due to the policies of stabilization and adjustment patterned by the IMF, which had been implemented since the end of 1980 and then formalized in the letter of intentions of December 1982. The second difference is that the 1983 maxidevaluation was not annulled in the following month as had happened in 1979-1980.

Monetary expansion was contained at a level of 74.7 percent and 69.7 percent in 1981 and 1982, for inflation of 95.2 percent and 99.7 percent respectively, thereby causing a strong reduction in real liquidity. The total deficit of the public sector was reduced from 6.6 percent in 1982 to 2.5 percent in 1983. The real interest rate reached levels over 30 percent per annum, and the industrial employment level suffered a strong contraction, going down to the same level as in 1973. Industrial idle capacity reached almost 30 percent.

In respect to anti-inflationary policy, the wage law was changed at the beginning of 1983, with a reduction for workers earning more than three minimum wages. On the other hand, as the workers who earned more than 11.5 minimum wages did not have the replacement of their real purchasing power guaranteed, wages became partially deindexed. With the passage of law 2065 in November, which created an even more accentuated deindexation, the coefficient of the average readjustment fell to 87 percent of the national consumer price index (INPC). On top of this, price controls were reestablished, imposing a readjustment for industrial prices of 80 percent of the change in the ORTN.[3] A similar reduction was applied to rents.

It was this environment of a very heavy contraction in aggregate demand because of a tight fiscal and monetary policy, unprecedented in recent Brazilian history, combined with wage and industrial price controls, that the inflation rate skyrocketed, leading to the great stagflation of 1983. Neither the Keynesian models nor the monetarist models of inflation can explain this phenomenon. It is necessary to develop an alternative model that clearly distinguishes the elements that cause inflation to accelerate, as opposed to those that maintain inflation or cause inflationary inertia, even when there is high unemployment.

The first accelerating factor to manifest itself in 1983 was the pressure of agricultural prices, caused by a decrease in supply. In 1983, the main Brazilian crops, except for sugar cane, were 5.5 percent less than in 1982. This drop in production was partially due to crop failures resulting from climatic factors (floods in the South and droughts in the Northeast). The main reason, however, was an almost 6 percent reduction in cultivated area, because of the recessive policy itself and a drop in the real prices of agricultural goods in 1981 and 1982. Another fact, which is not as important as those mentioned previously, was a reduction in agricultural credit and the elimination of credit subsidies.

Agricultural prices began to go up at the end of 1982, after having been repressed, in real terms, for two consecutive years. The average monthly increase in agricultural prices in the wholesale market jumped from 4.9 percent in the second semester of 1982 to 12.2 percent in the first semester of 1983, and to 20.3 percent in the third quarter of 1983, when it climaxed.

In 1981 and 1982, it was the price of industrial products that pushed up the inflation rate, with increases of 99.6 percent and 99.8 percent respectively, compared to increases of 70.7 percent and 89.5 percent for agricultural prices in the same period. In 1983, the agricultural prices took the lead, increasing 335.8 percent as opposed to 200.5 percent for industrial products. Agricultural products play an important role in the cost of living index (INPC) and in indexation in general. As a result, this recomposition of the profit margins of agricultural prices, which especially benefitted the middlemen, spread to all other sectors via wage indexation and the automatic passing on of the price of agricultural raw materials, causing a strong acceleration in the inflation rate.

At the same time as the shock of the agricultural prices, the government provoked a new brutal price shock by declaring a 30 percent maxidevaluation of the cruzeiro in February 1983. As mentioned earlier, agricultural prices had already begun to exert pressure on the prices in other sectors at the end of 1982 and in the beginning of 1983, increasing by 11.9 percent in December and 11.5 percent in January in the wholesale market. As this was a totally inopportune moment from an inflationary point of view, the maxidevaluation caused prices to skyrocket. This then provoked successive waves of acceleration through the propagation effect, raising the inflation rate from a level of 100 percent, prevalent after since the end of 1979, to a level of over 200 percent at the end of 1983. As a result of these two shocks and their side effects, the general price index (IGP) jumped from a monthly average of 5.3 percent in the last quarter of 1982, to 8.5 percent in the first quarter of 1983, 9.4 percent in the second quarter, and 12.1 percent in the third quarter.

A real exchange devaluation (above the inflation rate) has a strong accelerating influence on inflation even though there are few imported products that participate in the GNP. Given the fact that more than two-thirds of Brazilian imports are petroleum and other basic components, the impact of a real change in the exchange rate is much greater than one would at first imagine. Moreover, the ultimate impact on inflation is more than proportional to the imported products' participation in the costs of production because of the generalized indexation of the economy.

Price readjustments for products and services whose prices are controlled by the government make up a third factor that also contributed to the acceleration of the inflation rate. These readjustments, especially for petroleum, steel, electric energy, and wheat, were aimed at eliminating subsidies in accordance with the recently assumed commitments to the IMF. They also took place in the second quarter of 1983, right after the two previously mentioned shocks. The shocks provoked by "corrective inflation" occurred at a moment when the system of prices was just beginning a process of absorbing and dispersing the shocks of the agricultural price increases and of the maxidevaluation.

Actually, the partial elimination of subsidies, which had occurred so far, fed inflationary expectations rather than actually pressuring costs. As can be seen in Table 8.3, the price readjustments administered by the government in 1983, with the exception of diesel oil, were less than the

Table 8.3 Prices Controlled by the Government (%)

	1980	1981	1982	1983
Electric energy	67.0	112.4	103.1	156.9
Telephone	69.1	98.4	90.4	127.5
Petroleum products				
Gasoline	125.7	66.7	96.5	166.5
Fuel oil	66.7	150.0	104.0	194.1
Diesel oil	404.2	90.1	104.3	225.2
Gas	104.3	94.7	105.4	213.8
Coal	77.2	248.8	174.4	102.6
Steel	133.9	105.9	99.0	150.1
Mail and telegraph service	56.2	139.9	101.2	88.0
Railroad transportation	79.4	112.1	98.2	152.6
IGP/DI	110.2	95.2	99.7	211.0

Source: Getúlio Vargas Foundation and the Central Bank

average fluctuations measured by the IGP. What happened was that there was a concentration of price readjustments in the second quarter of the year, after they had been held down for months. This exacerbated inflationary expectations, thus provoking an elevation in the anticipated inflation rate much higher than that which would result from a simple passing on of costs.

There is no doubt that when the inflation rate reaches a level of 10 percent per month, inflationary expectations play a more important role. This is because the risks of a divergence between effective and anticipated inflation become greater as the inflation rate rises. Given this situation, in the short run, the business community begins to base its calculations on some unit of buying power other than the current nominal currency. In this case, the dollar and the ORTN took the place of the cruzeiro as the accounting unit. When readjusting prices, the businessmen were also more strongly influenced by these buying power units than by cost increases.

3

As seen in Chapter 2, the accelerating factor of inflation, P, can be summed up as: (1) the increase in nominal average wages, $\dot{w}$, above the increase in productivity, $\dot{q}$; (2) the increase in the profit margin over the increase in sales, $\dot{m}$; (3) the devaluation of the exchange rate, $\dot{e}$; (4) the increase in the international prices for imported goods, $\dot{z}$; (5) the increase in indirect taxes; and (6) the increase in the real interest rates.

The increases of profit margins and wages do not in themselves cause inflation to accelerate, but rather are consequences of one of the following factors: (a) a generalized excess of aggregate demand in relation to supply, when there is full employment and the idle capacity is exhausted; (b) sectorial bottlenecks of supply; (c) the monopolized power of businesses and trade unions; (d) a reduction of productivity and consequently the elevation of fixed unit costs; and (e) increases in direct taxes.

In analyzing an economy like that of Brazil, in which inflation is a chronic phenomenon and which is characterized by the strong presence of oligopolies and of the state, it is fundamental to integrate the mechanism of indexing prices into the analysis. When there is chronic inflation, all businessmen try to defend their real income by automatically passing on increases in costs to prices. Thus, not only does inflation acquire inertia, but price shocks are also spread throughout the whole economy, creating an inflationary multiplier. When indexation is complete and generalized, an increase in any price in the economy not only provokes an initial increase in the general level of prices proportional to its participation in costs, but it is also multiplied by a factor represented by the mechanism of indexation. This mechanism guarantees all agents an increase equal to that which began the process, thus maintaining real income and relative prices intact.

In order to develop a more concrete theoretical base to explain the recent phenomenon of inflationary acceleration, it is necessary to break down the general price index into its three components, each with distinct behavior: industrial prices, $\dot{p}_i$; agricultural prices, $\dot{p}_a$; and prices which are controlled by the government, $\dot{p}_g$:

$$\dot{p} = \gamma_1 \dot{p}_i + \gamma_2 \dot{p}_a + \gamma_3 \dot{p}_g \qquad 8.1$$

where the γ's are the weight given to the participation of each sector in the composition of the general price index, p.

In the Brazilian industrial sector, which is marked by the strong presence of oligopolies and large state enterprises, prices are administered and set according to a markup above direct or variable costs. This markup factor tends to maintain itself constant in normal conditions of demand. However, in the course of the economic cycle, and when the economy is submitted to deep shocks or changes, businesses adjust their markups with an eye to protecting their long-term profit rates. Under normal conditions, margins are stable, and any increase in direct costs, interest rates, or indirect taxes are passed on to the consumer. Margins vary when there is a significant increase in direct taxes, fixed unit costs, and the degree of monopoly.

In order to determine the fluctuations of industrial prices, we should consider the fluctuations of profit margins, $\dot{m}$, the fluctuation of the wage rate, $\dot{w}$, the dollar price of imported raw materials, $\dot{z}$, and the exchange rate, $\dot{e}$, that is:

$$\dot{p} = \dot{m} + \alpha (\dot{w} - \dot{q}) + (1 - \alpha) (\dot{z} + \dot{e}) \qquad 8.2$$

where α stands for the participation of the cost of labor in the total direct cost.

In the agricultural sector, prices are governed by the rules of competition, except in the commercialization of a few products. In this sector, there is free mobility of capital and, with this, the agricultural producers are not able to influence their prices in the market. Short-term agricultural prices depend on the conditions of supply and demand, and are therefore relatively deindexed. Agricultural prices are determined, on the one hand, by harvests and existing stocks and, on the other, by demand,

and there is almost nothing that agricultural producers can do to change them. In the long run, relative prices need to be balanced so that production prices can act as a center of gravity for the market prices. Long-term prices are structural parameters that accompany production costs as a way to guarantee a minimal profitability of capital. Therefore, agricultural prices, which are flexible and deindexed in the short run, are indexed in the long run.

In fact, as we will see later, the economic recession of 1981 and 1982 caused a strong contraction of agricultural prices, which contributed to a reduction of inflation in that period. It also resulted in a reduction of land cultivated in the following harvests. This fact, combined with crop failures due to climatic factors and with low stocks, caused supply to be insufficient in 1983, with consequent price increases. A reduction in cultivated area functions as a regulating mechanism that reestablishes relative prices, but it also implies an inflationary acceleration.

When discussing agricultural prices, it is also important to distinguish between prices that are determined in the international market and those in the internal market. The two prices will tend to move together, but their dependence on each other is generated by the degree of protectionism or liberalization of the market. The price of export products are almost completely dependent on the conditions of the international market and on the exchange rate policy unless the government develops control mechanisms, such as export quotas and internal price controls.

In simple terms, we can state that the variations in agricultural prices, $\dot{p}_a$, depend on supply, O, and on demand, D, in the short run and, in the medium run, on the general price index.

$$\dot{p}_a = f(D, O, \dot{p}) \qquad\qquad 8.3$$

In an economy in which inflation is a chronic phenomenon, economic agents and groups make an effort, both formally and informally, to protect their real earnings through the indexation of their prices according to the general price index. There are four administered prices that depend on the government, trade unions, or oligopolies: (1) the prices of products controlled or produced by the government, (2) the exchange rate, (3) wages, and (4) the profit margins of businesses. The rate of increase of these prices depends on a coefficient of price administration, A:

$$\dot{p}_g = A_1 \dot{p}_{-1} \qquad\qquad 8.4$$

$$\dot{e} = A_2 \dot{p} + M \qquad\qquad 8.5$$

$$\dot{w} = A_3 \, \dot{p}_{-1} \qquad\qquad 8.6$$

$$\dot{m} = A_4 \qquad\qquad 8.7$$

Note that A_1 and A_2 basically depend on government decisions. A_3 depends jointly on business, trade unions, and the government. A_4 depends on the decisions of the oligopolies as they try to adjust their profit margins to attain a long-term profit rate. Actually, all of these prices, with the exception of the profit margin (which is not exactly a price), are generally indexed to past or current rates of inflation. As for the exchange rate, we use A_2 as the coefficient of indexation that guarantees a given parity for the local currency and M to reflect an eventual maxidevaluation.

Inflationary acceleration or deceleration occurs in agricultural prices if supply or demand undergo variations that affect relative prices. For other prices, the acceleration or deceleration of inflation will depend on the coefficients of price administration, that is, if they are greater or smaller than 1. Generally, what happens with the prices controlled by the government, including the exchange rate, is that they tend to make A_1 and A_2 less than 1 during periods of decelerating inflation. Then corrective inflationary measures making A_1 and A_2 greater than 1, or a maxidevaluation of the exchange rate, reestablish relative price equilibrium, thus accelerating inflation. A_3 varies around 1 according to the bargaining power of the workers and the power of the workers and businesses over the government. In order for A_4 to be neutral in relation to inflationary acceleration or deceleration, it should be equal to zero. If this is the case, profit margins are satisfactory and allow businesses to attain their planned profit rate.

In the medium term, agricultural prices, controlled prices, the exchange rate, and wages should accompany the inflation rate in order to reestablish the equilibrium of the structure of relative prices. When the economy is formally indexed, price controls serve this purpose. In the short run, the pendular movements described above are the most common or probable, especially when inflation itself accelerates.

4

In terms of the previous model, the strong acceleration of inflation in 1979 can be summed up in terms of the three shocks mentioned above. The first is the increase of agricultural prices, which had been partially held down at the consumer level by various control mechanisms. Due to the end of controls and to poor crops, which are related, agricultural prices began to accelerate in the second semester of 1979. This expansion found a favorable environment in the new "developmentalist" policy adopted by the government at that time.

In this model, agricultural prices are related to the general price index, and these to nominal wages. Any increase in agricultural prices not only has an immediate impact on the general price index, according to its weight, γ_1, but it also has an indirect effect on industrial prices through the indexation of wages. Given that the participation of agricultural prices in the price index used for wage adjustments is high in Brazil, the indirect effect of the increase in agricultural prices on industrial prices is significant.[4] Also note that, as the shock of agricultural prices spreads throughout the economy through the indexation of wages, it has an inflationary impact much greater than that which corresponds to its participation in the GNP. This impact can be partially neutralized only if the factor of wage controls, A_3, is less than 1.

The impact of the second accelerating factor of inflation—the maxidevaluation of the cruzeiro in relation to the dollar in 1979, and particularly in 1983—can also be analyzed more clearly in terms of the above model. At first, the maxidevaluation converts itself into an increase in industrial prices, as the businesses try to maintain their profit margins at a constant level by passing on increases in the costs of raw materials, as can easily be seen in Equation 8.2. The extent of this effect depends on the rate of the exchange devaluation, and on the participation of the costs of imported raw materials in industrial costs $(1 - \alpha)$. Next, we have the effects of the spread of inflation via the impact of industrial prices on the price index used for wage and exchange correction. In other words, the maxidevaluation now converts itself into an increase in wages and of the exchange rate itself, as both are indexed. Obviously, these wage and exchange rate increases are immediately passed on to prices.

If we were to have a maxidevaluation of 30 percent, as occurred in Brazil in December 1979 and in February 1983, and if the rest of the economy were indexed, the effect of the maxidevaluation on the general index of prices would be equal to M, or to 30 percent. In reality, the inflationary effect would be less than 30 percent because agricultural prices are not directly indexed. Also, industrial prices of the competitive sectors are only partially indexed, and the correction coefficient is less than 1 for the prices controlled by the government and for wages. On the other hand, if a maxidevaluation occurred at the same time as an increase in agricultural prices and a "corrective inflation" of controlled prices, as happened in 1979 and 1983, the accelerating effects on inflation would tend to be above this 30 percent, even if the economy were not totally indexed.

The effect of a 30 percent maxidevaluation will also be greater than 30 percent if the economic agents do not accept the change in relative prices and try to increase their prices in order to reestablish their share in the income prior to the real devaluation. They will not succeed in this attempt if the subsequent minidevaluations follow inflation, but the price increases they make in the meantime will have a powerful multiplying effect on inflation. It was probably this type of mechanism that had the most weight in the extraordinary acceleration of inflation in 1983.

5

The inflationary acceleration that happened in Brazil in 1979 and 1983 can, however, be explained perfectly by the model of autonomous or inertial inflation. In these two years, neither the public deficit nor the increase in the monetary supply had an accelerating effect on inflation. They were limited to sanctioning acceleration that had already occurred.

On the other hand, the Brazilian government and the International Monetary Fund applied an orthodox model of adjustment, based on the monetary approach to the balance of payments, which led to a recession in the Brazilian economy in 1983 unprecedented in its industrial history. Although the government also tried to partially deindex the economy, the emphasis of its anti-inflationary economic policy was put on a reduction of the public deficit and in controlling the monetary base.

They had success in reducing the public deficit and reasonable success in reducing the money supply, but the inflation rate still doubled in this period.

Faced with these results, it became normal in Brazil, including in official government documents such as the fifth letter of intentions to the International Monetary Fund, to attribute the inflationary acceleration of 1983 to the three factors we examined in this chapter (increase of agricultural prices, maxidevaluation, and the "corrective inflation" of controlled prices).[5]

Based on this fact, it is clear that neither the Brazilian authorities at the time nor the International Monetary Fund have a theoretical model capable of explaining Brazilian inflation. Although they explained the inflationary acceleration of 1983 in nonmonetarist terms, they insisted on emphasizing a monetarist therapy.

April 1984

─────────────────────── **Notes** ───────────────────────

1. General prices index, internal availability (IGP-DI), calculated by the Getúlio Vargas Foundation. When we talk about inflation without any other reference, we are referring to this index, although there are other indexes that are also indicators of inflation.

2. *See* Fernando Homem de Mello, "Disponibilidade de alimentos e efeitos distributivos: Brasil 1967/79," *Pesquisa e Planejamento Econômico*, vol. 12, no. 2, August 1982.

3. ORTN—obrigações reajustáveis do tesouro nacional—are corrected monthly according to past inflation. The value of these federal bonds served as the basis for indexation in Brazil.

4. It is estimated that agricultural prices have a value of 0.43 in the INPC.

5. Central Bank of Brazil, "Brazil Economic Program—Internal and External Adjustment," March 1984, 23.

9

Inertial Inflation on
the Eve of the Shock

In January 1986, it was dramatically confirmed that inflation, with a rate of 16.2 percent (IPCA) or 17.8 percent (IGP), had undergone a new acceleration.[1] The fact that, in the last three years, inflation had stayed at an annual level of a little above 200 percent (corresponding to a monthly inflation of about 10 percent) had led many analysts, including government analysts, to imagine that this was the true level of present Brazilian inflation, around which monthly inflation rates would fluctuate. Actually, since the beginning of 1985, the level of inertial inflation in Brazil had already changed to an annual rate of almost 280 percent (an average of 12 percent per month). On the eve of the shock, after the accelerating factors that affected inflation in the second semester of 1985, this level was now nearly 350 percent a year (between 13 and 14 percent per month).

1

In 1985, a partial price freeze between April and July artificially lowered inflation for this period and altered the results for the year, helping to confirm the illusion that the real level of inflation continued to be a little above 200 percent. Actually, as we can see in Table 9.1, the annualized rate of inflation in terms of the IPCA between December 1984 and March 1985 (the previous government) was already 274.8 percent. It went down temporarily to 155.8 percent in the period of the sectorial price freeze, and then in the last six months (August 1985 to January 1986) rose to 305 percent. The results in terms of the IGP are similar, with the differences between the three periods more accentuated because of the greater weight of

Table 9.1 Inflation Annual Rates (%)

Periods	IPCA	IGP
December 1984 - March 1985	274.8	268.8
April 1985 - July 1985	155.8	149.6
August 1985 - January 1986	305.3	334.4
November 1985 - January 1986	360.2	453.7

Sources: FIBGE and Getúlio Vargas Foundation

intermediary goods. In the period after the freeze, annualized inflation rose to 334.4 percent in terms of the IGP.

Price freezes produce remarkable results while the controls are enforced. Even in an economy in which a chronic inflationary process has attained very high rates and is rooted deeply in the habits of the population, the results are spectacular. However, when the price freeze is partial and covers only some sectors, as soon as the controls are removed we have "corrective inflation" and the rate of inflation returns to the previous level. When the price freeze is partial, the "corrective inflation" becomes inevitable after some months in order to reestablish the struture of relative prices. We will have either shortages in the private sectors or an increase in the public sector deficit, if, as is usual, the prices of state-owned companies have been preferentially frozen. Therefore, the gains against inflation are temporary and, if the controlled sectors are able to recover the losses incurred during this period by increasing their profit margins, the final level of inflation may be even higher than the one previous to the partial freeze.[2]

The effect of a partial price freeze on the rate of inflation depends directly on the weight of these controlled prices in the overall price index and, indirectly, on their effect on the uncontrolled prices through increases in the cost of raw materials and in wages.

2

The change in the inflation level during 1985 from 280 percent to about 350 percent is the result of three accelerating factors: (1) an increase in the average real wage rate considerably above the increase in productivity (about 10 percent); (2) an increase in agricultural prices beginning in October; and (3) pressures from demand caused by a great expansion of exports in many of the industrial sectors. A fourth factor—"corrective inflation" aimed at reestablishing profit margins and recovering the losses suffered by the corporations during the freeze period—did not have its full effect because the government, through the CIP, only allowed a partial recovery of profit margins.

The increase in the monthly inflation level in 1985, from 12 percent to 13.5 percent, was not greater because two decelerating factors were neutralizing the above mentioned accelerating factors: (1) a reduction of the real interest rates, and (2) an increase in corporations' utilization of idle capacity. The first factor mainly reduced the variable costs and the second the fixed costs of the corporations, so that they did not have to pass on all of the increases in real wages to prices.

The acceleration of economic growth is a decelerating factor for inflation as long as there is idle capacity and, therefore, the possibility of reducing fixed costs. It turns into an accelerating factor for inflation (pressure from demand) when, as idle capacity and the reserve army of unemployed workers are exhausted, corporations begin to increase their profit margins and the workers their real wages. In the first three quarters of 1985, the acceleration of economic growth was a decelerating factor for inflation; in the last quarter of the year, as idle capacity and unemployment were declining, it became an accelerating factor for inflation.

------------------------------ 3 ------------------------------

The estimate of the inflation level on the eve of the shock at around 350 percent a year is, naturally, an approximation. If we annualize the inflation between November 1985 and February 1986, we will have an inflation of 360.2 percent according to the IPCA and of 453.7 percent according to the IGP. This last index shows the acceleration of inflation that occurred in the last quarter of 1985 more clearly because it reflects the increases in the prices of intermediary goods immediately. However, it exaggerates the increase of inflation, and thus cannot serve as a base for the definition of the new inflationary levels. On the other hand, the level of the inflation rate in January was clearly exceptional. For this reason, it seems to be more realistic to accept a trend level for inflation of 13.5 percent per month (corresponding to an annual inflation of 366.4 percent).

------------------------------ 4 ------------------------------

This high rate of inflation on the eve of the shock provoked a generalized fear that Brazil was entering an explosive inflationary spiral that would rapidly lead to hyperinflation. This fear, while understandable, did not make sense. One of the characteristics of Brazilian inertial or autonomous inflation is its inflexibility, not only downward, but also upward. Inflation accelerates in Brazil, but slowly, by stages, rather than in an explosive and uncontrolled way as happens with classic hyperinflation.

This relative upward rigidity of Brazilian inflation was mostly because of generalized indexation, that is, to the existence of legal monetary correction, which, among other things, allowed the real exchange rate to remain constant (the nominal exchange rate was devalued daily according to the inflation rate). In Germany and other countries where hyperinflation has occurred through an inflationary spiral, there were real devaluations daily, and the flight to more stable foreign currencies was possible. It was these continuous real devaluations and large-scale flight that produced the explosive inflationary spiral and led to hyperinflation. The mechanism was simple. Given the then inflation, the government was obliged to increase the money supply in order to cover its growing obligations and to minimally maintain the liquidity of the system. Money placed in the hands of the public was immediately changed into dollars or other foreign currencies. The demand for dollars was so intense that it provoked daily real devaluations of the local currency. Real devaluations of the local currency were a very powerful accelerating factor for inflation because they raised the costs of imported goods and, via the propagating effects, domestic costs (Gerald Merkin 1982).

In the case of Brazil, the situation was completely different. The government was also forced to expand the money supply, but cruzeiros were not changed into dollars. Given the existence of an indexed financial market, the cruzeiros were applied in this market: they financed the public deficit. Also, the real exchange rate remained constant except for when there was a maxidevaluation, as happened in February 1983.

5

Meanwhile, although we can remain reasonably calm about the small probability of an inflationary spiral, we should also be realistic enough to recognize that if inertial inflation is inflexible upwards, it is even more inflexible downwards. Because of this, it is completely unrealistic to imagine, as the then government seemed to do, that it is possible to return to a monthly inflation of 10 percent through the use of administrative price controls and a good administration of the stocks of agricultural products.[3] This strategy for fighting inflation is highly recommended, but its primary objective is not to reduce inflation, but to keep it under control, to prevent it from accelerating.

Actually, inertial inflation like Brazil's, which had already passed 300 percent, could not be fought with gradualist methods, be they orthodox or unorthodox. The only solution was a heterodox shock, the heroic policy for combatting inflation that we discussed in the last section of Chapter 3.

The gradualist orthodox policy is recommended by the IMF. It is based on fiscal and monetary contraction, cutting aggregate demand and leading the economy into a recession, which would provoke a reduction in real wages and in profit margins and, therefore, would decelerate inflation. The gradualist unorthodox policy is based on administrative control of prices, using a declining future inflation as a guideline.

Apart from the fact that the orthodox policy is inefficient because it is based on a generally incorrect diagnosis of inflation (demand inflation), both the orthodox and unorthodox gradualist policies are ineffective because, at this level of inflation, any supply shock cancels out all efforts to combat it through price controls, monetary and fiscal containment, or a combination of both these policies. An agricultural shock, a wage shock, a maxidevaluation, or "corrective inflation" measures cancel in one day what took months to attain.

This does not happen when inflation is much lower—at a level of 20 percent or 30 percent—because, at this level, the annual increase in productivity is an important instrument for decelerating inflation, and because the trade-off between unemployment and inflation is significant. Gradualist policies are effective as long as they make it possible that the increases in productivity are not immediately transformed into increases in nominal wages, but rather into reductions in costs and prices. One of the causes of inflationary deceleration in the central countries, beginning in 1980, was this capacity to take advantage of gains in productivity. However, it is clear that when inflation reaches levels above 300 percent, this utilization of the increases in productivity becomes marginal. If an orthodox policy is adopted, the loss in output necessary for a sensible effect on inflation is unbearable. It is also easily cancelled out by eventual offer or demand shocks.

6

If Brazilian inflation is inertial and has already passed the level of 300 percent, gradualist policies for combatting it, either orthodox or unorthodox, are ineffective. At this point, there is only one conclusion: only a heterodox shock can wipe out Brazilian inflation.

However, there are important obstacles to the adoption of a heterodox shock. In the first place, there is a lack of understanding of the nature of the Brazilian inflationary process. There is not yet a proper understanding of the inertial character of inflation. The government still insists on relating inflation to the public deficit and the increase in the money supply while both these phenomena have mainly been factors that sanction inflation, which is proceeding inertially and autonomously. Many officials do not clearly understand that, because of the distributive conflict and indexation, past inflation tends automatically to reproduce itself in the present. As the readjustments of prices are not synchronized, the economic agents have no other alternative than to pass on their cost increases to prices. Otherwise, they would lose their relative participation in the national income.

Second, lack of synchronization in the readjustment of prices, especially of wages, greatly complicates the choice of a D Day for the heterodox shock to freeze prices and wages. The alternative of creating a formula for the conversion of all wages to the average on D Day is theoretically correct but politically difficult to implement (Modiano 1986). In Argentina, where wages were increased monthly, the choice of the fifteenth of the month as the D Day satisfied all the needs for relative distributive neutrality. In Brazil, we either could have fused a conversion formula for wages or we would have had to wait for much higher inflation levels than the then present ones for the shock to be successful.

An increase in the inflation level is necessary for another reason. Because a policy of a general freeze of prices, wages, and the exchange rate presents certain risks, it demands a lot of political determination and popular collaboration. In other words, it demands general indignation against inflation, which, because of the mechanism of indexation, still is not strong in Brazil.[4]

It is also important to point out that the inflation rate can be broken down into three components: inertial, demand, and supply shocks. Obviously, if the price system is subject to a supply shock or demand pressure, these must be assimilated or removed for a heterodox shock to be successful. In this situation, the demand presssures are still weak, but the forecasts of bad harvests due to draught in the southern states generated an agricultural price shock at the beginning of 1986. This means that the price system is still absorbing the shock that provoked the disequilibrium in the structure of relative prices.

This fact can be observed in the wide dispersion of the sectorial rate of inflation. When inflation was essentially inertial in the second semester of 1984, the standard deviation of the rate of sectorial inflation was about 20.0, but, at beginning of 1986, it reached 52.0, thus showing the effects of the shock. Therefore, it is necessary to wait some months in order to reestablish the equilibrium of the structure of relative prices. Then we will have more viable conditions for a heterodox shock.

Finally, there is the misgiving that a heterodox shock would be accompanied by a serious recession, as happened in Argentina. Actually, this risk does exist. It is difficult to imagine getting rid of inflation without any sacrifices. Although the government deficit is a result rather than a cause of inflation, it should be reduced. An exchange devaluation should take place on the eve of the D Day. Interest rates should be kept at relatively high levels in order to avoid the flight of capital. But it is necessary to consider that the situation of Brazil is very different from that of Argentina. Brazil's industrial complex is very solid, its export surplus has structural characteristics, its public sector borrowing requirements (operational public deficit) are smaller, and the risk of capital flight much less. Therefore, there is no reason to fear a strong recession in Brazil.

———————————————— 7 ————————————————

The great problem of the Brazilian government in these next months will be to continue its gradualist administrative policy of fighting inflation, even though it knows that the results of this kind of policy are limited, given the high level of inflation. At the same time, it must prepare for a heterodox shock.

The government has a few factors in its favor, especially the large trade surplus, the successful negotiations of the foreign debt, a fiscal reform that allows for a reduction of the operational public deficit, and the improvement of the financial situation of the state-owned corporations. Meanwhile, there is no need for pessimism or alarmism. Inflation has moved to a higher level, but it is not out of control. It is a cause for concern and keeps the government and society under strain, but it can be tamed.

February 1986

———————————————— Notes ————————————————

1. IGP is the general price index calculated by the Getúlio Vargas Foundation traditionally used as the measure of inflation and indexation in Brazil, except for wage indexation. IPCA is the amplified consumer price index calculated by the Brazilian Institute of Geography and Statistics (IBGE). The IPCA has replaced the INPC, the national consumer price index,

and the IGP as the basis for official indexation in Brazil since November 1985. The INPC measures cost-of-living increases for families earning up to five minimum wages, and the IPCA for families earning up to thirty minimum wages. Starting in March 1986, the IPCA was replaced by the IPC, the consumer price index. The objective of this substitution was not to include about fifteen days of the inflation in February in the calculation of the inflation in March.

2. *See* Luiz Bresser Pereira and Fernando Maida Dall'Acqua (1985) for a more complete and formal development of this argument.

3. This chapter was originally written in February 1986, a few days before the shock.

4. This indignation began to be shown at the beginning of 1986. *See*, for example, Geraldo Forbes, "O santo guerreiro e o dragão da maldade", in *O Estado de São Paulo*, 2 February 1986.

10

The Difficulties of the Cruzado and the Austral Plans

Six months after the Cruzado Plan was implemented on 28 February 1986, its success in solving the specific problem for which it was created—the elimination of inertial inflation—is undeniable. Inflation, which was around 350 percent a year, fell to a figure of somewhere between 15 and 20 percent. However, strong inflationary pressures threatening the continuity of the success of the plan persist. Conversely, fourteen months after its implementation (on 16 June 1985) the Austral Plan has failed to eliminate inflation, while Israel's second heterodox stabilization plan, thirteen months after its D Day in July 1985 has succeeded in eliminating inertial inflation.

After fluctuating at around 4.5 percent a month between March and June 1986, Argentine inflation reached 6.8 percent in July and 8.8 percent in August. The annualized inflation for June, July, and August reached 118 percent, and that of August, 175 percent. The situation for the Cruzado Plan is more favorable for the moment, but if urgent measures are not taken to reestablish the micro- and macroeconomic balance of the plan, the freeze by itself will certainly not be capable of preventing the resurgence of inflation. In Israel, the success of the reform is more solid. About half of the price controls have been removed and the monthly rate of inflation is below 1.5 percent. The public deficit has been severely reduced while the level of production and employment has been kept stable.

Given those inflation rates, the freeze in Argentina has definitely been broken. Inflation is in full acceleration, which will only end when the new readjustments of prices and wages are relatively able to neutralize the most recent price increases. At this point, the inertial component of inflation would then become dominant again and, as has already happened in Israel, a new shock could be attempted.

--------------------------------- 1 ---------------------------------

There are those who mistakenly attribute the failure of the Austral Plan to the relative lifting of the price freeze that took place in April. This partial price liberalization, however, was already a consequence of inflationary pressures that had not been resolved. In a capitalist economy, it is impossible to maintain a price freeze for a long time. Either the government eliminates the main inflationary pressures and then proceeds with a planned lifting of the freeze, or else it does not manage to eliminate the accelerating factors of inflation and thus is forced to liberate prices because of the irresistable pressures from imbalances in the market. It was the latter alternative that prevailed in Argentina.

It is important, therefore, to know what these imbalances were and what the origin of these inflationary pressures was. Theoretically, we can have two kinds of imbalances: the macroeconomic ones that are represented by an excess of aggregate demand and the microeconomic ones that are explicit in the imbalances of relative prices.

Everything indicates that the Argentines were not dealing with a macroeconomic imbalance or, more specifically, with excess demand. Even though the public deficit had not been completely eliminated, it was significantly reduced. However, the economy definitely remained in recession until the beginning of 1986. In the first quarter of 1986, the growth of the GNP was only 0.4 percent, as compared to the same period in the previous year. Recently, a clear process of expansion has taken place, registering growth of 5.7 percent in the second quarter, but the levels of unemployment and idle capacity are still very high.

The imbalances that were not resolved, therefore, could only have been microeconomic. The economic authorities were unable to resolve the distortions in relative prices that existed on 16 June 1985, when the shock was applied. When the pressures from the sectors that suffered losses became unbearable, the floodgates began to open. The heating up of demand that took place at this point probably helped this process along—the freeze began to break. As a result, the pressures from workers for wage readjustments and exporters for exchange devaluations became stronger and stronger. When there was no other alternative except to give in to the pressures from wages and the exchange rate, the freeze lost its force and inflation entered into a straightforward process of acceleration, which probably has not yet ended.

————————————————————— 2 —————————————————————

The same thing does not necessarily have to happen in Brazil. The present situation of the Brazilian economy is much more favorable than that of Argentina's. Production is expanding. Although it is investing with moderation, industry is incorporating technical progress at an accelerated pace. The trade superavit is still very high. The Brazilian financial system is much better organized and developed than Argentina's. Its industry is more modern and competitive, and the fiscal system is much more developed. Last, the state bureaucratic apparatus is much better equipped. For all of these reasons, the Brazilian government has more effective means for carrying out its economic policy and controlling its economy. Perhaps it is for these reasons that inflation, in the first six months of the Cruzado Plan, was considerably lower than the corresponding inflation of the Austral Plan: 6.4 percent from March to August 1986 in Brazil as opposed to 20.1 percent from July to December 1985 in Argentina.

However, there is no question that the Brazilian economy is faced with serious macroeconomic and microeconomic imbalances. At first, the economic expansion, which reduced fixed unitary costs, and the reduction of the interest rates helped to neutralize the imbalances in relative prices, which the government itself did not feel able to solve. Next, however, an extraordinary increase in consumption changed the economic expansion into a serious macroeconomic distortion, which the compulsory loan and raising of the internal interest rate are not capable of resolving.

There is no question that the Cruzado Plan finds itself in a dangerous situation now. Part of the support that it initially received does not exist anymore. Consumers are irritated and disappointed with the lack of merchandise, with waiting lines and overpricing. Even though they are earning good profits, businessmen feel that their control over their own activities is threatened. Those who are the most conservative or who have lost the most say that the economy is being nationalized, that Brazil is being turned into a police state, and they place themselves more and more against the freeze.

In this situation, the mere insistence of the government in maintaining the freeze does not resolve the problem. It is essential to maintain the freeze for now, but it is also essential to reestablish the microeconomic balance of relative prices and the macroeconomic balance of aggregate supply and demand.

3

The Brazilian economy as a whole, which should not be confused with the Cruzado Plan, continues to show an extremely favorable performance. Between March and June of 1986, industrial production grew 12.4 percent and wholesale sales were up 29.9 percent in relation to the same period in the previous year. The unemployment level fell from 5.6 percent in June 1985 to 3.8 percent in June 1986. Real wages increased 14.6 percent from one year to the next. The foreign commercial superavit accumulated in this year continued at around $13 billion, although an increase in imports and a fall in the prices of some primary export products are begining to threaten this favorable result and make us remember that the external debt is still a serious unsolved problem.

Actually, this excellent performance of the real sector of the economy is the first problem of the Cruzado Plan. The extraordinary increase in consumption, widely overtaking the increase in production, implies shortages of supplies, waiting lines, and inflationary pressure translated into an increase of profit margins through either overpricing or the elimination of financial discounts on term sales. Contrary to what is generally stated, there is still idle capacity in the economy, but this does not prevent the inflationary pressures that come from the appearance of bottlenecks, especially in the supply of raw materials and meat. The new expansive cycle of the Brazilian economy, which began in 1984, has reached a peak in 1986—which the Cruzado Plan had favored.

The question of demand should be put into proper terms. Demand has not reached an excessively high level, but rather has had an excessively rapid recovery. According to the survey of the Getúlio Vargas Foundation of July 1986, the average degree of capacity utilization reached 82 percent, less than the record levels of 1972 and 1973—89 and 90 percent respectively. Industrial production only recovered to the average level of 1980. It is true that some sectors had already reached almost full capacity, such as nonferrous metals, cellulose, textiles, plastic containers, etc. It is also true that the level of demand became excessive in those sectors in which the flow of goods and services depends on stocks (which were greatly depressed after almost four years of recession), as in the case of beef herds. But the biggest problems are occurring in the sectors that still have some idle capacity, but which are faced with a scarcity of raw materials and thus are unable to expand production. This happens basically because demand has grown explosively and, in many segments, it is not possible to simply double production every two or three months, as has been happening with the demand for certain consumer goods. That is why the

Getúlio Vargas Foundation survey shows that the consumer goods sector is utilizing only 72 percent of its capacity and that 45 percent of the corporations have had difficulty in expanding production because of a scarcity of raw materials.

The situation will probably get worse in the last quarter of the year, as industry traditionally operates at levels 10 to 15 percent higher in this period than the average for the rest of the year in order to meet the end-of-year demand. Demand should also continue to expand in order to restore stocks, which are at a very low level. Faced with this situation, the government's hesitation in taking urgent fiscal policy measures to decelerate the growth of demand is hard to understand. Given a diagnosis that the problem is not an excessive and generalized level of demand in relation to productive capacity, but rather an excessive rhythm of expansion, a fiscal policy should contain this growth without the need to reduce the level of employment.

The second problem is the new outbreak of pressure from the trade unions for higher wages, which is added to the pressure from the market itself, especially for specialized labor. The explosion in the demand for labor and the higher demands of the trade unions has led to real increases in wages, which are considerably higher than the increase in productivity. These wage increases will not be translated into a reduction of profits only if they result in increased prices instead.

The Cruzado Plan' s third problem is the micreconomic imbalance of relative prices, or prices which have been "ahead" or "behind" since the day of the shock. The shortage of merchandise in the stores is not due only to excess demand, but also to the fact that the producers, especially those who can substitute products, stopped making a series of goods whose prices were behind on 28 February. Almost half of the products with set prices (all prices have been frozen, and about 500 products had their prices set in order to make the control easier), for example, are disappearing from the retail stores because their producers stopped making them, substituting for them whenever possible with new products. When the producer manages to substitute for the controlled goods, he solves his problem by provoking a small amount of inflationary acceleration; when he cannot do this, it appears immediately as a focus of repressed inflationary pressure.

The problem of the retail companies, on the other hand, is far from being solved. The financial discount they were supposed to receive from their suppliers in order to compensate for the end of inflation (since these suppliers had built an average monthly inflation of 14.6 percent into their term sales) should be 12.6 percent a month, but, in practice, ended up being an average of 5 percent. Those suppliers that gave greater discounts are now taking advantage of the excess demand, without formally disregarding the freeze, to reduce or eliminate the discounts, leaving the retailers in a difficult situation in spite of the increase in sales.

On the other hand, the corporations whose prices were ahead on 28 February and those that gave an insufficient financial discount to their customers saw their profit margins increase substantially. The increase in margins, together with the increase in sales, has led to an incredible increase in profits. The auditing companies have calculated that, in the first half of 1986, the profits of the industrial corporations would be, in real terms, approximately double the profits for the same period of 1985. This increase in profits allowed the corporations to concede significant real wage increases to their workers, which, in turn, stimulated consumption even more and therefore accentuated the imbalance between aggregate supply and demand.

These inflationary pressures built into the macroeconomic imbalance between aggregate supply and demand, the pressures from wages, and the unresolved distortions in relative prices will accelerate inflation as soon as the price freeze is lifted.

On the other hand, given an operational public deficit of between 4 and 5 percent of the GNP, while the economy is operating at close to full capacity, the public finances are still unbalanced, thus creating a fourth focus of inflationary acceleration. In 1986, this deficit is being partially financed by the monetization of the economy. The same level of deficit is predicted for 1987, during which the contribution of the compulsory loan should be less than 1.5 percent of the GNP. Assuming that bonds will be issued, corresponding to another 1.5 percent of the GNP, there is still between a 1 and 2 percent deficit that will either be financed by new international loans and/or by an increase in taxes.

Faced with these inflationary pressures, the government has taken some steps, such as the compulsory loan on the purchase of gasoline, cars, trips abroad, and raising interest rates. Its basic strategy, however, is too simple. It consists of trying to maintain the price freeze at all costs, even by using the police. For some members of the government, "the Cruzado Plan is the freeze," which therefore should be maintained indefinitely.

The Cruzado Plan is not the freeze, and the freeze should not be maintained indefinitely; it is a shock that was applied to the economy to try to eliminate inertial inflation. However, it cannot show a lack of respect for the law of value that rules the functioning of the market. The freeze succeeds in eliminating the factors that maintain inflation; it does not eliminate the accelerating factors of inflation that operate in the market: excess demand, uncontrolled increases in wages, and imbalances in relative prices. In order to control these accelerating factors, additional measures of economic policy are needed. These factors can only be temporarily repressed until the imbalances in the market are solved or until the moment that these pressures become irresistible and the freeze is broken.

The second alternative is the one that prevailed in Argentina. Although the Austral Plan was not faced with the problem of excess demand, it was neither able to contain wages nor resolve the problems of relative prices.

It is still too early to predict what the level of inflation will be in Brazil when the price freeze is lifted. The government will try to put this moment off as long as possible while it tries to correct the macroeconomic imbalance between aggregate supply and demand and the microeconomic imbalance of the relative prices. Meanwhile, if it does not show more energy in solving the problem of excess demand and in correcting the lagging prices, the Brazilian economy will be faced with a new inflationary acceleration in 1987. As for the lagging prices, it will have to make a choice between a little more inflation now or uncontrolled inflation in the near future. And, as for the macroeconomic imbalance, it will have to increase taxes and cut public spending. If these micro- and macroeconomic imbalances are not corrected rapidly the pressures from the market will be so strong that the freeze will break up, and, after a transitional period of acceleration of inflation, a high level of inertial inflation will be necessary. In this case the only reasonable alternative will be a second heterodox shock followed by a more firm conduction of aggregate demand and of relative prices.

September 1986

Statistical Appendix

Table 1 BRAZIL'S INTERNAL SECTOR (Annual rate of growth %)

Years	GDP (Gross Domestic Product)	Real Average Wages in Industry[a]	INFLATION		Money Supply (MI)	Real Public Deficit (% of GDP)
			General Price Index-Domestic Supply (GPI-DS)	Consumer Price Index[b]		
1970	8.3	1.0	19.2	22.7	26.5	-
1971	12.1	3.2	19.8	20.2	32.3	-
1972	11.1	4.1	15.7	16.4	38.3	-
1973	13.5	4.8	15.5	13.7	47.0	-
1974	9.7	0	34.5	33.9	33.5	-
1975	5.4	7.9	29.4	31.2	42.8	-
1976	9.7	4.7	46.3	44.8	37.2	-
1977	5.7	6.7	38.8	43.1	37.5	-
1978	5.0	8.4	40.8	38.2	42.2	-
1979	6.4	4.6	77.2	76.0	73.6	8.3
1980	7.2	− 0.3	110.2	94.6	70.2	6.7
1981	− 1.6	10.2	95.2	92.7	87.2	5.2
1982	0.9	10.9	99.7	103.3	65.0	6.2
1983	− 3.2	−10.1	211.0	164.4	96.4	3.0
1984	4.5	1.3	223.8	208.9	201.0	1.6
1985	8.0	5.0	235.1	233.7	312.0	3.2

Source: Central Bank of Brazil
(a) Between 1970/1974 the real rates were obtained from a survey of 18 unions in São Paulo (Source: Bacha and Taylor, Models of Growth and Distribution for Brazil, Washington, World Bank, 1980). From 1975 to 1985, the sources is IBGE Foundation. Nominal wages were deflated by the consumer Price Index of DIEESE.
(b) Until 1979 the variation was obtained from the Consumer Price Index for Rio de Janeiro, Getúlio Vargas Foundation. From 1980 to 1985, the variation refers to the extended national price index of the IBGE Foundation.

Table 2 BRAZIL'S EXTERNAL SECTOR   (US$ millions)

Years	Exports	Trade Balance	Deficit in Balance of Real Transactions	Interest Payments	Current Transactions	Liquid External Debt
1970	2,738.9	232.0	299.0	284.0	− 562.0	4,108.5
1971	2,903.9	− 343.5	979.5	344.0	− 1,307.0	4,898.7
1972	3,991.2	− 244.1	1,005.0	489.0	− 1,489.0	5,337.8
1973	6,199.2	7.0	875.5	839.5	− 1,688.0	6,155.7
1974	7,951.0	− 4,690.3	5,752.3	1,370.1	− 7,122.4	11,896.6
1975	8,669.9	− 3,540.4	4,909.9	1,804.3	− 6,712.2	17,130.9
1976	10,128.3	− 2,254.7	3,978.6	2,039.4	− 6,017.0	19,441.5
1977	12,120.2	96.8	1,574.9	2,462.4	− 4,037.3	24,781.1
1978	12,658.9	− 1,024.2	2,657.2	3,342.4	− 5,927.4	31,615.6
1979	15,244.4	− 2,839.5	5,412.0	5,347.5	− 10,741.6	40,215.5
1980	20,132.4	− 2,822.8	5,517.8	7,457.0	− 12,807.0	46,934.9
1981	23,293.0	1,202.4	1,627.6	10,305.2	− 11,734.3	53,904.0
1982	20,175.1	780.1	3,751.8	12,550.6	− 16,310.5	66,204.0
1983	21,899.3	6,470.4	− 3,318.3	10,263.2	− 6,837.4	76,756.3
1984	27,005.3	13,089.5	− 11,323.1	11,448.8	44.8	79,095.7
1985	25,639.0	12,450.0	− 9,600.0	11,092.0	267.8	81,453.0

Source: Central Bank of Brazil

Bibliography

Arida, Pérsio
  1982 - "Reajuste salarial e inflação," *Pesquisa e Planejamento econômico*, vol. 12, no. 2 (August).
  1984 - "Economic Stabilization in Brazil," text for discussion, no. 84, mimeo, Pontifícia Universidade Católica of Rio de Janeiro, (December).
  1986 - *Inflação Zero. Brazil, Argentina, Israel*, editor. Rio de Janeiro: Paz e Terra.
Argy, Victor
  1981 - *The Postwar International Money Crisis—An Analysis*. London: George Allen & Unwin.
Bacha, Edmar
  1980 - "Notas sobre inflação e crescimento," in *Revista Brasileira de Economia*, vol. 34, no. 4 (October-December).
  1982 - *Introdução à Macroeconomia. Uma Perspectiva Brasileira*. Rio de Janeiro: Editora Campus.
Ball, R.J., and Peter Doyle, editors
  1969 - *Inflation*. Harmondsworth: Penguin Books.
Banco Central do Brasil
  1984 - "Brazil's Economic Program—Internal and External Adjustment" (March).
Belluzzo, Luiz Gonzaga de Mello
  1977 - "A intervenção do estado no período recente," Ensaios de Opinião, no. 2-3.
Bhalla, Surgit S.
  1981 - "The Transmission of Inflation in Developing Countries," in William R. Cline, editor, *World Inflation and the Developing Countries*, Washington: The Brookings Institution.
Bomberger, W. A., and G. E. Makinen

1983 - "The Hungarian Hyperinflation and Stabilization of 1945-1946," *Journal of Political Economy*, vol. 91, no. 5 (December).

Bresser Pereira, Luiz

1968 - *Desenvolvimento e Crise no Brasil: 1930-1967*. Rio de Janeiro: Zahar (1970), second edition (1972), third edition (1984); first English edition, Boulder: Westview Press.

1970 - "Dividir ou multiplicar: a concentração da renda e a recuperação da economia brasileira," *Visão* (November); republished in Luiz Bresser Pereira, *Desenvolvimento e Crise no Brasil*, third amplified edition, (1972).

1977a - "O estado na economia brasileira," *Ensaios de Opinião*, no. 2-2.

1977b - *Estado e Subdesenvolvimento Industrializado*. São Paulo: Editora Brasiliense.

1980 - "As contradições da inflação brasileira," *Encontros com a Civilização Brasileira*, no. 21, (March); republished in Bresser Pereira and Nakano (1984b).

1981 - "A inflação no capitalismo de estado (e a experiéncia brasileira recente)," *Revista de Economia Política*, vol. 1, no. 2, (April-June); republished in Bresser Pereira and Nakano (1984b).

1986 - *Lucro, Acumulação e Crise*, São Paulo: Editora Brasiliense.

Bresser Pereira, Luiz, and Fernando Maida Dall'Acqua

1985 - "Congelamento setorial de preços e inflação corretiva," *Economia em Perspectiva, Carta de Conjuntura*, no. 17 (September).

Bresser Pereira, Luiz, and Yoshiaki Nakano

1983 - "Fatores aceleradores, mantenedores e sancionadores da inflação," mimeo, X Encontro Nacional de Economia. Belém: Associação Nacional de Centros de Pós-Graduação em Economia, ANPEC, published in *Revista de Economia Política*, vol. 4, no. 1 (January-March 1984); republished in Bresser Pereira and Nakano (1984b).

1984a - "Política administrativa de controle da inflação," *Revista de Economia Política*, vol. 4, no. 3 (July-September); republished in Bresser Pereira and Nakano (1984b).

1984b - *Inflação e Recessão*. São Paulo: Editora Brasiliense.

1986 - "Inflação inercial e curva de Phillips," *Revista de Economia Política*, vol. 6, no. 2, (April-June).

Bronfenbrenner, Martin, and F. D. Holzman

1963 - "Survey of Inflation Theory," *The American Economic Review*, vol. LIII, no. 4 (September).

Cardoso, Fernando Henrique

1977 - "Estado capitalista e marxismo," *Estudos CEBRAP*, no. 21 (July-September).

Castells, Manoel

1977 - "Crise do estado, consumo coletivo e contradições urbanas," in Nicos Poulantzas (1977).

Coutinho, Luciano G.

1977 - "O setor produtivo estatal: autonomia e limites," *Ensaios de Opinião*, no. 2-3.

Cripps, Francis
1977 - "The Money Supply, Wages and Inflation," *Cambridge Journal of Economics*, vol. 1, no. 1 (March).

Cunha, Paulo Vieira da
1983 - "Reajustes salariais na indústria e a lei salarial de 1979: uma nota empírica," *Dados Revista de Ciências Sociais*, vol. 26, no. 3.

Dall'Acqua, Fernando Maida
1986 - "Pressão inflacionária e desafio para o plano," *Folha de São Paulo*, 1 June.

Davidson, Paul
1978 - "Why Money Matters," *Journal of Post-Keynesian Economics*, vol. 1, no. 1 Autumn.

Delfim Netto, Antonio, Afonso Celso Pastore, Pedro Cipolari, and Eduardo Pereira de Carvalho
1965 - *Alguns Aspectos da Inflação Brasileira*, São Paulo: Estudos ANPES, no. 9.

Desai, Meghnad
1981 - *Testing Monetarism*. London: Frances Pinter Publishers Ltd.

Dornbusch, Rudiger
1986 - "Reforma monetária no Brasil," *Folha de São Paulo*, 3 January.

Eckstein, Otto
1981 - *Core Inflation*. Englewood Cliffs: Prentice Hall.

Eckstein, Otto, and James A. Girola
1978 - "Long-term Properties of the Price-Wage Mechanism the United States," *Review of Economics and Statistics*, no. 60 (August).

Fazio, Antonio
1981 - "Inflation and Wage Indexation in Italy," *Banca Nazionale del Lavoro Quarterly Review*, no. 137 (June).

Flanders, M. June, and Assaf Razin, editors
1981 - *Development in an Inflationary World*. New York: Academic Press.

Fonseca, Marcos G.
1979 - "Contra o desaquecimento, crescimento seletivo," *Exame* (14 March).

Forbes, Geraldo
1986 - "O santo guerreiro e o dragão da maldade," *O Estado de São Paulo* (2 February).

Friedman, Milton
1956 - "The Quantity Theory of Money - A Restatement," Milton Friedman, editor, *Studies in the Quantity Theory of Money*. Chicago: University of Chicago Press.
1968 - "The Role of Monetary Policy," *The American Economic Review*, vol. LVIII, no. 1 (March).

Frisch, Helmut
  1977 - "Inflation Theory, 1963-1975: A 'Second Generation' Survey,"
  Journal of Economic Literature, vol. XV, no. 4, (December).
Furtado, Celso
  1959 - *Formação Econômica do Brasil.* Rio de Janeiro: Fundo de Cultura.
  1976 - *A Economia Latino-americana.* São Paulo: Companhia Editora
  Nacional, cap. XII.
Galbraith, John K.
  1968 - *O Novo Estado Industrial.* Rio de Janeiro: Civilização Brasileira,
  translated from *The New Industrial State,* first U.S. edition (1967).
Gapinski, James, and Charles R. Lockwood, editors
  1979 - *Essays in Post-Keynesian Inflation.* Cambridge, Mass.: Ballinger
  Publishing Co.
Hagger, A. J.
  1977 - *Inflation: Theory and Policy.* London: Macmillan. Robert E. Hall,
  editor,
  1982 - *Inflation: Causes and Effects.* Chicago: University of Chicago
  Press.
Hegedus, Georges
  1986 - "A hiperinflação húngara de 1945-1946," *Revista de Economia
  Política,* vol. 6, no 2 (April-June).
Hirschman, Albert O.
  1982 - *Shifting Involvements.* Princeton: Princeton University Press.
Johnson, Harry G.
  1963 - "A Survey of Theories of Inflation," *Indian Economic Review,*
  vol. VI, no. 4, (August); republished in Harry G. Johnson, *Essays in
  Monetary Economics.* London: George Allen and Unwin (1969).
Kaldor, Nicholas
  1970 - "The New Monetarism," *Lloyd's Bank Review* (July).
  1982 - *The Scourge of Monetarism.* Oxford: Oxford University Press.
Kalecki, Michael
  1971 - "Political Aspects of Full Employment," *Selected Essays on the
  Dynamic of the Capitalist Economy, 1933-1970.* Cambridge:
  Cambridge University Press, published article (1942).
Keynes, John Maynard
  1930 - *A Treatise on Money.* New York: Harcourt, Brace.
Labinini, Paolo Sylos
  1979 - "Prices and Income Distribution," in *Journal of Post-Keynesian
  Economics,* vol. II, no 1 (Autumn).
Leite, Antonio Dias
  1985 - "Idéia fundamental de um plano de domínio da inflação em cem
  dias," *Boletim de Conjuntura Industrial* of the Instituto de Economia
  Industrial of the Universidade Federal of Rio de Janeiro, vol. 5, no.
  1, (January); republished in Antonio Dias Leite, *A Transição para a
  Nova Republica.* Rio de Janeiro: Nova Fronteira (1985).

Lima, Luiz Antonio de Oliveira
 1977 - "Salários, inflação e balanço de pagamentos," *Folha de São Paulo* (5 June).
Lipietz, Alain
 1982 - "Credit Money: A Condition Permitting Inflationary Crisis," *Review of Radical Political Economics*, vol. 14, no. 2 (Summer).
Lockwood, Charles E.
 1979 - "The Anti-inflationary Value of Direct Controls," Gapinski and Lockwood (1979).
Lopes, Francisco Lafayete
 1978 - "Teoria e política da inflação brasileira: uma revisão crítica da literatura," Gramado (December 1980); ANPEC mimeo; republished in João Sayad (1979).
 1984a - "Só um choque heterodoxo pode derrubar a inflação," *Economia em Perspectiva*. Conselho Regional de Economia (August).
 1984b - "Inflação inercial, hiperinflação e desinflação: notas e conjecturas," *Revista da ANPEC*, no. 7 (December); republished in *Revista de Economia Política*, vol. 5, no. 2 (April-June 1985).
 1986 - *Choque Heterodoxo. Combate à Inflação e Reforma Monetária.* Rio de Janeiro: Editora Campus.
Lopes, Francisco L., and André Lara Rezende
 1980 - "Sobre as causas da recente aceleração inflacionária," *VII Encontro Nacional de Economia*. Nova Friburgo: Associação Nacional de Centros de Pós-Graduação em Economia, ANPEC, mimeo, (December).
Lopes, Francisco L., and Edmar Bacha
 1981 - "Inflation, Growth and Wage Policy," discussion text no. 10, Departamento de Economia of Pontifícia Universidade Católica of Rio de Janeiro.
Martinelli, Alberto, editor
 1977 - *Stato e Acumulazione del Capital.* Milan: Mazzota.
Martins, Carlos Estevam
 1977 - *Capitalismo de Estado e Modelo Político no Brasil.* São Paulo: Graal. Carlos Estevam Martins, editor
 1977 - *Estado e Capitalismo no Brasil.* São Paulo: Hucitec-CEBRAP.
Marx, Karl
 1867 - *O Capital, I.* Rio de Janeiro, Editora Civilização Brasileira (translation of the fourth German edition), first edition.
Mello, Fernando Homem de
 1982 - "Disponibilidade de alimentos e efeitos distributivos: Brasil 1967-79," *Pesquisa e Planejamento Econômico*, vol. 12, no. 2, (August).
Mello, João Manuel Cardoso de
 1977 - "O estado brasileiro e os limites da estatização," *Ensaios de Opinião*, no. 2-3.
Merkin, Gerald

1982 - "Towards a Theory of the German Inflation," Gerald Feldman et al., *The German Inflation*. Berlin: Walter de Gruyter.

Modiano, Eduardo

1983 - "A dinâmica de salários e preços na economia brasileira: 1966/81," *Pesquisa e Planejamento Econômico*, vol. 13, no. 1, (April).

1985 - "O choque argentino e o dilema brasileiro," discussion text no. 12, mimeo, Pontifícia Universidade Católica of Rio de Janeiro; published in *Revista de Economia Política*, vol. 6, no. 2 (April-June 1986).

Montoro Filho, André Franco

1977 - "Inflação e desequilíbrios," *Estudos Economicos*, vol. 7, no. 3 (September-December).

Moore, Basil J.

1979 - "The Endogenous Money Stocks," *Journal of Post-Keynesian Economics*, vol. II, no. 1 (October).

Morgan Guaranty Trust Company

1979 - "World Financial Markets" (May).

Moura da Silva, Adroaldo

1978 - "Inflação: uma visão heterodoxa," Estudos Econômicos, vol. 8, no. 1 (January-April).

1981 - "Inflação: Reflexões à margem da experiência brasileira," *Revista de Economia Política*, vol. 1, no. 3 (July-September).

1983 - "Regras de reajuste de preços e salários e a inércia inflacionária," Estudos Econômicos, vol. 12, no. 2 (May-August).

Nakano, Yoshiaki

1982 - "Recessão e inflação," *Revista de Economia Política*, vol. 2, no. 2 (April-June).

Neuhaus, Paulo

1978 - "A inflação brasileira em perspectiva histórica", *Revista Brasileira de Economia*, vol. 32, no. 2 (April-June).

Noyola, Juan F.

1956 - "El desarrollo económico y la inflación en Mexico y otros paises latinoamericanos," *Investigación Económica* (1956); republished in the same journal, no. 169 (July 1984).

O' Connor, James

1977 - *USA: A Crise do Estado Capitalista*. Rio de Janeiro: Paz e Terra; English original: *The Fiscal Crisis of the State* (1973).

Offe, Claus

1977 - *Lo Stato Nel Capitalismo Maturo*, Milan: Etas Libri.

Oliveira, Francisco de

1977 - "Estado e crença econômica: a contribuição da economia para uma ciência do estado," *Ensaios de Opiniao*, no. 2-3.

Oliveira, Julio G.

1964 - "La inflación estructural y el estructuralismo latinoamericano," O. Sunkel et al. *Inflación y Estructura Económica*. Buenos Aires: Paidos, (1967); originally published in English in *Oxford Economic Papers*, vol. XVI, no. 3 (November 1964).

Pastore, Afonso Celso
1968 - *A Resposta da Produção Agrícola aos Preços no Brasil*. São Paulo: Faculdade de Economia e Administração da Universidade de S. Paulo, bulletin 55.

Phillips, A. W.
1958 - "The Relationship Between Unemployment and the Rate of Change of Money Wage Rates in the United Kingdom, 1861-1957," *Economica*, vol. 25, transcribed in Ball and Doyle (1969).

Pinto, Aníbal
1973 - *Inflación: Raices Estructurales*. Mexico: Fondo de Cultura, serie Lecturas, no. 3.
1978 - *Inflação Recente no Brasil e na América Latina*. Rio de Janeiro: Graal.

Poulantzas, Nicos, editor
1977 - *O Estado em Crise*, São Paulo: Graal.

Ramos, Joseph R.
1977 - "Inflación persistente, inflación reprimida y hiperstanflación. Lecciones de inflación y estabilización en Chile," in *Cuadernos de Economía*, no. 43, Instituto de Economía of the Pontificía Universidad Católica de Chile (December 1977); republished in *Desarrollo económico*.

Rangel, Ignácio
1963 - *A Inflação Brasileira*. Rio de Janeiro: Tempo Brasileiro; third edition: São Paulo: Editora Brasiliense (1978).

Rezende, André Lara
1979 - "Incompatibilidade distributiva e inflação estrutural," mimeo, VII Encontro Nacional de Economia. Atibaia: Associação Nacional de Centros de Pós-Graduação em Economia, ANPEC (December); published in *Estudos Econômicos*, vol. 11, no. 3 (September-December 1981).
1984 - "A moeda indexada: Uma proposta para eliminar a inflação inercial," *Gazeta Mercantil* (26, 27 and 28 September).
1985 - "Moeda indexada: nem mágica nem panacéia," *Revista de Economia Política*, vol. 5, no. 2 (April-June).

Rezende, André Lara, and Pérsio Arida
1984 - "Inertial Inflation and Monetary Reform in Brazil," mimeo, Pontifícia Universidade Católica of Rio de Janeiro (January); presented at a seminar in Washington, D.C. sponsored by the Institute of International Economics (December 1984); published in Pérsio Arida (1986).

Sá, Francisco, Jr., et al.

- Inflação e desenvolvimento. Rio de Janeiro: Editora Vozes (n.d.)

Samuelson, Paul, and Robert Solow
1960 - "Analytical Aspects of Anti-inflation policy," *The American Economic Review*, vol. I, no. 2, (May).

Sargent, Thomas J.
1982 - "The Ends of Four Big Inflations," in Robert E. Hall (1982).

Sayad, João, editor
1979 - *Resenhas de Economia Brasileira*. São Paulo: Saraiva.

Sherman, Howard J.
1983 - *Stagflation—An Introduction to Traditional and Radical Macroeconomics*. New York: Harper and Row.

Silveira, Carlos Eduardo
1974 - A experiência brasileira da inflação, 1930-1961, mimeo, Escola de Administração de Empresas de São Paulo of Fundação Getúlio Vargas: EC-BRAS-2-91.

Simonsen, Mário Henrique
1969 - *Brasil 2001*. Rio de Janeiro: ANPEC.
1970 - *Inflação: Gradualismo x Tratamento de Choque*. Rio de Janeiro: ANPEC.
1978 - "O indigente cardápio econômico," in *Folha de São Paulo* (16 July).
1979 - "A inflação brasileira e a atual política inflacionária," mimeo, Brasília.
1980 - "A teoria da inflação e a controvérsia sobre a indexação," in *Estudos Econômicos*, vol. 10, no. 2 (May).
1984 - "Desindexação e reforma monetária," *Conjuntura Econômica*, vol. 38, no. 11 (November).

Sonntag, Heinz Rudolf, and Hector Valecillos, editors,
1977 - *El Estado en el Capitalismo Contemporaneo*. Mexico: Siglo XXI.

Sunkel, Oswaldo
1958 - "La inflación chilena: Un enfoque heterodoxo," *El Trimestre económico*, vol. XXV, no. 4 (October-December); transcribed in O. Sunkel et al. (1967).

Sunkel, Oswaldo, et al.
1967 - *Inflación y Estructura Económica*. Buenos Aires: Paidos.

Suplicy, Eduardo Matarazzo
1977 - "Administrador de cartéis?" *Folha de São Paulo* (22 March).

Tobin, James
1981 - "Diagnosing Inflation: A Taxonomy," Flanders and Razin (1981).

Vellutini, Roberto de Arnaldo Silva
1985 - "Política administrativa de controle da inflação: alguns comentários," *Revista de Economia Política*, vol. 5, no. 3 (July-September).

Vincent, J. M., J. Hirsch et al.
1975 - *L' Etat Contemporain et le Marxisme*. Paris: Maspéro.

Wachtel, Howard M., and Peter D. Adelsheim

    1977 - "How Recession Feeds Inflation: Price Markups in a Concentrated Economy," *Challenge* (September-October).

Weintraub, Sidney

    1978 - *Capitalism's Inflation and Unemployment Crisis: Beyond Monetarism and Keynesianism.* Reading, Mass.: Addisson-Wesley Publishing Co.

Yeager, Leland B., and associates

    1981 - *Experiences with Stopping Inflation,* Washington, D.C.: American Enterprise Institute for Public Policy Research.

Index

Accumulation, 124, 126, 139, 140(n11)
Administered inflation, 27, 33, 47, 62(n9), 69, 122, 123-124, 128-129, 130, 134; characteristics, 52-53; defined, 40-41; economy, 127-128; oil prices, 43-44
Administration, 59, 131; inflationary controls, 14-15; of prices, 22, 45-47, 53, 57, 74, 164-165, 172, 100-101, 103, 138. *See also* Administered inflation; Administrative policy
Administrative policy, 93, 106(n10); gradualist, 96-97; price controls, 94, 97, 100-101, 102, 104; shock policy, 104-105
Aggregate demand, 87, 90, 91, 93, 94, 159-160, 179. *See also* Demand
Agriculture, 126, 148, 160; inflation rates, 143, 144; price elasticity, 126-127; prices, 17, 88, 101, 102, 153, 158-159, 163-164, 165, 166, 167, 170; production, 153-154

Amplified consumer price index (IPCA), 171, 175-176(nl)
Animal products, 101
Anti-inflationary policy, 83, 86, 87, 121, 123, 124, 129, 137; adjustment, 94-95; administration, 93-94, 96-97; demand management, 91-93; monetarist, 88-91; price controls, 100, 104; wages, 84-85
Argentina, 8, 15, 16, 48, 85. *See also* Austral Plan
Arida, Pérsio, 15
Austral Plan, 8, 15, 16, 177, 178, 183

Balance of payments, 85, 95; adjustments, 56, 57; deficits, 92, 94. *See also* Debt; Deficits
Black market, 106
Bresser Pereira, Luiz, 15
Buffer stocks, 101
Businesses, 38, 157. *See also* Cartels; Corporations; Multinational corporations
Buying power, 17

Capital, 36, 37, 48. *See also*

Capital flight; Capitalism
Capital flight, 175
Capitalism, 66, 67, 96;
    corporations, 36, 144;
    inflation, 27, 65, 80; money
    supply, 75-76; stagflation,
    51-52; technobureaucratic,
    42-43, 49-50, 57, 59
Cartels, 119, 128. *See also*
    Corporations; Multinational
    corporations
Castelo Branco administration,
    121, 122-123
Chile, 48, 85
CIP. *See* Interministerial Price
    Control
Commodities, 70, 75
Compensatory inflation, 47, 49,
    50-51
Consumer price index (IPC), 2, 4,
    17, 176(n1). *See also*
    Amplified consumer price
    index
Consumers, 42-43, 44
Consumption, 21, 154
Corporations, 41, 51, 52, 81,
    100, 102, 119, 132, 144;
    consumers, 42-43; costs,
    148-149; margins and, 54,
    61-62(n8), 171;
    oligopolization, 36-37, 53,
    78-79, 80, 129, 130; price
    controls, 106(n6), 97, 124;
    prices, 37, 39-40, 44, 182;
    profit margins, 69, 112, 114,
    145, 148; public, 137-138;
    wages, 136-137. *See also*
    Businesses; Cartels;
    Multinational corporations
Corrective inflation, 46-47, 52,
    53, 62-63(n13), 69, 87, 156,
    170
Cost inflation. *See* Administered
    inflation
Costs, 63(n17), 122, 128; pass

ons, 148-149; prices, 40,
    148-149
Credit, 95, 124, 133, 137, 156;
    money supply, 75-76;
    subsidized, 131-132. *See also*
    Credit policy
Credit policy, 124, 158
Cruzado Plan, 15, 21, 177, 179;
    effects, 16, 22-23, 180, 183;
    measures, 2-3; problems,
    180-182
Cruzados; conversion, 3-4, 6, 17.
    See also Cruzado Plan;
    Cruzeiros
Cruzeiros; conversion, 6, 17;
    devaluation, 3, 131, 157,
    160, 166
Currency, *See* Cruzado; Cruzeiros;
    Devaluation; Exchange rate

D Day, 2, 3, 5-6, 15, 16, 17, 105,
    174
Debt, 56, 62(n12), 77-78. *See also*
    Deficits
Deceleration, 54
Deficits, 56, 95, 104, 125, 136;
    balance of payments, 92, 94;
    inflation rate, 77-78; public,
    7, 22, 47-48, 63(n15), 76-
    77, 78, 80, 84, 95, 182. *See
    also* Debt
Deflation, 22, 29
Deindexation, 14, 96, 101;
    economic, 2, 4, 15, 94, 104.
    See also Indexation
Delfim Netto, Antonio, 123, 156
Demand, 116, 123, 134, 143, 148;
    expansion, 180-181;
    inflation rate, 121-122. *See
    also* Aggregate demand;
    Demand inflation; Demand
    management; Demand shock;
    Supply
Demand inflation, 54, 134. *See
    also* Demand

Demand management, 88; policy, 91-93
Demand shock, 110-111, 128
Devaluation, 16, 88, 90; cruzeiros, 131, 160; exchange rates, 56, 95, 161. *See also* Maxidevaluation
Development programs, 123
Dias Leite, Antonio, 15
Dictatorships, 48-49
Dissynchronization, 12
Distributive policy, 140(n5)
Dornbusch, Rudiger, 15

Economic growth, 7, 21, 34, 103, 137, 171; inflation, 10, 129; rates, 3, 67. *See also* Economic policy; Economic systems; Economy
Economic policy, 3, 14, 55-56, 67, 82, 138; austerity, 154-156; demand, 121-122; effect, 56-57, 58, 60; inflation, 1, 2, 12, 39-40, 55, 58-59; recession, 133-134; state and, 49-50; validity, 38-39. *See also* Macroeconomic policy
Economic systems, 75; defined, 36-37; government, 49-51. *See also* Economic growth; Economic policy; Economy
Economy, 11, 56, 74, 119, 131, 156, 180; deindexation, 2, 104; inflation rate, 66-67; oligopolization, 96, 103, 127-128; stabilization, 125-126; stimulation, 123-124. *See also* Economic growth; Economic policy; Economic systems
Employment, 34, 66, 84, 91. *See also* Trade unions; Underemployment; Unemployment; Workers
Exchange rate, 69, 84, 95, 97,
153, 165, 172; devaluation, 56, 159, 161, 175; freeze, 1, 2, 14; indexation, 100, 158; setting, 45, 46-47; variations, 85, 114-115
Expenditures, 136
Exports, 158, 164, 170; credit subsidies, 131-132; price setting, 43, 44, 46. *See also* Imports; Import substitution; Trade; Trade balance
External debt, 3. *See also* Debt

"Feedback components," 71-72
Figueiredo government, 2
Financial assets, 100
Fixed margins, 52, 53
Food, 154, 156. *See also* Agriculture

GDP. *See* Gross domestic product
General price index (IGP), 137, 160-161, 162, 163, 168(n1); agriculture, 166, 175(n1); inflation rates, 169-170, 171
Getúlio Vargas Foundation, 137
GNP, *See* Gross national product
Gouveia de Bulhões, Octávio, 15
Gradualist policy, 122, 173
Gross domestic product (GDP), 7, 10, 34, 47
Gross national product (GNP), 30, 122, 161, 166, 182

Heterodox shock, 1, 2, 7, 15, 106-107(n11), 173, 174

IGP. *See* General price index
IMF. *See* International Monetary Fund
Imported inflation, 44, 130
Imports, 94, 123, 124, 126, 131, 158, 161. *See also* Exports; Import substitution; Trade;

Trade balance
Import substitution, 130-131. *See also* Imports; Trade; Trade balance
Income, 41, 67, 71, 72, 93, 98, 104, 119; money supply, 60, 75; transfer, 131, 138-139. *See also* Income distribution; Salaries; Wages
Income distribution, 3, 41, 70, 72, 119. *See also* Income
Indexation, 96, 101, 110, 114, 115-116, 156, 158, 172; alternative, 99-100; effects, 72-73; prices, 97-98, 174; process, 70-71; wages, 55-56, 98-99. *See also* Deindexation
Indexed currency, 15
Industry, 8, 123, 131, 180; inflation rates, 143, 144; prices, 17, 156, 160, 163, 166
Inertial inflation, 12, 13, 21, 27, 83; theory, 8-9, 10, 11
Inflation; theories of, 1-2, 8-9, 10-12, 28-29, 33-34, 63(n18). *See also* Inflation rates; *individual types of inflation*
Inflation rates, 16, 22, 28-29, 30, 87, 88, 104, 110, 111, 120-122, 124, 138, 139-140(nnl, 4), 141(n15), 143, 151, 162, 171, 179; components, 115-116; credit subsidies, 131, 132; deficits, 77-78; economy, 66-67; general price index, 169-170; indexation, 99-100; recession, 133-134; sectorial, 174-175; wages, 78-79, 90
INPC. *See* National consumer price index
Interest rates, 8, 22, 45, 91, 114,

129, 138, 156, 159, 175, 179; lowering, 94, 171
Interindustrial relations, 17, 21
Interministerial Price Control (CIP), 103, 123, 124, 137, 140(n9), 156, 171
International Monetary Fund (IMF), 167
Investment, 8, 51, 134
IPC. *See* consumer price index
IPCA. *See* Amplified consumer price index

Kaleckian theory, 14
Keynesian theory, 33, 34, 66, 73, 85, 95; fiscal policy, 50, 69; model, 79, 80, 116
Kubitschek government, 131

Labor. *See* Employment; Trade unions; Workers
Lara Rezende, André, 15
Law 6708, 156
Legitimacy, 48-49, 54, 56, 103
Liquidity, 32, 47-48, 54, 133, 136
Lopes, Francisco, 15

Macroeconomic policy, 38-39, 66
Margins, 61-62(n8). *See also* Profit margins
Market, 36, 37, 69, 81, 91, 101, 127, 164, 178; competitive, 96-97; economic policy, 58, 59; inflation, 37-38, 52, 61(n3); price control, 22, 45
Maxidevaluation, 115, 116, 153, 157-158, 159, 160, 166-167, 172
Mexico, 85
Mineral industry, 101
Modernization, 153-154
Modiano, Eduardo, 15
Monetarist model, 82(n2), 91, 92, 93, 122, 127, 143; theory, 88-90, 95

Monetary policy, 94, 136, 154, 156, 158. *See also* Monetary reform
Monetary reform, 1, 2-3, 4, 14, 15, 154. *See also* Monetary policy
Money supply, 35, 52, 60, 75, 84, 90, 95, 133, 139(n2); capitalism, 75-76; demand, 22, 31-32; inflation, 11, 12, 32-33, 54, 61(nn2, 3), 73-74, 127, 136; need, 12-13; prices, 13, 73; public deficit, 76-77, 78
Multinational corporations, 36. *See also* Cartels; Corporations

Nakano, Yoshiaki, 15
National consumer price index (INPC), 156, 159, 160, 175-176(n1)
National treasury bonds (OTNs), 4
Neostructuralist theory, 11-12, 14

Oil prices, 43-44, 54, 56, 124, 130, 151, 154. *See also* Petroleum products
Oligopolies, 144-145, 149. *See also* Corporations, oligopolization
ORTNs. *See* Readjustable national treasury bonds
OTNs. *See* National treasury bonds

Petroleum products, 156, 161, 162. *See also* Oil prices
Phillips curve, 10, 11, 34, 61(n6), 79, 81, 85, 86, 88, 116; function, 110-111; inertial inflation, 109-110; inflation rate, 112-113
PIP. *See* Prices and income policy
Planning system, 36, 37, 38, 39-40, 45

Policies, 58, 59, 60. *See also* individual policies
Post-Keynesian model, 14
Price controls, 59, 74, 104, 105, 124, 138, 154, 156, 165, 172, 177; administrative policy, 94, 96, 97, 100, 101; effectiveness, 102-103, 106(n6), 137. *See also* Price freezes
Price elasticity, 126-127
Price freezes, 1, 2, 5, 14, 15, 134, 169, 170, 174, 178, 179. *See also* Price controls
Prices; adjustments, 5-6, 71, 125, 143, 151, 153; administration, 43, 45-47, 129, 164-165; agricultural, 126-127, 160, 163-164, 165, 166, 167, 170; controls, 14, 53, 57-58; corporations, 37, 39-40, 53, 182; costs, 40, 148-149; distortion, 101-102; formation, 144; growth rate, 17, 18(fig.); imbalances, 16-17, 21; increases, 28-30, 71-72, 120, 128, 129, 130, 137, 157; indexation, 97-98; industrial, 160, 163, 166; inflation, 12, 31, 35, 144; money supply, 13, 22, 52, 54, 73; readjustments, 161-162, 174; shocks, 158-159, 162-163; stabilization, 4, 7; theories, 33-34. *See also* Price controls; Price elasticity; Price freezes
Prices and income policy (PIP), 103
Private sector, 51. *See also* Businesses; Corporations; Multinational corporations
Production, 39, 54; agricultural, 153-154, 160; costs, 148-149; expansion, 179, 180-

181; market and, 38, 164.
See also Productivity
Productivity, 85, 129, 140(n12),
173; prices, 39, 45; wages,
68, 69, 100. *See also*
Production
Profit margins, 69, 71, 74, 84,
85, 106(n3), 130, 157, 180;
corporate, 69, 80-81, 109,
114, 130, 144, 148;
increasing, 68, 112, 134,
149, 162; inflation, 70, 78-
79, 87; reduction, 81, 95
Profits, 67, 68, 128, 148. *See also*
Profit margins
Programa estratégico de
desenvolvimento, 123
PSBR. *See* Public sector borrowing
requirements
Psychological inflation, 130
Public sector borrowing
requirements (PSBR), 87

Raw materials, 69, 143, 148, 180,
181
Readjustable national treasury
bonds (ORTNs), 4, 159,
168(n3)
Recession, 15, 16, 61-62(n8), 91,
92, 133, 148, 149, 159; cost
controls, 122-123; inflation,
33, 87-88, 122
Remonetization, 6
Resources, 73
Retail companies, 181-182

Salaries, 63(n17), 131. *See also*
Wages
Simonsen, Mário Henrique, 15,
124, 133, 134, 138, 154
Stabilization Plan, 2, 6, 8
Stagflation, 9, 29-30, 35, 39, 51-
52, 83, 92, 96, 103, 113
Structural inflation, 9, 33, 54, 55,
61(n7), 69, 132-133, 136,
140-141(nn8, 14); theory,

10, 35, 126-127
Supply, 160, 134, 179. *See also*
Demand
Supply and demand. *See* Demand;
Supply
Supply shock, 62(n11), 116, 124,
128, 174

Taxation, 50-51, 126, 129, 159
Technobureaucracies, 51, 63(n15),
131; capitalism 42-43, 57,
59; development, 36, 37;
state, 49-50
Terms of trade, 44. *See also* Trade
balance
Trade, 95, 158. *See also* Exports;
Imports; Import substitution;
Terms of trade; Trade balance
Trade balance, 56, 123. *See also*
Exports; Imports; Import
substitution; Terms of trade
Trade unions, .37, 55, 81, 114,
128-129, 181. *See also*
Wages; Workers

Underemployment, 137. *See also*
Employment; Unemployment
Unemployment, 35, 50, 61(n7),
74, 78, 86, 87, 109, 112,
116, 136, 149; demand
shock, 110-111; price
controls, 103, 106(n10);
wages and, 34, 61(n6), 79,
81. *See also* Employment
United Kingdom, 29, 30, 103
United States, 29-30, 106(n6), 154

Wages, 17, 95, 128, 159, 165;
adjustments, 3, 55-56, 71,
114, 156-157; bargaining,
70, 181; controls, 14, 97,
102-103, 105, 106(n6);
freezes, 1, 2, 5, 14, 174;
increases, 84, 90, 98-99,
134, 136-137, 162, 170;

indexing, 9, 42, 55, 98-99;
inflation, 62(n10), 78-79,
129, 131; negotiations, 4-5;
prices, 45, 97; production,
54, 69; profit margins, 84-
85; real, 68, 90;
unemployment, 34, 61(n6),
79, 81, 86, 149. *See also*
Salaries
Workers, 41-42, 64(n19), 67, 69,
70, 131. *See also*
Employment; Trade unions

About the Book and the Authors

The theory of inertial inflation explains a phenomenon that neither monetarist nor Keynesian economics is able to illuminate. In addition to its roots in upward pressure on prices, inflation under contemporary capitalism has an inertial component, Given the distributive conflict, which leads economic agents automatically to pass cost increases through to prices, the level of inflation experienced in the past continues to be anticipated, and is therefore carried into the present. The level of inflation will be maintained even in the absence of such traditional explanatory factors as public deficits and excess demand. This book clarifies the analytical concepts and variables necessary to understand inertial inflation and its policy implication.

The authors emphasize the distinction between the accelerating (supply or demand shocks) and maintaining (inertial) aspects of inflation. They perceive an increased money supply as a consequence rather than a cause of inflation—a validation of inflation that has already taken place—and demonstrate that the inertial component becomes more pronounced as the rate of inflation increases. When faced with high levels of inflation, policymakers must adopt a policy of heterodox shock: the instantaneous freezing of all prices, wages, and exchange rates. It is this theory that served as the basis for the Austral Plan (1985, Argentina) and Cruzado Plan (1986, Brazil), which interrupted annual rates of inflation of 1000 percent and 350 percent respectively, The chapters on Brazil's economy provide an analysis of the Brazilian inflation based on this theoretical model.

Luiz Bresser Pereira, finance minister of Brazil since April 1987, has served also as chief of staff (Secretário do Governo) for the state of São

Paulo (BANESPA). Dr. Bresser Pereira is also professor of economics at the Getúlio Vargas Foundation. He began his professional life as a journalist in 1950 and was senior vice president of Brazil's Pão de Açucar Group from 1963 to 1983.

Yoshiaki Nakano is on the faculty of the School of Business Administration of the Getúlio Vargas Foundation and professor of economics in the foundation's Department of Planning and Economic Analysis. He has served as director of rural and industrial credit at BANESPA and vice president of the São Paulo State Development Bank. In April 1987 he became the head of the economic staff of the Ministry of Finance of Brazil.